Workshop on Language Technology for Cultural Heritage, Social Sciences, and Humanities 2011

(LaTeCH 2011)

Held at ACL HLT 2011

Portland, Oregon, USA
24 June 2011

ISBN: 978-1-61839-232-9

Printed from e-media with permission by:

Curran Associates, Inc.
57 Morehouse Lane
Red Hook, NY 12571

Some format issues inherent in the e-media version may also appear in this print version.

Printed by Curran Associates, Inc. (2011)

For permission requests, please contact the Association for Computational Linguistics at the address below.

Association for Computational Linguistics
209 N. Eighth Street
Stroudsburg, Pennsylvania 18360

Phone: 1-570-476-8006
Fax: 1-570-476-0860

acl@aclweb.org

Additional copies of this publication are available from:

Curran Associates, Inc.
57 Morehouse Lane
Red Hook, NY 12571 USA
Phone: 845-758-0400
Fax: 845-758-2634
Email: curran@proceedings.com
Web: www.proceedings.com

Preface

The LaTeCH (*Language Technology for Cultural Heritage, Social Sciences, and Humanities*) annual workshop series aims to provide a forum for researchers who are working on aspects of natural language and information technology applications that pertain to data from the humanities, social sciences, and cultural heritage. The LaTeCH workshops were initially motivated by the growing interest in language technology research and applications for the cultural heritage domain. The scope has soon nevertheless broadened to also include the humanities and the social sciences.

Current developments in web and information access have triggered a series of digitisation efforts by museums, archives, libraries and other cultural heritage institutions. Similar developments in humanities and social sciences have resulted in large amounts of data becoming available in electronic format, either as digitised, or as born-digital data. The natural next step to digitisation is the intelligent processing of this data. To this end, the humanities, social sciences, and cultural heritage domains draw an increasing interest from researchers in NLP aiming at developing methods for semantic enrichment and information discovery and access. Language technology has been conventionally focused on certain domains, such as newswire. These fairly novel domains of cultural heritage, social sciences, and humanities entail new challenges to NLP research, such as noisy text (e.g., due to OCR problems), non-standard, or archaic language varieties (e.g., historic language, dialects, mixed use of languages, ellipsis, transcription errors), literary or figurative writing style and lack of knowledge resources, such as dictionaries. Furthermore, often neither annotated domain data is available, nor the required funds to manually create it, thus forcing researchers to investigate (semi-) automatic resource development and domain adaptation approaches involving the least possible manual effort.

In the current edition of the LaTeCH workshop, we have received a record number of submissions, a subset of which has been selected based on a thorough peer-review process. A central issue for the majority of contributions to this LaTeCH workshop has been the problem of linguistic processing for historical language varieties (e.g., Spanish, Czech, German, Slovene and Swedish) and the respective resource development and tool adaptation. In terms of applications, the contributions attempt to provide language technology solutions for cultural heritage and humanities researchers ranging from historians and architecture historians to linguists, cultural heritage curators, ethnologists and literary critics. The text types targeted for analysis range from full-text to semi-structured text, while the domains addressed range from the analysis of historical text and encrypted medieval manuscripts, to novels and fairy tales and modern academic journals, online blogs and fora. The variety of topics and the increased number of submissions illustrate the growing interest in this exciting and expanding research area.

We would like to thank all authors for the hard work that went into their submissions. We are also grateful to the members of the programme committee for their thorough reviews, and to the ACL-HLT 2011 organisers, especially the Workshop Co-chairs, Hal Daumé III and John Carroll for their help with administrative matters.

Kalliopi Zervanou & Piroska Lendvai

Organizers:

Kalliopi Zervanou (Co-chair), University of Tilburg (The Netherlands)
Piroska Lendvai (Co-chair), Research Institute for Linguistics (Hungary)
Caroline Sporleder, Saarland University (Germany)
Antal van den Bosch, University of Tilburg (The Netherlands)

Program Committee:

Ion Androutsopoulos, Athens University of Economics and Business (Greece)
Tim Baldwin, University of Melbourne (Australia)
David Bamman, Tufts University (USA)
Toine Bogers, Royal School of Library & Information Science, Copenhagen (Denmark)
Paul Buitelaar, DERI Galway (Ireland)
Kate Byrne, University of Edinburgh (Scotland)
Milena Dobreva, HATII, University of Glasgow (Scotland)
Mick O'Donnell, Universidad Autonoma de Madrid (Spain)
Julio Gonzalo, Universidad Nacional de Educacion a Distancia (Spain)
Claire Grover, University of Edinburgh (Scotland)
Ben Hachey, Macquarie University (Australia)
Eduard Hovy, USC Information Sciences Institute (USA)
Jaap Kamps, University of Amsterdam (The Netherlands)
Vangelis Karkaletsis, NCSR Demokritos (Greece)
Stasinos Konstantopoulos, NCSR Demokritos (Greece)
Ioannis Korkontzelos, National Centre for Text Mining – NaCTeM (UK)
Véronique Malaisé, Elsevier, Content Enrichment Center
Barbara McGillivray, Oxford University Press
John Nerbonne, Rijksuniversiteit Groningen (The Netherlands)
Katerina Pastra, CSRI (Greece)
Michael Piotrowski, University of Zurich (Switzerland)
Georg Rehm, DFKI (Germany)
Martin Reynaert, University of Tilburg (The Netherlands)
Svitlana Zinger, TU Eindhoven (The Netherlands)

Table of Contents

Conference Program

Friday June 24, 2011

9:00–9:10	Welcome
9:10–9:40	*Extending the tool, or how to annotate historical language varieties* Cristina Sánchez-Marco, Gemma Boleda and Lluís Padró
9:40–10:10	*A low-budget tagger for Old Czech* Jirka Hana, Anna Feldman and Katsiaryna Aharodnik
10:10–10:30	*Evaluating an 'off-the-shelf' POS-tagger on Early Modern German text* Silke Scheible, Richard J. Whitt, Martin Durrell and Paul Bennett
10:30–11:00	Coffee break
11:00–11:10	*e-Research for Linguists* Dorothee Beermann and Pavel Mihaylov
11:10–11:15	*Automatic linguistic annotation of historical language: ToTrTaLe and XIX century Slovene* Tomaž Erjavec
11:15–11:20	*Historical Event Extraction from Text* Agata Katarzyna Cybulska and Piek Vossen
11:20–11:30	*Enrichment and Structuring of Archival Description Metadata* Kalliopi Zervanou, Ioannis Korkontzelos, Antal van den Bosch and Sophia Ananiadou
11:30–11:40	*Structure-Preserving Pipelines for Digital Libraries* Massimo Poesio, Eduard Barbu, Egon Stemle and Christian Girardi
11:40–11:45	*The ARC Project: Creating logical models of Gothic cathedrals using natural language processing* Charles Hollingsworth, Stefaan Van Liefferinge, Rebecca A. Smith, Michael A. Covington and Walter D. Potter
11:45–11:55	*Crowdsourcing syntactic relatedness judgements for opinion mining in the study of information technology adoption* Asad Sayeed, Bryan Rusk, Martin Petrov, Hieu Nguyen, Timothy Meyer and Amy Weinberg
12:00–13:00	Poster Session
13:00–14:00	Lunch break

Extending the tool, or how to annotate historical language varieties

Cristina Sánchez-Marco
Universitat Pompeu Fabra
Barcelona, Spain
cristina.sanchezm@upf.edu

Gemma Boleda, Lluís Padró
Universitat Politècnica de Catalunya
Barcelona, Spain
{gboleda,padro}@lsi.upc.edu

Abstract

We present a general and simple method to adapt an existing NLP tool in order to enable it to deal with historical varieties of languages. This approach consists basically in expanding the dictionary with the old word variants and in retraining the tagger with a small training corpus. We implement this approach for Old Spanish.

The results of a thorough evaluation over the extended tool show that using this method an almost state-of-the-art performance is obtained, adequate to carry out quantitative studies in the humanities: 94.5% accuracy for the main part of speech and 92.6% for lemma. To our knowledge, this is the first time that such a strategy is adopted to annotate historical language varieties and we believe that it could be used as well to deal with other non-standard varieties of languages.

1 Introduction

In the last few years, there has been a growing interest in all disciplines of the humanities to study historical varieties of languages using quantitative methods (Sagi et al., 2009; Lüdeling et al., to appear). Large corpora are necessary to conduct this type of studies, so as to smooth the great data sparseness problem affecting non-standard varieties of languages, and thus guarantee the validity of the generalizations based on these data.

Historical language varieties bear similarities to standard varieties, but they also exhibit remarkable differences in a number of respects, such as their morphology, syntax, and semantics. In addition, as orthographic rules were not established until later centuries, a great amount of graphemic variation is found in historical texts, such that one word can be written using many different graphemic variants. This variation increases considerably the number of different words and therefore the lexicon of the corresponding language variety. For instance, searching for the infinitival verb form *haber* 'have' in a historical corpus for Spanish can be a difficult task if there are, say, 5 variants of the same word (*auer, aver, hauer, haver, haber*) and the corpus does not contain any other linguistic information, such as lemma and part of speech (PoS).

In this paper we propose a strategy to automatically enrich texts from historical language varieties with linguistic information, namely to expand a pre-existing NLP tool for standard varieties of a language. To our knowledge, it is the first time that such an approach is proposed and evaluated. In particular, we describe the method followed to extend a library (FreeLing[1]) for the linguistic analysis of Standard Spanish to enable it to deal with Old Spanish[2].

This general approach has four main advantages over the state-of-the-art strategies (described in section 2). First, the resulting tool can be reused (with the consequent saving of resources). Second, the tool can be further improved by other researchers. Third, it is the tool that is adapted, instead of forc-

[1] http://nlp.lsi.upc.edu/freeling. The tool for Old Spanish is available in the development version 3.0-devel, accessible via SVN.

[2] As it is considered by most scholars, we consider Old Spanish the period from the 12th to the 16th century.

ing standardisation on the original texts (see section 2). Also, the strategy can be used to extend other existing tools.

The specific case study in this paper presents additional advantages. On the one hand, FreeLing is an open source resource that is well documented and actively maintained. In addition, due to the modularity of this tool, it is relatively easy to adapt. On the other hand, the result of the extension is a tool for Old Spanish across different centuries, that is to say, the tool can be used to accurately tag not only Spanish from a particular century but also to tag the language over a long period of time (from the 12th to the 16th century). The resulting tool achieves almost state-of-the-art performance for PoS-taggers: a tagging accuracy of 94.5% on the part of speech, 92.6% on lemmas, and 89.9% on the complete morphological tag including detailed information such as gender or number for nouns and tense and person for verbs.

Plan of the paper. In Section 2 we review the state of the art. In Sections 3 through 5 we describe FreeLing and the data and methodology used for its adaptation to Old Spanish. Then the results of the evaluation and error analysis are presented (Sections 6 and 7). We conclude with some discussion and suggestions for future work (Section 8).

2 Related work

Up to now, three main approaches have been followed to automatically enrich historical corpora with linguistic information: (i) automatic tagging using existing tools followed by human correction, (ii) standardisation of the words followed by automatic tagging with existing tools, and (ii) re-training of a tagger on historical texts.

The first approach has been adopted in projects such as the *Penn Historical Corpora*[3] , *The York-Toronto-Helsinki Parsed Corpus of Old English Prose* (Taylor, 2007), and the *Corpus of Early English Correspondence* or *CEEEC* (Raumolin-Brunberg and Nevalainen, 2007). The second strategy, namely, to standardize the corpora prior to their annotation with NLP tools, has also been followed by other scholars (Rayson et al., 2007; Ernst-Gerlach and Fuhr, 2007; Baron and Rayson, 2008). In this approach, graphemic variants in Old English and German texts are identified and subsequently mapped onto their modern equivalents (i.e., the standardized forms). This approach is adequate for tasks such as information retrieval (Ernst-Gerlach and Fuhr, 2007), but not quite so for quantitative research for historical variants. For example, there are many words in historical varieties of languages for which a corresponding standard variant does not exist (e.g., *maguer* 'although' in Old Spanish). As reported in Rayson et al. (2007) the PoS tagging accuracy obtained with this method in texts from the Early Modern English period is around 85%.

Recently there have been some experiments with morphosyntactic tagging of historical data by training a model on old texts (Rögnvaldsson and Helgadóttir, 2008; Dipper, 2010). For example, Rögnvaldsson and Helgadóttir (2008) use this approach to tag Old Norse texts (sagas from the 13th and 14th century) yielding 92.7% accuracy on the tag, almost 3 points higher than that obtained in our case.

Our approach is similar in spirit to the latter, as we also train a tagger using an annotated historical corpus. However, it differs in that we consistently extend the whole resource (not only the tagger, but also the dictionary and other modules such as the tokenization). Thus, we build a complete set of tools to handle Old Spanish. Also, our work covers a larger time span, and it is able to tag texts from a wide variety of genres (hence the difference in accuracy with respect to Rögnvaldsson and Helgadóttir (2008)).

As noted in the Introduction, in comparison to state-of-the-art approaches the strategy proposed in this paper requires fewer resources, it is easily portable and reusable for other corpora and languages and yields a satisfactory accuracy.

3 The analyzer

FreeLing is a developer-oriented library providing a number of language analysis services, such as morphosyntactic tagging, sense annotation or dependency parsing (Padró et al., 2010). As mentioned in the Introduction, this tool, being open source, actively developed and maintained, and highly modular, is particularly well suited for our purposes. In addition, it provides an application programming

[3] `http://www.ling.upenn.edu/hist-corpora.`

interface (API) which allows the desired language analyses to be integrated into a more complex processing. In its current version (2.2), this resource provides services (to different extents) for the following languages: English, Spanish, Portuguese, Italian, Galician, Catalan, Asturian, and Welsh. In this paper we have focused on the adaptation of the resources for morphosyntactic tagging, but the syntactic and semantic modules can also be customized. The FreeLing processing pipeline for morphosyntactic tagging is illustrated in Figure 1. As shown in the figure, a set of texts is submitted to the analyzer, which processes and enriches the texts with linguistic information using the different modules: tokenization, dictionary, affixation, probability assignment and unknown-word guesser[4], and PoS tagger.

The tagset used by this tool is based on the EAGLES standard[5]. The first letter of each tag indicates the morphological class of the word. The remaining letters (up to 6) specify more fine-grained morphosyntactic and semantic information, such as the gender and number of nouns or the tense, mode and type (main or auxiliary) of verbs.

4 The Data

4.1 Old Spanish Corpus

In order to adapt the tool, we have worked with the electronic texts compiled, transcribed and edited by the Hispanic Seminary of Medieval Studies (*HSMS*).[6] We will refer to the set of texts used to adapt the tool as *Old Spanish Corpus*. These texts, all critical editions of the original manuscripts, comprise a variety of genres (fiction and non-fiction) from the 12th until the 16th century and consist of more than 20 million tokens and 470 thousand types. The original texts in these compilations render the copy very closely (diplomatic transcriptions)

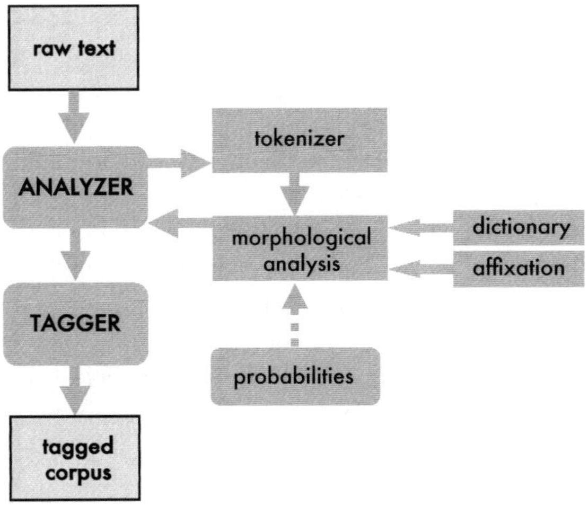

Figure 1: Processing pipeline in FreeLing.

and contain annotations encoding paleographic information, for instance about the physical characteristics of the manuscript or marks and notes by different scribes. These annotations were removed, and the original transcription of the words has been mantained preserving the similarity to the original copies.

As is the case for most languages keeping data from historical varieties, the number and type or genre of texts which have been preserved for each century varies. From this perspective, the Old Spanish Corpus used to extend the tool is representative of the language, since it covers the language of the Middle Age period, containing samples of most genres and centuries from the 12th century up to the 16th century. As shown in the first row of Table 1, the corpus contains a much lower number of tokens for the 12th century compared to the remaining centuries, as only one document from this century is included in the corpus. The 13th to 15th centuries are fairly well represented, while comparably less tokens are available for the 16th century, due to the design of the *HSMS* collections. To get an impression on the types of texts covered in the Old Spanish Corpus, the documents have been classified according to their genre or topic in *CORDE*[7]. 8 types of genres or topics have been considered: fiction (including

[4]This module has two functions: first, it assigns an *a priori* probability to each analysis of each word. Second, if a word has no analysis (none of the previously applied modules succeeded to analyze it), a statistical guesser is used to find out the most likely PoS tags, based on the word ending.

[5]Expert Advisory Group on Language Engineering Standards (`http://www.ilc.cnr.it/EAGLES96/home.html`).

[6]Corfis et al. (1997), Herrera and de Fauve (1997), Kasten et al. (1997), Nitti and Kasten (1997), O'Neill (1999).

[7]*CORDE* is a reference corpus of diachronic Spanish containing texts from the 8th century up to 1975 (`http://www.rae.es`).

novels and also other narrative books), law, didactics (treatises, sapiential literature), history (chronicles, letters and other historical documentation), society (hunting, fashion), poetry, science (medicine, astrology, astronomy), and religion (Bible). Figure 2 illustrates the distribution of texts according to their genre or topic in each century. The width and height of rows represent the proportion of texts of each genre-topic for each century. Each box corresponds to a particular type of text. On the x-axis the centuries are represented, from the 13th to the 16th century.[8] As can be seen from the size of the corresponding boxes, there is a higher number of fiction books in the later centuries. In contrast, the proportion of law and religion books decreases in time. All in all, the corpus contains a fair variety of genres and topics present in Old Spanish literature, so the language used in these types of documents is represented in the expanded tool as well.

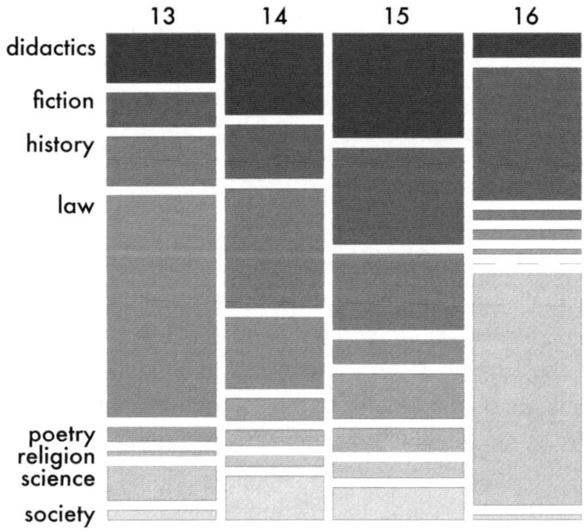

Figure 2: Distribution of genres in the Old Spanish Corpus from 13th to 16th century.

4.2 Gold Standard Corpus

A *Gold Standard Corpus* has been created in order to retrain the tagger and to carry out the evaluation and the error analysis. This corpus consists of 30,000 tokens which have been pre-annotated with the Standard Spanish tagger and manually corrected. Texts composing the Gold Standard Corpus have been selected from the Old Spanish Corpus so as to mirror the data in the whole corpus as far as possible. The token distribution of the Gold Standard Corpus is shown in the second row of Table 1, and the distribution of text types in the second row of Table 2.

4.3 Standard Spanish Corpus

A *Standard Spanish Corpus* has been used to establish a baseline performance for the tagger, namely, the *LexEsp* corpus (Sebastián et al., 2000), consisting of texts from 1975 to 1995 and totalling more than 5 million words. The corpus comprises a representative sample of the Spanish written variety in the 20th century (40% of the tokens in this corpus correspond to fiction, 20% science and didactics, and 40% different classes of press –sports, weekly magazines, and newspapers).

5 Method

The method proposed consists in using the existing Standard Spanish tool as a basis to create an Old Spanish processor to automatically enrich Old Spanish texts with lemma and morphosyntactic tag information. The adaptation of the existing Standard Spanish tool involves the expansion of the dictionary (section 5.1), the modification of other modules which are part of the library, such as the tokenization and the affixation modules (section 5.2), and the retraining of the tagger (section 5.3).

5.1 Dictionary expansion

Data. The Standard Spanish dictionary contains 556,210 words. This dictionary has been expanded with 32,015 new word forms, totalling more than 55,000 lemma-tag pairs, and thus increasing the number of word forms in the dictionary to 588,225. For example, the word form *y* in the expanded dictionary has 4 different lemma-tag pairs, corresponding to a coordinate conjunction, a noun, a pronoun, and an adverb, whereas in the Standard Spanish dictionary it has only 2 lemma-tag pairs, corresponding to the coordinate conjunction and noun uses. Table 3 illustrates the distribution of the categories of words which have been added to the dictionary. As could be expected from the general distribution of words across PoS categories, verbs and nouns account for more than half of the words added.

[8]The document in the 12th century data, belonging to poetry, is not represented in this graph because of its small size.

Corpus	12th c.	13th c.	14th c.	15th c.	16th c.	Total
Old Spanish	0.1	32.2	21.5	31.6	14.6	22,805,699
Gold Standard	4.5	31.3	35.1	20.5	8.6	30,000

Table 1: Size of the Old Spanish and the Gold Standard Corpus, respectively, in tokens (percentages over the *Total* column).

Corpus	Fiction	Law	Didactics	History	Society	Poetry	Science	Religion	Total
Old Spanish	22.4	21.8	18.5	17.5	6.3	6.6	3.6	3.3	22,805,699
Gold Standard	39.9	13.0	13.0	13.0	0.0	8.7	8.7	4.3	30,000

Table 2: Text type distribution in the Old Spanish and the Gold Standard Corpus, respectively, in tokens (percentages over the *Total* column).

Verbs	48.8%	Adverbs	0.4%
Nouns	20.8%	Determiners	0.3%
Adjectives	7.0%	Conjunctions	0.3%
Pronouns	0.6%	Interjections	0.2%
Prepositions	0.5%	Numbers	0.2%
		Punctuation	0.01%

Table 3: Distribution of words added to the dictionary.

Method. Two different types of mapping rules have been used in order to automatically generate the types of words to be added to the dictionary: substring rules and word rules. *Substring rules* map 54 sequences of characters from an old variant onto the corresponding standard variant. These mapping rules are based on the observed regularities in the spelling of Old Spanish texts (Sánchez-Prieto, 2005; Sánchez-Marco et al., 2010). These rules are independent of the morphophonological context, except that 18% of them are restricted to the beginning or the end of a word. Table 4 shows some examples of these rules. 81.4% of the types added to the dictionary have been generated using these rules. All words generated by this method are added to the dictionary if and only if they are contained in the corpus. This avoids the automatic generation of a very high number of variants.

Old	Modern	Example
euo	*evo*	*nueuo* → *nuevo* 'new'
uio	*vio*	*uio* → *vio* 'saw'

Table 4: Examples of the substring rules.

The remaining 18.5% of the types incorporated into the dictionary have been created using *word rules*. These are mappings from an old variant of a word to its corresponding standard variant (created manually), to deal with the most frequent types not covered by the substring rules, such as for instance words without an accent (*consul* → *cónsul* 'consul'), or other graphemic variants (*yglesia* → *iglesia* 'church', *catholica* → *católica* 'catholic').

5.2 Adapting other modules

The *tokenization* of some symbols has been customized, in order to deal with the particular characteristics of the original data, for instance to account for the fact that in most cases the letter *ç* is written in the texts of the *HSMS* as *c'*, and *ñ* as *n˜* (*yac'e* 'lay', *cin˜o* 'adhered'). Also, FreeLing analyzes forms not found in the dictionary through an *affixation* module that checks whether they are derived forms, such as adverbs ending in *-mente* or clitic pronouns (*-lo*, *-la*) attached to verbs. This module has also been adapted, incorporating Old Spanish clitics (*-gela*, *-li*) and other variants of derivation affixes (adverbs in *-mientre* or *-mjentre*).

5.3 Retraining the tagger

FreeLing includes 2 different modules able to perform PoS tagging: a hybrid tagger (*relax*), integrating statistical and hand-coded grammatical rules, and a Hidden Markov Model tagger (*hmm*), which is a classical trigram markovian tagger, based on TnT (Brants, 2000). As mentioned in Section 4, the tagger for Standard Spanish has been used to pre-annotate the Gold Standard Corpus, which has subsequently been corrected to be able to carry out the retraining. The effort of correcting the corpus is much lower compared to annotating from scratch. In this paper we present the evaluation of the performance of the extended resource using the *hmm* tagger with the probabilities generated automatically from the trigrams in the Gold Standard Corpus.

6 Evaluation

In this section we evaluate the dictionary (Section 6.1) and present the overall tagging results (Section 6.2). The resources for Standard Spanish have been used as a baseline.

6.1 Dictionary

In order to evaluate the expanded dictionary, we use three different measures: ambiguity, coverage, and accuracy and recall of automatically generated entries.

Ambiguity measures the average number of lemma-tag pairs per word form. To compute average ambiguity, each word form is assigned a score corresponding to the number of lemma-tag pairs in its dictionary entry. We have checked ambiguity in two different ways: (i) in the dictionary (type-based), (ii) in the corpus (token-based). *Coverage* measures the percentage of tokens in the corpus which are analysed by the dictionary. Uncovered or unknown words are those forms which are not included in the dictionary or analysed by the affixation module. We also evaluated the *precision* and *recall* of *automatically generated entries*, that is the percentage of correct words among those added to the dictionary by the substring rules,[9] and the percentage of the expected lemmas for those words actually added by the rules. Both measures have been obtained by checking a random sample of 512 types (corresponding to 2% of the types added with the substring rules). As only the words added to the dictionary are being evaluated, these measures have been obtained only over the Old Spanish dictionary.

The results of the evaluation are summarised in Table 5. As can be seen in this table, the Old Spanish Corpus is more ambiguous than the Standard Spanish Corpus, despite the fact that the dictionary is not (note that the 32,000 entries added are only a 5.8% increase in the Standard dictionary). The higher ambiguity in the corpus is probably due to the fact that many function words, such as the word *y* mentioned in section 5.1, have more entries in the expanded dictionary than in the Standard Spanish dictionary. The increase in ambiguity is also due to the large time span covered by the dictionary, as for instance forms that in the 13th century were lexical verbs and later changed to auxiliaries will bear both the old and the new morphosyntactic tag (*haber* changed its meaning from 'possess' or 'hold' to be the auxiliary in perfect tenses). Due to this increase in ambiguity, we can expect a higher number of errors due to ambiguity in Old Spanish than in Standard Spanish texts, as the tagger has more options to disambiguate in context and thus the overall error probability increases. As for coverage, 99.4% of the words in the Standard Spanish Corpus are covered by the Standard Spanish dictionary and affixation module. In contrast, 92.6% of the words in the Old Spanish Corpus are covered. If a word has no analysis, the probability assignment module tries to guess which are its possible PoS tags, based on the word ending. This also means that the adapted tool needs to guess the tag of a word more often, therefore increasing the number of potential errors.

As for precision, the lemmas and tags which have been automatically generated using substring rules and added to the dictionary achieve 99.2%. Only 0.8% of the lemmas and tags are incorrect. These are mostly cases either of Latin words (*sedeat*) or proper nouns (*maaçe*, *lameth*), which in any case are words not easily treated with automatic rules. Also in this evaluation sample, there are some incomplete entries, lacking 1 or more lemmas and tags. Cases of entries lacking some lemma (1.4% of the evaluation sample, yielding 98.6% recall) are proper nouns (*valenc'ia, thesis*), Latin words (*mjlites, euocat*), already incomplete entries in the Standard Spanish dictionary (*escanpado* 'cleared up'), and lemma-tag pairs not generated by any of the rules (*baiassen* 'went down'). Entries lacking some tags (5.3% of the evaluation sample, yielding 94.7% recall) are mostly cases of some verbal tenses, for example words in which the tag for the future or simple past is not included (*pessara* 'he will regret', *affronto* 'he faced'). The old variant typically lacks the diacritics,

[9] The word rules and manual mappings have not been evaluated, as they have been manually created.

	Old Spanish		Standard Spanish	
	Type-based	Token-based	Type-based	Token-based
Ambiguity	1.21	1.85	1.20	1.68
Coverage		92.6%		99.4%
Precision	99.2%			
Recall	98.6% (lemmas), 95% (PoS)			

Table 5: Evaluation of the dictionary.

so the morphosyntactic tag for the accented variants is not generated.

6.2 Tagging

In order to evaluate the performance of the tagger, the *accuracy* in the tagging of lemmas, PoS-1 (the whole label, containing detailed morphosyntactic information; 6 characters of the tag in total), and PoS-2 (word class; 1 character in total) has been checked. In all cases, this measure has been obtained as a result of a 5-fold cross-validation. As described in Section 5, the method proposed involves (a) adapting the dictionary and other modules, (b) retraining the tagger with Old Spanish texts. To assess the relative impact of these two adaptations, we report the results of evaluating the tagging under several conditions. To assess (a), we report two scores obtained using: (C0) original tools for Standard Spanish, and (C1) the expanded dictionary and other modules combined with the Standard Spanish tagger. To assess (b), and, specifically, the impact of the size of the tagger retraining corpus, we report the results of retraining the tagger with: (C2) 10,000-token, (C3) 20,000-token, and (C4) 30,000-token subsets of the Gold Standard Corpus, always using the expanded dictionary and other modules.

The accuracy scores obtained on the Gold Standard Corpus are summarised in Table 6. This table shows that in each of the conditions, the accuracy increases. As can be seen in Table 7, most of the improvements are significant at a 99% confidence level (χ^2 test, 1 d.f.). Exceptions are the lemma when comparing C2 and C1, and the lemma and tag when comparing C4 and C3, which do not obtain a significant improvement (not even at the 95% level).

The results indicate that both adapting the dictionary and other modules and retraining the tagger have a positive impact on the overall performance of the extended tool on Old Spanish texts. The factor that has the highest impact is the dictionary expansion (together with the adaptation of the tokenization and affixation modules), with improvements ranging from 13.6% for PoS-2 to 18.3% for lemma. However, retraining the tagger, even if it is with a small corpus, also pays off in terms of precision: With 30,000 words, the performance on PoS-identification increases from 91.0% to 94.5%. The best result with the full set of tags (PoS-1) is 89.0% and 94.5% for the main PoS.

To compare the Old Spanish and Standard Spanish taggers on the same basis, we retrained the FreeLing Standard Spanish tagger on a 30,000-token

	Lemma	PoS-1	PoS-2
C0	72.4	70.9	77.4
C1	90.7	86.0	91.0
C2	91.2	87.5	91.9
C3	92.3	89.5	93.7
C4	92.6	89.9	94.5
SS	99.1	94.0	97.6

Table 6: Accuracy obtained for lemma, PoS-1, and PoS-2 in the 5-fold cross-validation for the Old Spanish tagger on the Gold Standard Corpus (rows C0 to C4) and for Standard Spanish (row SS).

Condition	C0	C1	C2	C3
C1	l, p1, p2			
C2	l, p1, p2	p1, p2		
C3	l, p1, p2	l, p1, p2	l, p1, p2	
C4	l, p1, p2	l, p1, p2	l, p1, p2	p2

Table 7: Statistical significance in the tagging with the different conditions. If there is a statistically significant difference at a 99% confidence degree according to a χ^2 test with 1 d.f., *l* (for lemma), *p1* (for PoS-1), and *p2* (for PoS-2) are written.

fragment of the LexEsp corpus. The results for Standard Spanish, shown in the last row of Table 6, are still significantly higher (χ^2 test, 1 d.f., 99% conf. level) than those for the Old Spanish tagger: The accuracy over PoS-2 is 97.6%, 3 points higher than the 94.5% obtained for Old Spanish. The error analysis presented below shows the causes of these errors, giving clues as to how this performance could be improved.

7 Error analysis

The analysis of errors has been conducted over the 100 most frequent errors in tagging obtained with the Old Spanish tagger under condition C4. This analysis shows that most of the errors in the tagging are due to the ambiguity in the dictionary, as could be expected given the discussion in the previous section. Specifically, 90% of the errors corresponds to words for which the correct tag is available in the dictionary, but the tagger has not selected it. More than half of these errors (57.8%) are due to types which are also ambiguous in the Standard Spanish dictionary. The most frequent errors involve (i) function words such as determiner vs. clitic readings of *la, las* 'the/it' and relative pronoun vs. subordinating conjunction readings of *que* 'that', (ii) first and third person singular of verbal forms, which are homographs in Old Spanish (*queria* 'I|he wanted', *podia* 'I|he could'). The remaining 42.2% of the errors due to ambiguity are mostly words lacking the accent in Old Spanish. These are ambiguous verbal forms of the present and simple past (*llego* 'arrive|arrived'), pronouns (*que* 'what|that'), and adverbs (*mas* 'more|but'). Other errors correspond to types which were more ambiguous in Old Spanish, such as the already mentioned ambiguity for the coordinating conjunction (*y* 'and'). The 10% errors that are not due to ambiguity correspond to words which were not added by any of the methods used to expand the dictionary, mostly proper nouns (*pierres, antolinez*), but also other words not covered by any rule (*ovo* 'had', *coita* 'wish'). This low percentage shows that the dictionary expansion is quite thorough.

8 Discussion and future work

In this paper we have presented a method to extend an existing NLP tool in order to enable it to deal with historical varieties of a language. To our knowledge, this is the first time that such an strategy is pursued to automatically enrich Spanish historical texts with linguistic information. The modules for Standard Spanish of an existing tool, especially the dictionary and affixation modules, have been adapted using evidence from a large and representative Old Spanish corpus. Also the tagger has been retrained, using a 30,000-token Gold Standard Corpus. Thus, the tool for Standard Spanish has been extended, profiting from the similarity between the historical and standard varieties of Spanish, such that constructing a resource for Old Spanish required a relatively modest effort (around 6 person-months). As a result, we have obtained a reusable tool, which can be used to tag other corpora and be maintained and improved by other scholars.

The quality of the tagging is quite good: The tagger is able to correctly identify word lemmas in 92.6% of the cases, and in 94.5% the main PoS. The performance is still below the state-of-the-art for standard varieties of languages, and below the performance on a Corpus of Standard Spanish, but it is good enough to carry out quantitative analyses of historical data. We have shown that the lower performance is due to two factors: First, the increased ambiguity in the dictionary due to the large time span considered (the tool is able to tag texts from the 12th to the 16th centuries). Second, the small size of the training corpus. It is expected that the performance could improve by using the same methods to deal with PoS-disambiguation using context information in state-of-the-art tools. For instance, adding manual rules to the hybrid tagger included in FreeLing may improve the performance. Also, a spelling corrector could help solving the 10% of the errors which are not due to ambiguity but to orthographic variation.

The approach proposed could be followed to deal not only with historical varieties of languages, but also with other non-standard varieties, such as dialects or texts found in chats, blogs, or SMS texts. In the future, we will test it with so-called "Spanish 2.0".

Acknowledgments

This work is supported by the Ministry of Education and the Ministry of Science and Technology of Spain under contracts AP2006-03547 (FPU), FFI2010-15006 (OntoSem 2), TIN2009-14715-C04-04 (KNOW-II), and JCI2007-57-1479, and by the European Union via the EU PASCAL2 Network of Excellence (FP7-ICT-216886).

References

Alistair Baron and Paul Rayson. 2008. Vard 2: A tool for dealing with spelling variation in historical corpora. In *Proceedings of the Postgraduate Conference in Corpus Linguistics*, Birmingham, UK. Aston University.

Thorsten Brants. 2000. Tnt - a statistical part-of-speech tagger. In *Proceedings of the Sixth Applied Natural Language Processing Conference ANLP-2000*, Seattle, WA.

Ivy A. Corfis, John O'Neill, and Jr. Theodore S. Beardsley. 1997. *Early Celestina Electronic Texts and Concordances*. Hispanic Seminary of Medieval Studies, Ltd. Madison, Wisconsin.

Stefanie Dipper. 2010. Pos-tagging of historical language data: First experiments. In *emantic Approaches in Natural Language Processing: Proceedings of the Conference on Natural Language Processing (KONVENS 2010)*.

Andrea Ernst-Gerlach and Norbert Fuhr. 2007. Retrieval in text collections with historic spelling using linguistic and spelling variants. In *Proceedings of the 7th ACM IEEE Joint Conference on Digital Libraries (JCDL)*, Vancouver, British Columbia, Canada.

María Teresa Herrera and María Estela González de Fauve. 1997. *Concordancias Electrónicos del Corpus Médico Español*. Hispanic Seminary of Medieval Studies, Ltd. Madison, Wisconsin.

Llyod Kasten, John Nitti, and Wilhemina Jonxis-Henkemens. 1997. *The Electronic Texts and Concordances of the Prose Works of Alfonso X, El Sabio*. Hispanic Seminary of Medieval Studies, Ltd. Madison, Wisconsin.

Anke Lüdeling, Hagen Hirschmann, and Amir Zeldes. to appear. Variationism and underuse statistics in the analysis of the development of relative clauses in german. In Yuji Kawaguchi, Makoto Minegishi, and Wolfgang Viereck, editors, *Corpus Analysis and Diachronic Linguistics*. John Benjamins, Amsterdam.

John Nitti and Lloyd Kasten. 1997. *The Electronic Texts and Concordances of Medieval Navarro-Aragonese Manuscripts*. Hispanic Seminary of Medieval Studies, Ltd. Madison, Wisconsin.

John O'Neill. 1999. *Electronic Texts and Concordances of the Madison Corpus of Early Spanish Manuscripts and Printings*. Hispanic Seminary of Medieval Studies, Ltd. Madison, Wisconsin.

Lluís Padró, Miquel Collado, Samuel Reese, Marina Lloberes, and Irene Castellón. 2010. Freeling 2.1: Five years of open-source language processing tools. In *Proceedings of 7th Language Resources and Evaluation Conference (LREC 2010), ELRA, La Valletta*, Malta, May 2010.

Helena Raumolin-Brunberg and Terttu Nevalainen. 2007. The York-Toronto-Helsinki Parsed Corpus of Old English Prose. In J.C. Beal, K. P. Corrigan, and H. L. Moisl, editors, *Creating and Digitizing Language Corpora. Volume 2: Diachronic Databases*, pages 148–171. Palgrave Macmillan, Hampshire.

P. Rayson, D. Archer, A. Baron, and N. Smith. 2007. Tagging historical corpora - the problem of spelling variation. In *Proceedings of Digital Historical Corpora, Dagstuhl-Seminar 06491, International Conference and Research Center for Computer Science*, Schloss Dagstuhl, Wadern, Germany, 3rd-8th December 2006.

Eiríkur Rögnvaldsson and Sigrún Helgadóttir. 2008. Morphological tagging of old norse texts and its use in studying syntactic variation and change. In *2nd Workshop on Language Technology for Cultural Heritage Data, LREC 2008 workshop*, Marrakech.

Eyal Sagi, Stefan Kaufmann, and Brady Clark. 2009. Semantic density analysis: Comparing word meaning across time and phonetic space. In Roberto Basili and Marco Pennacchiotti, editors, *Proceedings of the EACL 2009 Workshop on GEMS: GEometrical Models of Natural Language Semantics*, Athens.

Cristina Sánchez-Marco, Gemma Boleda, Josep Maria Fontana, and Judith Domingo. 2010. Annotation and representation of a diachronic corpus of spanish. In *Proceedings of Language Resources and Evaluation (LREC)*, Malta, May 2010.

Pedro Sánchez-Prieto. 2005. La normalización del castellano escrito en el siglo xiii. Los caracteres de la lengua: grafías y fonemas. In Rafael Cano, editor, *Historia de la lengua española*, pages 199–213. Ariel, Barcelona.

Núria Sebastián, M. Antònia Martí, Manuel Francisco Carreiras, and Fernando Cuetos. 2000. *Léxico informatizado del español*. Edicions Universitat de Barcelona, Barcelona.

Ann Taylor. 2007. The York-Toronto-Helsinki Parsed Corpus of Old English Prose. In J.C. Beal, K. P. Corrigan, and H. L. Moisl, editors, *Creating and Digitizing Language Corpora. Volume 2: Diachronic Databases*, pages 196–227. Palgrave Macmillan, Hampshire.

A Low-budget Tagger for Old Czech

Jirka Hana
Charles University, MFF
Czech Republic
first.last@gmail.com

Anna Feldman
Montclair State University
USA
first.last@montclair.edu

Katsiaryna Aharodnik
Montclair State University
USA
ogorodnichek@gmail.com

Abstract

The paper describes a tagger for Old Czech (1200-1500 AD), a fusional language with rich morphology. The practical restrictions (no native speakers, limited corpora and lexicons, limited funding) make Old Czech an ideal candidate for a resource-light cross-lingual method that we have been developing (e.g. Hana et al., 2004; Feldman and Hana, 2010).

We use a traditional supervised tagger. However, instead of spending years of effort to create a large annotated corpus of Old Czech, we approximate it by a corpus of Modern Czech. We perform a series of simple transformations to make a modern text look more like a text in Old Czech and vice versa. We also use a resource-light morphological analyzer to provide candidate tags. The results are worse than the results of traditional taggers, but the amount of language-specific work needed is minimal.

1 Introduction

This paper describes a series of experiments in an attempt to create morphosyntactic resources for Old Czech (OC) on the basis of Modern Czech (MC) resources. The purpose of this work is two-fold. The practical goal is to create a morphologically annotated corpus of OC which will help in investigation of various morphosyntactic patterns underpinning the evolution of Czech. Our second goal is more theoretical in nature. We wanted to test the resource-light cross-lingual method that we have been developing (e.g. Hana et al., 2004; Feldman and Hana, 2010) on a source-target language pair that is divided by time instead of space. The practical restrictions (no native speakers, limited corpora and lexicons, limited funding) make OC an ideal candidate for a resource-light approach.

We understand that the task we chose is hard given the 500+ years of language evolution. We are aware of the fact that all layers of the language have changed, including phonology and graphemics, syntax and vocabulary. Even words that are still used in MC are often used with different distributions, with different declensions, with different gender, etc.

Our paper is structured as follows. We first briefly describe related work and motivate our approach. Then we outline the relevant aspects of the Czech language and compare its Modern and Old forms. Then we describe the corpora and tagsets used in our experiments. The rest of the paper describes the actual experiments, the performance of various models and concludes with a discussion of the results.

2 Related Work

Since there are no morphological taggers developed specifically for OC, we compare our work with those for MC. Morče (`http://ufal.mff.cuni.cz/morce/`) is currently the best tagger, with accuracy slightly above 95%. It is based on a statistical (averaged perceptron) algorithm which relies on a large morphological lexicon containing around 300K entries. The tool has been trained and tuned on data from the Prague Dependency Treebank (PDT; Bémova et al., 1999; Böhmová et al., 2001). The best set of features was selected after hundreds of experiments were performed. In contrast, the resource-light system we developed is not as accurate, but the amount of language-specific work needed is incomparable to that of the state-of-the-art systems. Language specific work on our OC tagger, for example, was completed in about 20 hours, instead of several years.

Research in resource-light learning of morphosyntactic properties of languages is not new. Some have assumed only partially tagged training corpora (Merialdo, 1994); some have begun with small tagged seed wordlists (Cucerzan and Yarowsky, 2002) for named-entity tagging, while others have exploited the automatic transfer of an already existing annotated resource in a different genre or a different language (e.g. cross-language projection of morphological and syntactic information as in (Cucerzan and Yarowsky, 2000; Yarowsky et al., 2001), requiring no direct supervision in the target language). The performance of our system is comparable to the results cited by these researchers.

In our work we wanted to connect to pre-existing knowledge that has been acquired and systematized by traditional linguists, e.g. morphological paradigms, sound changes, and other well-established facts about MC and OC.

3 Czech Language

Czech is a West Slavic language with significant influences from German, Latin and (in modern times) English. It is a fusional (flective) language with rich morphology and a high degree of homonymy of endings.

3.1 Old Czech

As a separate language, Czech forms between 1000-1150 AD; there are very few written documents from that time. The term Old Czech usually refers to Czech roughly between 1150 and 1500. It is followed by Humanistic Czech (1500-1650), Baroque Czech (1650-1780) and then Czech of the so-called National Revival. Old Czech was significantly influenced by Old Church Slavonic, Latin and German. Spelling during this period was not standardized, therefore the same word can have many different spelling variants. However, our corpus was transliterated – its pronunciation was recorded using the rules of the Modern Czech spelling (see Lehečka and Voleková, 2011, for more details).

change	example	
ú > *ou* non-init.	*múka* > *mouka*	'flour'
sě > *se*	*sěno* > *seno*	'hay'
ó > *uo* > *ů*	*kóň* > *kuoň* > *kůň*	'horse'
šč > *šť*	*ščír* > *štír*	'scorpion'
čs > *c*	*čso* > *co*	'what'

Table 1: Examples of sound/spelling changes from OC to MC

3.2 Modern Czech

Modern Czech is spoken by roughly 10 million speakers, mostly in the Czech Republic. For a more detailed discussion, see for example (Naughton, 2005; Short, 1993; Janda and Townsend, 2002; Karlík et al., 1996). For historical reasons, there are two variants of Czech: Official (Literary, Standard) Czech and Common (Colloquial) Czech. The official variant is based on the 19th-century resurrection of the 16th-century Czech. Sometimes it is claimed, with some exaggeration, that it is the first foreign language the Czechs learn. The differences are mainly in phonology, morphology and lexicon. The two variants are influencing each other, resulting in a significant amount of irregularity, especially in morphology. The Czech writing system is mostly phonological.

3.3 Differences

Providing a systematic description of differences between Old and Modern Czech is well beyond the scope of this paper. Therefore, we just briefly mention a few illustrative examples. For a more detailed description see (Vážný, 1964; Dostál, 1967; Mann, 1977).

3.3.1 Phonology and Spelling

Examples of some of the more regular changes between OC and MC spelling can be found in Table 1 (Mann (1977), Boris Lehečka p.c.).

3.3.2 Nominal Morphology

The nouns of OC have three genders: feminine, masculine, and neuter. In declension they distinguish three numbers: singular, plural, and dual, and seven cases: nominative, genitive, dative, accusative, vocative, locative and instrumental. Voca-

category		Old Czech	Modern Czech
infinitive		péc-i	péc-t 'bake'
present	1sg	pek-u	peč-u
	1du	peč-evě	–
	1pl	peč-em(e/y)	peč-eme
	⋮		
imperfect	1sg	peč-iech	–
	1du	peč-iechově	–
	1pl	peč-iechom(e/y)	–
	⋮		
imperative	2sg	pec-i	peč
	2du	pec-ta	–
	2pl	pec-te	peč-te
	⋮		
verbal noun		peč-enie	peč-ení

Table 2: A fragment of the conjugation of the verb *péci/péct* 'bake' (OC based on (Dostál, 1967, 74-77))

tive is distinct only for some nouns and only in singular.

MC nouns preserved most of the features of OC, but the dual number survives only in a few paired names of parts of the body, in the declensions of the words "two" and "both" and in the word for "two hundred". In Common Czech the dual plural distinction is completely neutralized. On the other hand, MC distinguishes animacy in masculine gender, while this distinction is only emerging in late OC.

3.3.3 Verbal Morphology

The system of verbal forms and constructions was far more elaborate in OC than in MC. Many forms disappeared all together (three simple past tenses, supinum), and some are archaic (verbal adverbs, plusquamperfectum). Obviously, all dual forms are no longer in MC. See Table 2 for an example.

4 Corpora

4.1 Modern Czech Corpus

Our MC *training* corpus is a portion (700K tokens) of PDT. The corpus contains texts from daily newspapers, business and popular scientific magazines. It is manually morphologically annotated.

The tagset (Hajič (2004)) has more than 4200 tags encoding detailed morphological information. It is a positional tagset, meaning the tags are sequences of values encoding individual morphological features and all tags have the same length, encoding all the features distinguished by the tagset. Features not applicable for a particular word have a N/A value. For example, when a word is annotated as `AAFS4----2A----` it is an adjective (`A`), long form (`A`), feminine (`F`), singular (`S`), accusative (`4`), comparative (`2`), not-negated (`A`).

4.2 Old Czech Corpora

Several steps (e.g., lexicon acquisition) of our method require a plain text corpus. We used texts from the Old-Czech Text Bank (STB, `http://vokabular.ujc.cas.cz/banka.aspx`), in total about 740K tokens. This is significantly less than we have used in other experiments (e.g., 39M tokens for Czech or 63M tokens for Catalan (Feldman and Hana, 2010)).

A small portion (about 1000 words) of the corpus was manually annotated for testing purposes. Again this is much less than what we would like to have, and we plan to increase the size in the near future. The tagset is a modification of the modern tagset using the same categories.

5 Method

The main assumption of our method (Feldman and Hana, 2010) is that a model for the target language can be approximated by language models from one or more related source languages and that inclusion of a limited amount of high-impact and/or low-cost manual resources is greatly beneficial and desirable.

We use TnT (Brants, 2000), a second order Markov Model tagger. The language model of such a tagger consists of emission probabilities (corresponding to a lexicon with usage frequency information) and transition probabilities (roughly corresponding to syntax rules with strong emphasis on local word-order). We approximate the emission and transition probabilities by those trained on a modified corpus of a related language. Below, we describe our approach in more detail.

6 Experiments

We describe three different taggers:

1. a TnT tagger using modified MC corpus as a source of both transition and emission probabilities (section 6.1);

2. a TnT tagger using modern transitions but approximating emissions by a uniformly distributed output of a morphological analyzer (MA) (sections 6.2 and 6.3); and

3. a combination of both (section 6.4).

6.1 Translation Model

6.1.1 Modernizing OC and Aging MC

Theoretically, we can take the MC corpus, translate it to OC and then train a tagger, which would probably be a good OC tagger. However, we do not need this sophisticated, costly translation because we only deal with morphology.

A more plausible idea is to modify the MC corpus so that it looks more like the OC just in the aspects relevant for morphological tagging. In this case, the translation would include the tagset, reverse phonological/graphemic changes, etc. Unfortunately, even this is not always possible or practical. For example, historical linguists usually describe phonological changes from old to new, not from new to old.[1] In addition, it is not possible to deterministically translate the modern tagset to the older one. So, we modify the MC training corpus to look more like the OC corpus (the process we call 'aging') and also the target OC corpus to look more like the MC corpus ('modernizing').

6.1.2 Creating the Translation Tagger

Below we describe the process of creating a tagger. As an example we discuss the details for the *Translation* tagger. Figure 1 summarizes the discussion.

1. Aging the MC training (annotated) corpus:

   - MC to OC tag translation:
     Dropping animacy distinction (OC did not distinguish animacy).

   - Simple MC to OC form transformations:
     E.g., modern infinitives end in *-t*, OC infinitives ended in *-ti*;
     (we implemented 3 transformations)

2. Training an MC tagger. The tagger is trained on the result of the previous step.

3. Modernizing an OC plain corpus. In this step we modernize OC forms by applying sound/graphemic changes such as those in Table 1. Obviously, these transformations are not without problems. First, the OC-to-MC translations do not always result in correct MC forms; even worse, they do not always provide forms that ever existed. Sometimes these transformations lead to forms that do exist in MC, but are unrelated to the source form. Nevertheless, we think that these cases are true exceptions from the rule and that in the majority of cases, these OC translated forms will result in existing MC words and have a similar distribution.

4. Tagging. The modernized corpus is tagged with the aged tagger.

5. Reverting modernizations. Modernized words are replaced with their original forms. This gives us a tagged OC corpus, which can be used for training.

6. Training an OC tagger. The tagger is trained on the result of the previous step. The result of this training is an OC tagger.

The results of the translation model are provided in Tables 3 (for each individual tag position) and 4 (across various POS categories). What is evident from these numbers is that the Translation tagger is already quite good at predicting the POS, subPOS and number categories. The most challenging POS category is the category of verbs and the most difficult feature is case. Based on our previous experience with other fusional languages, getting the case feature right is always challenging. Even though case participates in syntactic agreement in both OC and MC, this category is more idiosyncratic than, say, person or tense. Therefore, the MC syntactic and lexical information provided by the translation

[1] Note that one cannot simply reverse the rules, as in general, the function is not a bijection.

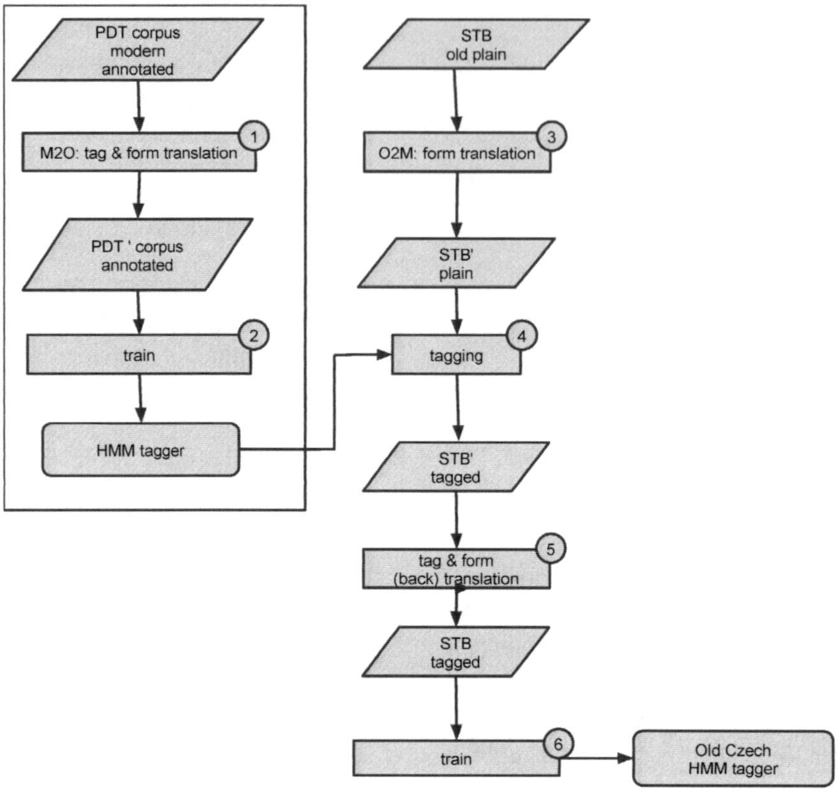

Figure 1: Schema of the Translation Tagger

model might not be sufficient to compute case correctly. One of the solutions that we explore in this paper is approximating the OC lexical distribution by the resource-light morphological analyzer (see section 6.3).

While most nominal forms and their morphological categories (apart from dual) survived in MC, OC and MC departed in verbs significantly. Thus, for example, three OC tenses disappeared in MC and other tenses replaced them. These include the OC two aorists, supinum and imperfectum. The transgressive forms are almost not used in MC anymore either. Instead MC has periphrastic past, periphrastic conditional and also future. In addition, these OC verbal forms that disappeared in MC are unique and non-ambiguous, which makes it even more difficult to guess if the model is trained on the MC data. The tagger, in fact, has no way of providing the right answer. In the subsequent sections we use a morphological analyzer to address this problem. Our morphological analyzer uses very basic hand-encoded facts about the target language.

6.2 Resource-light Morphological Analysis

The *Even* tagger described in the following section relies on a morphological analyzer. While it can use any analyzer, to stay within a resource light paradigm, we have used our resource-light analyzer (Hana, 2008; Feldman and Hana, 2010). Our approach to morphological analysis (Hana, 2008) takes the middle road between completely unsupervised systems on the one hand and systems with extensive manually-created resources on the other. It exploits Zipf's law (Zipf, 1935, 1949): not all words and morphemes matter equally. A small number of words are extremely frequent, while most words are rare. For example, in PDT, 10% most frequent noun lemmas cover about 75% of all noun tokens in the corpus. On the other hand, the less frequent 50% of noun lemmas cover only 5% of all noun tokens.

Therefore, in our approach, those resources that are easy to provide and that matter most are created

Tags:	70.6
Position 0 (POS):	91.5
Position 1 (SubPOS):	88.9
Position 2 (Gender):	87.4
Position 3 (Number):	91.0
Position 4 (case):	82.6
Position 5 (PossGen):	99.5
Position 6 (PossNr):	99.5
Position 7 (person):	93.2
Position 8 (tense):	94.4
Position 9 (grade):	98.0
Position 10 (negation):	94.4
Position 11 (voice):	95.9

Table 3: Accuracy of the Translation Model on individual positions (in %).

All	Full:	70.6
	SubPOS	88.9
Nouns	Full	63.1
	SubPOS	99.3
Adjs	Full:	60.3
	SubPos	93.7
Verbs	Full	47.8
	SubPOS	62.2

Table 4: Performance of the Translation Model on major POS categories (in %).

manually or semi-automatically and the rest is acquired automatically. For more discussion see (Feldman and Hana, 2010).

Structure The system uses a cascade of modules. The general strategy is to run "sure thing" modules (ones that make fewer errors and that overgenerate less) before "guessing" modules that are more error-prone and given to overgeneration. Simplifying somewhat the current system for OC contains the following three levels:

1. Word list – a list of 250 most frequent OC words accompanied with their possible analyses. Most of these words are closed class.

2. Lexicon-based analyzer – the lexicon has been automatically acquired from a plain corpus using the knowledge of manually provided information about paradigms (see below).

3a. Guesser – this module analyzes words relying purely on the analysis of possible endings and their relations to the known paradigms. Thus the English word *goes* would be analyzed not only as a verb, but also as plural of the potential noun *goe*, as a singular noun (with the presumed plural *goeses*), etc. In Slavic languages the situation is complicated by high incidence of homonymous endings. For example, the Modern Czech ending *a* has 14 different analyses (and that assumes one knows the morpheme boundary).

Obviously, the guesser has low precision, and fails to use all kinds of knowledge that it potentially could use. Crucially, however, it has high recall, so it can be used as a safety net when the more precise modules fail. It is also used during lexicon acquisition, another context where its low precision turns out not to be a major problem.

3b. Modern Czech word list – a simple analyzer of Modern Czech; for some words this module gives the correct answer (e.g., *svátek* 'holiday', some proper names).

The total amount of language-specific work needed to provide OC data for the analyzer (information about paradigms, analyses of frequent forms) is about 12 hours and was done by a non-linguist on the basis of (Vážný, 1964; Dostál, 1967).

The results of the analyzer are summarized in Table 5. They show a similar pattern to the results we have obtained for other fusional languages. As can be seen, morphological analysis without any filters (the first two columns) gives good recall but also very high average ambiguity. When the automatically acquired lexicon and the longest-ending filter (analyses involving the longest endings are preferred) are used, the ambiguity is reduced significantly but recall drops as well. As with other languages, even for OC, it turns out that the drop in recall is worth the ambiguity reduction when the results are used by our MA-based taggers. Moreover, as we mentioned in the previous section, the tagger based purely on the MC corpus has no chance on verbal forms that disappeared from the language completely.

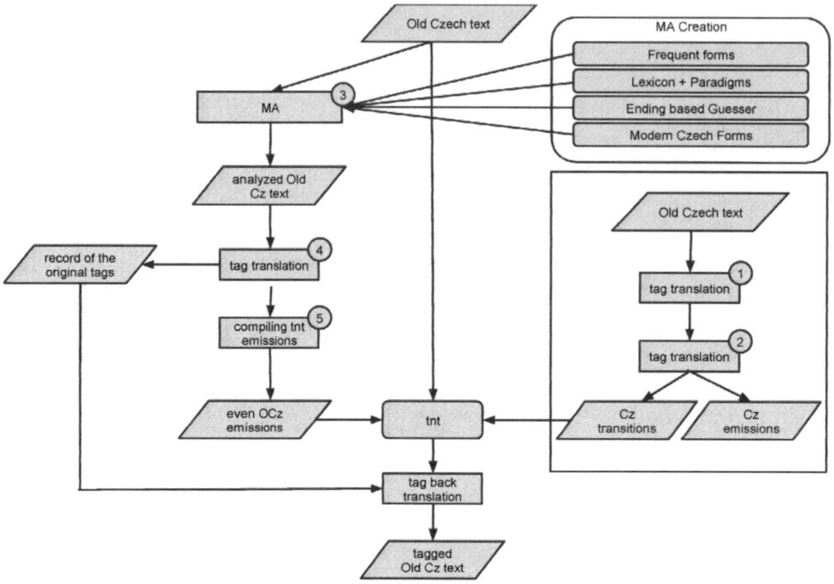

Figure 2: Schema of the MA Based Even Tagger

Lexicon & leo	no		yes	
	Recall	Ambi	Recall	Ambi
Overall	96.9	14.8	91.5	5.7
Nouns	99.9	26.1	83.9	10.1
Adjectives	96.8	26.5	96.8	8.8
Verbs	97.8	22.1	95.6	6.2

Table 5: Evaluation of the morphological analyzer on Old Czech

All	Full:	67.7
	SubPOS	87.0
Nouns	Full	44.3
	SubPOS	88.6
Adjs	Full:	50.8
	SubPos	87.3
Verbs	Full	74.4
	SubPOS	78.9

Table 6: Performance of the Even Tagger on major POS categories (in %)

6.3 Even Tagger

The *Even* tagger (see Figure 2) approximates emissions by using the output of the morphological analyzer described in the previous section.

The transition probabilities are based on the Aged Modern Czech corpus (result of step 2 of Figure 1). This means that the transitions are produced during the training phase and are independent of the tagged text. However, the emissions are produced by the morphological analyzer on the basis of the tagged text during tagging. The reason why the model is called *Even* is that the emissions are distributed evenly (uniformly; which is a crude approximation of reality).

The overall performance of the Even tagger drops down, but it improves on verbs significantly. Intuitively, this seems natural, because there is a relatively small homonymy among many OC verbal endings (see Table 2 for an example) so they are predicted by the morphological analyzer with low or even no ambiguity.

6.4 Combining the Translation and Even Taggers

The *TranslEven* tagger is a combination of the Translation and Even models. The Even model clearly performs better on the verbs, while the Translation model predicts other categories much better. So, we decided to combine the two models in the following way. The Even model predicts verbs, while the Translation model predicts the other categories. The TranslEven Tagger gives us a better overall performance and improves the prediction on each individual position of the tag. Unfortunately, it slightly reduces the performance on nouns (see Tables 7 and 8).

All	Full:	74.1
	SubPOS	90.6
Nouns	Full	57.0
	SubPOS	91.3
Adjs	Full:	60.3
	SubPos	93.7
Verbs	Full	80.0
	SubPOS	86.7

Table 7: Performance of the TranslEven tagger on major POS categories (in %)

Full tags:	74.1
Position 0 (POS):	93.0
Position 1 (SubPOS):	90.6
Position 2 (Gender):	89.6
Position 3 (Number):	92.5
Position 4 (case):	83.6
Position 5 (PossGen):	99.5
Position 6 (PossNr):	94.9
Position 7 (person):	94.9
Position 8 (tense):	95.6
Position 9 (grade):	98.6
Position 10 (negation):	96.1
Position 11 (voice):	96.4

Table 8: Performance of the TranslEven tagger on individual positions (in %).

7 Discussion

We have described a series of experiments to create a tagger for OC. Traditional statistical taggers rely on large amounts of training (annotated) data. There is no realistic prospect of annotation for OC. The practical restrictions (no native speakers, limited corpora and lexicons, limited funding) make OC an ideal candidate for a resource-light cross-lingual method that we have been developing. OC and MC departed significantly over the 500+ years, at all language layers, including phonology, syntax and vocabulary. Words that are still used in MC are often used with different distributions and have different morphological forms from OC.

Additional difficulty of this task arises from the fact that our MC and OC corpora belong to different genres. While the OC corpus includes poetry, cookbooks, medical and liturgical texts, the MC corpus is mainly comprised of newspaper texts. We cannot possibly expect a significant overlap in lexicon or syntactic constructions. For example, the cookbooks contain a lot of imperatives and second person pronouns which are rare or non-existent in the newspaper texts.

Even though our tagger does not perform as the state-of-the-art tagger for Czech, the results are already useful. Remember that the tag is a combination of 12 morphological features and if only one of them is incorrect, the whole positional tag is marked as incorrect. So, the performance of the tagger (74%) on the whole tag is not as low in reality. For example, if one is only interested in detailed POS information (the tagset that roughly corresponds to the English Penn Treebank tagset in size), the performance of our system is over 90%.

Acknowledgments

This research was generously supported by the Grant Agency Czech Republic (project ID: P406/10/P328) and by the U.S. NSF grants #0916280, #1033275, and #1048406. We would like to thank Alena M. Černá and Boris Lehečka for annotating the testing corpus and for answering questions about Old Czech. We also thank Institute of Czech Language of the Academy of Sciences of the Czech Republic for the plain text corpus of Old Czech. Finally, we thank anonymous reviewers for their insightful comments. All mistakes are ours.

References

Bémova, A., J. Hajic, B. Hladká, and J. Panevová (1999). Morphological and Syntactic Tagging of the Prague Dependency Treebank. In *Proceedings of ATALA Workshop*, pp. 21–29. Paris, France.

Böhmová, A., J. Hajic, E. Hajičová, and B. Hladká (2001). The Prague Dependency Treebank: Three-Level Annotation Scenario. In A. Abeillé (Ed.), *Treebanks: Building and Using Syntacti-*

cally Annotated Corpora. Kluwer Academic Publishers.

Brants, T. (2000). TnT – A Statistical Part-of-Speech Tagger. In *Proceedings of ANLP-NAACL*, pp. 224–231.

Cucerzan, S. and D. Yarowsky (2000). Language Independent Minimally Supervised Induction of Lexical Probabilities. In *Proceedings of the 38th Meeting of the Association for Computational Linguistics (ACL)*, Hong Kong, pp. 270–277.

Cucerzan, S. and D. Yarowsky (2002). Bootstrapping a Multilingual Part-of-speech Tagger in One Person-day. In *Proceedings of the 6th Conference on Natural Language Learning (CoNLL)*, pp. 132–138. Taipei, Taiwan.

Dostál, A. (1967). *Historická mluvnice česká II – Tvarosloví. 2. Časování [Historical Czech Grammar II - Morphology. 2. Conjugation]*. Prague: SPN.

Feldman, A. and J. Hana (2010). *A resource-light approach to morpho-syntactic tagging*. Amsterdam/New York, NY: Rodopi.

Hajič, J. (2004). *Disambiguation of Rich Inflection: Computational Morphology of Czech*. Praha: Karolinum, Charles University Press.

Hana, J. (2008). Knowledge- and labor-light morphological analysis. *OSUWPL 58*, 52–84.

Hana, J., A. Feldman, and C. Brew (2004, July). A resource-light approach to Russian morphology: Tagging Russian using Czech resources. In D. Lin and D. Wu (Eds.), *Proceedings of EMNLP 2004*, Barcelona, Spain, pp. 222–229. Association for Computational Linguistics.

Janda, L. A. and C. E. Townsend (2002). Czech.

Karlík, P., M. Nekula, and Z. Rusínová (1996). *Příruční mluvnice češtiny [Concise Grammar of Czech]*. Praha: Nakladatelství Lidové Noviny.

Lehečka, B. and K. Voleková (2011). (polo)automatická počítačová transkripce [(semi)automatic computational transcription]. In *Proceedings of the Conference Dějiny českého pravopisu (do r. 1902) [History of the Czech spelling (before 1902)]*. in press.

Mann, S. E. (1977). *Czech Historical Grammar*. Hamburg: Buske.

Merialdo, B. (1994). Tagging English Text with a Probabilistic Model. *Computational Linguistics 20*(2), 155–171.

Naughton, J. (2005). *Czech: An Essential Grammar*. Oxon, Great Britain and New York, NY, USA: Routledge.

Short, D. (1993). Czech. In B. Comrie and G. G. Corbett (Eds.), *The Slavonic Languages*, Routledge Language Family Descriptions, pp. 455–532. Routledge.

Vážný, V. (1964). *Historická mluvnice česká II – Tvarosloví. 1. Skloňování [Historical Czech Grammar II - Morphology. 1. Declension]*. Prague: SPN.

Yarowsky, D., G. Ngai, and R. Wicentowski (2001). Inducing Multilingual Text Analysis via Robust Projection across Aligned Corpora. In *Proceedings of the First International Conference on Human Language Technology Research (HLT)*, pp. 161–168.

Zipf, G. K. (1935). *The Psychobiology of Language*. Houghton-Mifflin.

Zipf, G. K. (1949). *Human Behavior and the Principle of Least-Effort*. Addison-Wesley.

Evaluating an 'off-the-shelf' POS-tagger on Early Modern German text

Silke Scheible, Richard J. Whitt, Martin Durrell and **Paul Bennett**
School of Languages, Linguistics, and Cultures
University of Manchester
Silke.Scheible, Richard.Whitt@manchester.ac.uk
Martin.Durrell, Paul.Bennett@manchester.ac.uk

Abstract

The goal of this study is to evaluate an 'off-the-shelf' POS-tagger for modern German on historical data from the Early Modern period (1650-1800). With no specialised tagger available for this particular stage of the language, our findings will be of particular interest to smaller, humanities-based projects wishing to add POS annotations to their historical data but which lack the means or resources to train a POS tagger themselves. Our study assesses the effects of spelling variation on the performance of the tagger, and investigates to what extent tagger performance can be improved by using 'normalised' input, where spelling variants in the corpus are standardised to a modern form. Our findings show that adding such a normalisation layer improves tagger performance considerably.

1 Introduction

The work described in this paper is part of a larger investigation whose goal is to create a representative corpus of Early Modern German from 1650-1800. The GerManC corpus, which is due to be completed this summer, was developed to allow for comparative studies of the development and standardisation of English and German in the 17th and 18th centuries. In order to facilitate corpus-linguistic investigations, one of the major goals of the project is to annotate the corpus with POS tags. However, no specialised tools are yet available for processing data from this period. The goal of this study is therefore to evaluate the performance of an 'off-the-shelf' POS-tagger for modern German on data from the Early Modern period, in order to assess if modern tools are suitable for a semi-automatic approach, and how much manual post-processing work would be necessary to obtain gold standard POS annotations.

We report on our results of running the TreeTagger (Schmid, 1994) on a subcorpus of GerManC containing over 50,000 tokens of text annotated with gold standard POS tags. This subcorpus is the first resource of its kind for this variant of German, and due to its complex structure it represents an ideal test bed for evaluating and adapting existing NLP tools on data from the Early Modern period. The study described in this paper represents a first step towards this goal. Furthermore, as spelling variants in our corpus have been manually normalised to a modern standard, this paper also aims to explore the extent to which tagger performance is affected by spelling variation, and to what degree performance can be improved by using 'normalised' input. Our findings promise to be of considerable interest to other current corpus-based projects of earlier periods of German (Jurish, 2010; Fasshauer, 2011; Dipper, 2010). Before presenting the results in Section 4, we describe the corpus design (Section 2), and the preprocessing steps necessary to create the gold standard annotations, including adaptations to the POS tagset (Section 3).

2 Corpus design

In order to be as representative of Early Modern German as possible, the GerManC corpus design considers three different levels. First, the corpus includes a range of text types: four orally-oriented genres (dramas, newspapers, letters, and sermons), and four print-oriented ones (narrative prose, and humanities, scientific, and legal texts). Secondly, in order to enable historical developments to be traced, the period is divided into three fifty year sections (1650-1700, 1700-1750, and 1750-1800). Finally, the corpus also aims to be representative with respect to region, including five broad areas: North German, West Central, East Central, West Upper (including Switzerland), and East Upper German (including Austria). Three extracts of around 2000 words were selected per genre, period, and region, yielding a corpus size of nearly a million words.

The experiments described in this paper were carried out on a manually annotated gold standard subcorpus of GerManC, GerManC-GS. The subcorpus was developed to enable an assessment of the suitability of existing NLP tools on historical data, with a view to adapting them to improve their performance. For this reason, GerManC-GS aims to be as representative of the main corpus as possible. However, to remain manageable in terms of annotation times and cost, the subcorpus only considers two of the three corpus variables, 'genre' and 'time', as they alone were found to display as much if not more variation than 'region'. GerManC-GS thus includes texts from the North German region, with one sample file per genre and time period. The corpus contains 57,845 tokens in total, and was annotated with gold standard POS tags, lemmas, and normalised word forms (Scheible et al., to appear).

3 Creating the gold standard annotations

This section provides an overview of the preprocessing work necessary to obtain the gold standard annotations in GerManC-GS. We used the GATE platform to produce the initial annotations, which facilitates automatic as well as manual annotation (Cunningham et al., 2002). First, GATE's German Language plugin[1] was used to obtain word tokens and sentence boundaries. The output was manually inspected and corrected by one annotator, who further added a layer of normalised spelling variants. This annotation layer was then used as input for the TreeTagger (Schmid, 1994), obtaining annotations in terms of POS tags and lemmas. All annotations were subsequently corrected by two annotators, and disagreements were reconciled to produce the gold standard.

3.1 Tokenisation

As German orthography was not yet codified in the Early Modern period, a number of specific decisions had to be made in respect of tokenisation. For example, clitics can occur in various non-standard forms. To allow for accurate POS tagging, clitics should be tokenised as separate items, similar to the negative particle *n't* in *can't* in English, which is conventionally tokenised as *ca|n't*. A case in point is *hastu*, a clitic version of *hast du* ('have you'), which we tokenise as *has|tu*. Furthermore, German '*to*-infinitive' verb forms are often directly appended to the infinitival marker *zu* without intervening whitespace (e.g. *zugehen* instead of *zu gehen*, 'to go'). Such cases are tokenised as separate forms (*zu|gehen*) to allow for their accurate tagging as *zu*/PTKZU *gehen*/VVINF.

A further problem can be found in multi-word tokens, where the same expression is sometimes treated as a compound (e.g. *obgleich*), but at other times written separately (*ob gleich*). Such cases represent a problem for POS-tagging as the variants have to be treated differently even though their function in the sentence is the same. Our tokenisation scheme deals with these in a similar way to normal conjunctions consisting of two words, where the most suitable tags are assigned to each token (e.g. *als*/KOKOM *wenn*/KOUS). Thus, the compound *obgleich* is tagged KOUS, while the multiword variant *ob gleich* is tagged as *ob*/KOUS *gleich*/ADV.

3.2 Normalising spelling variants

All spelling variants in GerManC-GS were normalised to a modern standard. We view the task of normalising spelling variation as a type of prelemmatisation, where each word token occurring in a text is labelled with a normalised head variant. As linguistic searches require a historically accurate treatment of spelling variation, our scheme has a preference for treating two seemingly similar tokens as separate items on historical grounds (e.g. *etwan* vs. *etwa*). On the other hand, the scheme normalises variants to a modernised form

[1] http://gate.ac.uk/sale/tao/splitch15.html

even where the given lexical item has since died out (e.g. obsolete verbs ending in *-iren* are normalised to *-ieren*), in order to support automatic tools using morphological strategies such as suffix probabilities (Schmid, 1994). Inter-annotator agreement for annotating spelling variation was 96.9%, which indicates that normalisation is a relatively easy task.

Figure 1 shows the proportion of normalised word tokens in the individual corpus files plotted against time. The graph clearly shows a decline of spelling variants over time: while the earlier texts contain 35-40% of normalised tokens, the proportion is lower in later texts (11.3% in 1790, and 5.4% in 1798). This suggests that by the end of the period (1800) codification of the German language was already at an advanced stage.

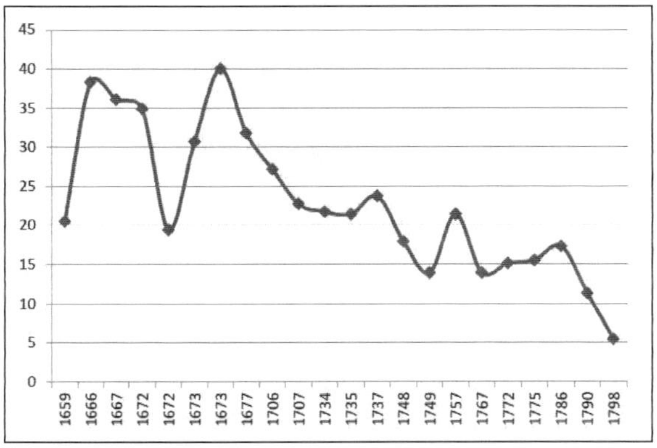

Figure 1: Proportion of normalised tokens (plotted against time)

3.3 Adapting the POS tagset (STTS)

To account for important differences between modern and Early Modern German (EMG), and to facilitate more accurate searches, we adapted the STTS tagset (Schiller et al., 1999). The STTS-EMG tagset merges two categories, as the criteria for distinguishing them are not applicable in EMG (1.), and provides a number of additional ones to account for special EMG constructions (2. to 6.):

1. **PIAT** (merged with **PIDAT**): Indefinite determiner, as in *'**viele solche** Bemerkungen'* (*'many such remarks'*)
2. **NA**: Adjectives used as nouns, as in *'der **Gesandte**'* (*'the ambassador'*)
3. **PAVREL**: Pronominal adverb used as relative, as in *'die Puppe, **damit** sie spielt'* (*'the doll with which she plays'*)
4. **PTKREL**: Indeclinable relative particle, as in *'die Fälle, **so** aus Schwachheit entstehen'* (*'the cases which arise from weakness'*)
5. **PWAVREL**: Interrogative adverb used as relative, as in *'der Zaun, **worüber** sie springt'* (*'the fence over which she jumps'*)
6. **PWREL**: Interrogative pronoun used as relative, as in *'etwas, **was** er sieht'* (*'something which he sees'*)

Around 2.0% (1132) of all tokens in the corpus were tagged with one of the above POS categories. Inter-annotator agreement for the POS tagging task was 91.6%.

4 'Off-the-shelf' tagger evaluation on Early Modern German data

The evaluation described in this section aims to complement the findings of Rayson et al. (2007) for Early Modern English, and a recent study by Dipper (2010), in which the TreeTagger is applied to a corpus of texts from Middle High German (MHG) - i.e. a period earlier than ours, from 1050-1350. Both studies report considerable improvement of POS-tagging accuracy on normalised data. However, unlike Dipper (2010), whose experiments involve retraining the TreeTagger on a modified version of STTS, our experiments assess the "off-the-shelf" performance of the modern tagger on historical data. We further explore the question of what effect spelling variation has on the performance of a tagger, and what improvement can be achieved when running the tool on normalised data.

Table 1 shows the results of running the TreeTagger on the original data vs. normalised data in our corpus using the parameter file for modern German supplied with the tagger[2]. The results show that while overall accuracy for running the tagger on the original input is relatively low at 69.6%, using the normalised tokens as input results in an overall improvement of 10% (79.7%).

[2]`http://www.ims.uni-stuttgart.de/projekte/corplex/TreeTagger/DecisionTreeTagger.html`

	O	N
Accuracy	69.6%	79.7%

Table 1: TreeTagger accuracy on original (O) vs. normalised (N) input

However, improvement through normalisation is not distributed evenly across the corpus. Figure 2 shows the performance curves of using TreeTagger on original (O) and normalised (N) input plotted against publication date. While both curves gradually rise over time, the improvement curve (measured as difference in accuracy between N and O) diminishes, a direct result of spelling variation being more prominent in earlier texts (cf. Figure 1).

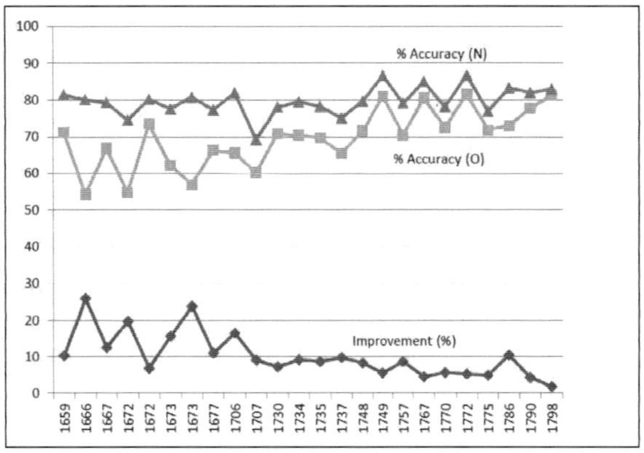

Figure 2: Tagger performance plotted against publication date

Compared with the performance of the TreeTagger on modern data (ca. 97%; Schmid, (1995)), the current results seem relatively low. However, two issues should be taken into account when interpreting these findings: First, the modern accuracy figures result from an evaluation of the tagger on the text type it was developed on (newspaper text), while GerManC-GS includes a variety of genres, which is bound to result in lower performance. Secondly, inter-annotator agreement was also found to be considerably lower in the present task (91.6%) than in one reported for modern German (98.6%; Brants, 2000a). This is likely to be due to the large number of unfamiliar word forms and variants in the corpus, which represent a problem for human annotators.

Finally, Figure 3 provides a more detailed overview of the effects of spelling variation on POS tagger performance. Of 12,744 normalised tokens in the corpus, almost half (5981; 47%) are only tagged correctly when using the normalised variants as input. Using the original word form as input results in a false POS tag in these cases. Overall, this accounts for an improvement of around 10.3% (5981 out of 57,845 tokens in the corpus). However, 32% (4119) of normalised tokens are tagged correctly using both N and O input, while 18% (2339) of tokens are tagged incorrectly using both types of input. This means that for 50% of all annotated spelling variants, normalisation has no effect on POS tagger performance. In a minority of cases (305; 3%) normalisation has a negative effect on tagger accuracy.

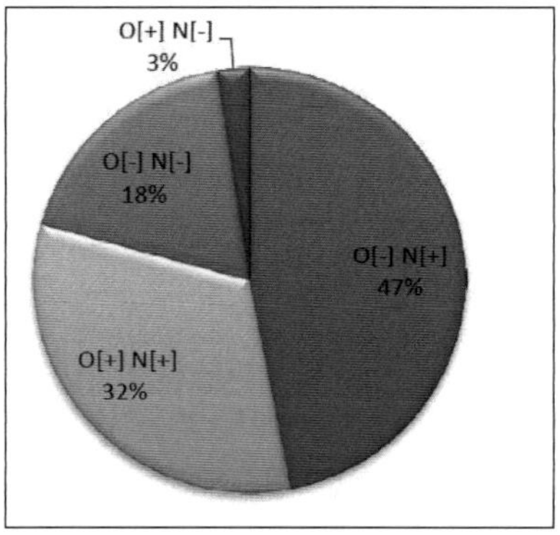

Figure 3: Effect of using original (O)/normalised (N) input on tagger accuracy for normalised tokens (+: correctly tagged; -: incorrectly tagged)

5 Conclusion and future work

The results of our study show that using an 'off-the shelf' German POS tagger on data from the Early Modern period achieves reasonable results (69.6% on average), but requires a substantial amount of manual post-editing. We further demonstrated that adding a normalisation layer can improve results by 10%. However, using the current manual normalisation scheme only half of all annotations carried out have a positive effect on tagger performance. In future work we plan to investigate if the scheme can be adapted to account for more cases, and to what extent normalisation can be reliably automated (Jurish, 2010). Finally, we plan to retrain state-of-the-art POS taggers such as the TreeTagger and TnT Tagger (Brants, 2000b) on our data and compare the results to the findings of this study.

References

Torsten Brants. 2000a. Inter-annotator agreement for a German newspaper corpus. *Second International Conference on Language Resources and Evaluation (LREC 2000), Athens, Greece.*

Torsten Brants. 2000b. TnT – a statistical part-of-speech tagger. *Proceedings of the 6th Applied NLP Conference, ANLP-2000, Seattle, WA.*

Hamish Cunningham, Diana Maynard, Kalina Bontcheva, and Valentin Tablan. 2002. GATE: A framework and graphical development environment for robust NLP tools and applications. *Proceedings of the 40th Anniversary Meeting of the Association for Computational Linguistics.*

Stefanie Dipper. 2010. POS-Tagging of historical language data: First experiments in semantic approaches in Natural Language Processing. *Proceedings of the 10th Conference on Natural Language Processing (KONVENS-10). Saarbrücken, Germany. 117-121.*

Vera Fasshauer. 2011. http://www.indogermanistik.uni-jena.de/index.php?auswahl=184
Accessed 30/03/2011.

Bryan Jurish. 2010. Comparing canonicalizations of historical German text. *Proceedings of the 11th Meeting of the ACL Special Interest Group on Computational Morphology and Phonology (SIGMORPHON), Uppsala, Sweden. 72-77.*

Paul Rayson, Dawn Archer, Alistair Baron, Jonathan Culpeper, and Nicholas Smith. 2007. Tagging the Bard: Evaluating the accuracy of a modern POS tagger on Early Modern English corpora. *Proceedings of the Corpus Linguistics Conference (CL2007), University of Birmingham, UK.*

Silke Scheible, Richard J. Whitt, Martin Durrell, and Paul Bennett. To appear. A Gold Standard Corpus of Early Modern German. *Proceedings of the Fifth Linguistic Annotation Workshop (LAW V), Portland, Oregon.*

Anne Schiller, Simone Teufel, Christine Stöckert, and Christine Thielen. 1999. Guidelines für das Tagging deutscher Textcorpora mit STTS. *Technical Report. Institut für maschinelle Sprachverarbeitung, Stuttgart.*

Helmut Schmid. 1994. Probabilistic part-of-speech tagging using decision trees. *International Conference on New Methods in Language Processing, Manchester, UK. 44–49.*

Helmut Schmid. 1995. Improvements in Part-of-Speech Tagging with an Application to German. *Proceedings of the ACL SIGDAT-Workshop. 47–50.*

e-Research for Linguists

Dorothee Beermann
Norwegian University of Science and Technology
Trondheim, Norway
dorothee.beermann@hf.ntnu.no

Pavel Mihaylov
Ontotext,
Sofia, Bulgaria
pavel@ontotext.com

Abstract

e-Research explores the possibilities offered by ICT for science and technology. Its goal is to allow a better access to computing power, data and library resources. In essence e-Research is all about cyberstructure and being connected in ways that might change how we perceive scientific creation. The present work advocates open access to scientific data for linguists and language experts working within the Humanities. By describing the modules of an online application, we would like to outline how a linguistic tool can help the linguist. Work with data, from its creation to its integration into a publication is not rarely perceived as a chore. Given the right tools however, it can become a meaningful part of the linguistic investigation. The standard format for linguistic data in the Humanities is Interlinear Glosses. As such they represent a valuable resource even though linguists tend to disagree about the role and the methods by which data should influence linguistic exploration (Lehmann, 2004). In describing the components of our system we focus on the potential that this tool holds for real-time data-sharing and continuous dissemination of research results throughout the life-cycle of a linguistic project.

1 Introduction

Within linguistics the management of research data has become of increasing interest. This is partially due to the growing number of linguists that feel committed to the documentation and preservation of endangered and minority languages (Rice, 1994). Modern approaches to Language Description and Documentation are not possible without the technology that allows the creation, retrieval and storage of diverse data types. A field whose main aim is to provide a **comprehensive** record of language constructions and rules (Himmelmann, 1998) is crucially dependent on software that supports the effort. Talking to the language documentation community Bird (2009) lists as some of the immediate tasks that linguists need help with; interlinearization of text, validation issues and, what he calls, the handling of uncertain data. In fact, computers always have played an important role in linguistic research. Starting out as machines that were able to increase the efficiency of text and data management, they have become tools that allow linguists to pursue research in ways that were not previously possible.[1] Given an increased interest in work with naturally occurring language, a new generation of search engines for online corpora have appeared with more features that facilitate a linguistic analysis (Biemann et al., 2004). The creation of annotated corpora from private data collections, is however, still mainly seen as a task that is only relevant to smaller groups of linguists and anthropologists engaged in Field Work. Shoebox/Toolbox is probably the oldest software especially designed for this user group.Together with the Fieldwork Language Explorer (FLEx), also devel-

[1] We would like to cite Tognini-Bonelli (2001) who speaks for corpus linguistics and (Bird, 2009) who discusses Natural Language Processing and its connection to the field of Language Documentation as sources describing this process.

oped by SIL[2], and ELAN[3] which helps with multimedia annotation, this group of applications is probably the best known set of linguistic tools specialised in supporting Field Linguists.

A central task for linguistic field workers is the interlinearization of text which is needed for the systematisation of hand-written notes and transcripts of audio material. The other central concern of linguists working with small and endangered languages is the creation of lexica. FLEx therefore integrates a lexicon (a word component), and a grammar (a text interlinearization component).

The system that is described here, assists with the creation of interlinear glosses. However, the focus is on data exchange and data excavation. Data from the Humanities, including linguistic data, is time-consuming to produce. However, in spite of the effort, this data is often not particularly reusable. Standardly it exists exclusively as an example in a publication. Glosses tend to be elementary and relative to a specific research question. Some grammatical properties are annotated but others that are essential for the understanding of the examples in isolation might have been left out, or are only mentioned in the surrounding text. Source information is rarely provided.

The tool presented in this paper tries to facilitate the idea of creating re-usable data gathered from standard linguistic practices, including collections reflecting the researcher's intuition and her linguistic competence, as well as data derived from directed linguistic interviews and discussions with other linguists or native speakers resulting in sentence collection derived from hand-written notes or transcripts of recordings. Different from natural language processing tools and on a par with other linguistic tools our target user group is "non-technologically oriented linguists" (Schmidt, 2010) who tend to work with small, noisy data collections.

2 General system description

Our tool consists of a relational database combined with a tabular text editor for the manual creation of text annotations wrapped into a wiki which serves as a general entrance port and collaboration tool. The system is loaded in a browser. The customised wiki serves as an access point to the database. Using standard wiki functionality we direct the user to the database via *New text*, *My texts*, and *Text- or Phrase search*. *My texts* displays the user's repository of annotations called 'Texts'. The notion of Text does not only refer to coherent texts, but to any collection of individual phrases. *My texts*, the user's private space, is divided into two sections: *Own texts* and *Shared texts*. This reflects the graded access design of the system. Users administer their own data in their private space, but they can also make use of other users' shared data. In addition texts can be shared within groups of users.[4]

Interlinear Glosses can be loaded to the systems wiki where they can be displayed publically or printed out as part of a customized wiki page. As an additional feature the exported data automatically updates when the natural language database changes.

Comparing the present tool with other linguistic tools without a RDBMS in the background, it seems that the latter tools falter when it comes to data queries. Although both the present system and FLEx share some features, technically they are quite distinct. FLEx is a single-user desktop system with a well designed integration of interlinear glossing and dictionary creation facilities (Rogers, 2010), while the present system is an online application for the creation of interlinear glosses specialised in the exchange of interlinear glosses. The system not only 'moves data around' easily, its *Interlinear Glosser*, described in the following section, makes also data creation easier. The system tries to utilise the effect of collaboration between individual users and linguistic resource integration to support the further standardisation of linguistic data. Our tag sets for word and morpheme glossing are rooted in the Leipzig Glossing Rules, but have been extended and connected to ontological grammatical information. In addition we offer sentence level annotations.

Glossing rules are conventional standards and one way to spread them is (a) to make already existing

[2]SIL today stands for *International Partners in Language Development*.

[3]http://www.lat-mpi.eu/tools/elan/

[4]At present data sets can only be shared with one pre-defined group of users at the time.

standards easily accessible at the point where they are actively used and (b) to connect the people engaged in e-Research to create a community. Glossing standards as part of linguistic research must be pre- defined, yet remain negotiable. Scientific data in the Humanities is mainly used for qualitative analysis and has an inbuilt factor of uncertainty, that is, linguists compare, contrast and analyse data where where uncertainty about the relation between actual occurring formatives and grammatical concepts is part of the research process and needs to be accommodated also by annotation tools and when it comes to standardisation.

2.1 Interlinear Glossing Online

After having imported a text into the Editor which is easily accessed from the site's navigation bar (*New text*), the text is run through a simple, but efficient sentence splitter. The user can then select via mouse click one of the phrases and in such a way enter into the annotation mode. The editor's interface is shown in Figure 1.

The system is designed for annotation in a multilingual setting. The user starts annotating by choosing the language for the text that she has loaded to the system from an integrated ISO-language list. Many languages of Africa are known under different names and it therefore is useful to find a direct link to the web version of Ethnologue, a SIL International resource. Ethnologue can for example help with identifying alternative language names and offers useful pointers to SIL publications. The present system distinguishes between different levels of annotation. Free translational glosses, standard for all interlinear glosses, and what we call construction descriptions are sentence level annotations; so is Global Tagging. These global tags can be selected in the form of eight construction parameters

Construction kernel: transitiveVerb, reflexiveVerb, multiplePredicate, transitiveObliqueVerb,...

Situation: causation, intention, communication, emotional-experienced, ...

Frame alternation: passive, middle, reflexive, passive+applicative, ...

Secondary predicates: infinitivial, free gerund, resultative,...

Discourse function: topicalisation, presentationals, rightReordering,...

Modality: deontic, episthemic, optative, realis, irrealis,...

Force: declarative, hortative, imperative, ...

Polarity: positive, negative

The field *Construction description* is meant for keeping notes, for example in those cases where the categorisation of grammatical units poses problems for the annotator. Meta data information is not entered using the Interlinear Glosser but the systems wiki where it is stored relative to texts. The texts can then fully or partially be loaded to the Interlinear Glosser. Using the wiki's Corpus namespace the user can import texts up to an individual size of 3500 words. We use an expandable Metadata template to prompt to user for the standard bibliographic information, as well as information about *Text type*, *Annotator* and *Contributor*. At present the corpus texts and the annotated data needs to be linked manually.

Word- and morpheme level annotation represents the centre piece of the annotation interface which appears as a simple table. Information is ordered horizontally and vertically, so that words and morphs are aligned vertically with their Baseform, Meaning, Gloss and Part of speech information. From the annotation table the user can chose one of the words and mark it as *Head* adding some basic syntactic information. Annotation can be partial and the idea is that free class morphemes are annotated for meaning while closed class items receive a gloss. Morphs may be accompanied by null to many glosses leading to enumerations of gloss symbols when necessary.

Each phrase has a unique identifier. This means that a data token can be shared freely online. The use case in Figure 2 illustrates this point.

Next to real-time data-sharing it is mainly the easy access to the relevant linguistic resources that facilitates manual annotation.[5]

[5]With the Lazy Annotation Mode (LAM) we offer an additional function that automatically enriches annotation tables

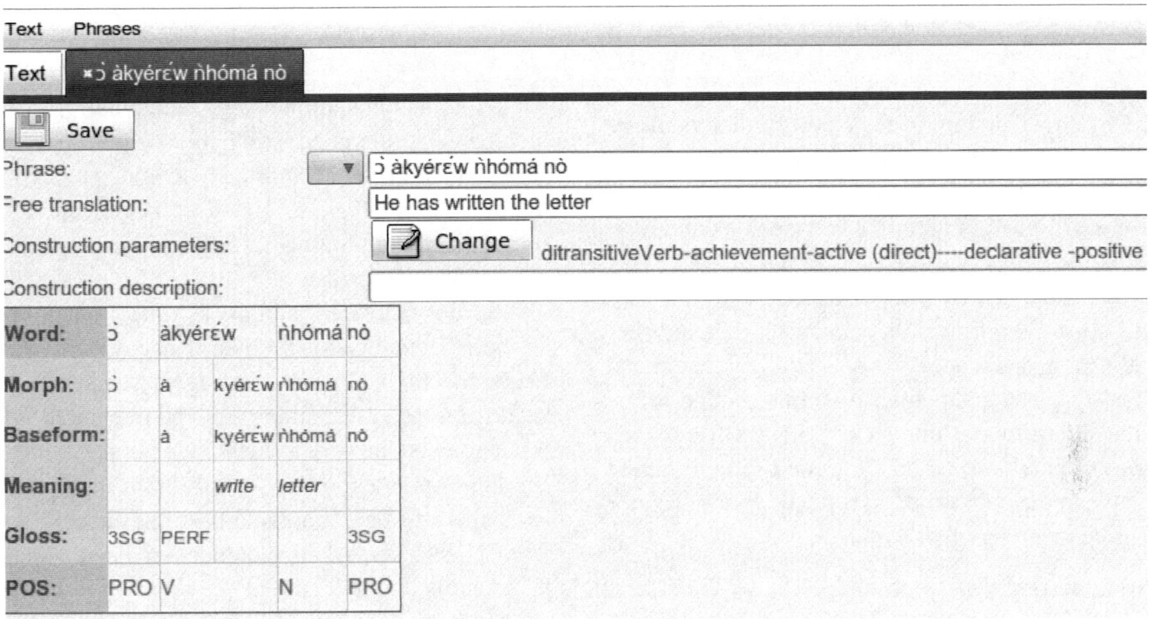

Figure 1: The Interlinear Glosser

Three users of our system work together on the Bantu language Runyankore-Rukiga, a Bantu language spoken in Uganda. The language has no digital resources and annotated text is hard to come by. The group members experience a a lot of uncertainty in the selection of gloss values. While one of them is a lecturer at Makerere University in Kampala the other two study abroad. Mulogo attends class today, the topic is Tense and Aspect. He remembers that Ojore who tends to work at home has recently annotated his Field Work transcripts for his thesis on Tense and Aspect. Ojore happens to be online. Mulogo quickly asks Ojore if he could link him the two examples that he had mentioned the other day. They illustrated the co-occurrences of the immediate past and the perfective marker *-ire*. Ojore links him the tokens in Skype. Mulogo opens them in his browser and asks the teacher if he could project the examples after the break for some discussion. Meanwhile Ojore discovers that Dembe had in some contexts identified a morpheme that he has glossed as the immediate past as a present tense marker. Dembe is not online right now, so he links the two crucial examples to her in an e-mail. Normally they talk online in the morning when the connection to Kampala is better. He also adds a note to the construction description of the tokens for Mulogo and Dembe to read later.

Figure 2: A use case illustrating real-time data sharing

First of all lists over tags can be accessed from the wiki navigation bar where they are automatically updated when the database changes. The tag lists can be ordered either according to Gloss class or alphabetically. Short explanations for the glosses are provided. We have grouped all glosses into annotation classes and mapped them to the GOLD (General Ontology for Linguistic Description) ontology (See Figure 3). The idea behind Gold (Farrar and Langendoen, 2003) is to facilitate a more standardised use of basic grammatical features. As an OWL ontology it presents features in terms of categories and their relations. At this point the integration with GOLD is only light-weight and meant to give users of the system direct access to an ontology over grammatical types supplemented by bibliographic information and further examples showing the use of categories. This way essential information is made available at the point where it is needed. Uncertainty about the meaning of gloss can be reduced this way.

An important feature of the Interlinear Glosser is that it allows export of data to some of the main text editors - Microsoft Word, OpenOffice.org Writer and LaTeX. The example below illustrates an exported interlinear gloss. In addition to export from the Interlinear Glosser, individual or sets of interlinear glosses can be exported from the SEARCH interface which we will discuss in the next section. Offering a solution to the issue of wrapping (Bow et al., 2003), which arises for the representation of interlinear glosses for long sentences,[6] the system allows a clean representation of annotated sentences of any length. In general the alignment of morphemes and glosses (optionally indicated by a dotted line) forms the body of the interlinear gloss, while the original string and the free translation are wrapped independently

with word related information already known to the database. LAM annotations need to be evaluated by the human annotator. They have only a limited value for languages with a rich system of allomorphic variation, but they are quite helpful otherwise even for languages with a rich portmanteau morphemes. In Toolbox this function is called 'sentence parsing'

[6]What is a long sentence is a relative issue which is not only determined by the number of words that a sentence consists of, but also by the length of the enumeration of gloss tags that are aligned with each of the individual morphemes.

Omu nju hakataahamu abagyenyi

m	nj		hkthm					bgyngy		
Omu	n	ju	ha	ka	taah	a	mu	a	ba	gyenyi
in	CL9	*house*	CL16	PST	*enter*	IND	LOC	IV	CL2	*visitor*
PREP	N		V					N		

'In the house entered visitors'

The example illustrates locative inversion in Ruyankore-Rukiga, a Bantu language spoken in Uganda. The translational and functional glosses, which belong to two distinct tiers in our editor, appear as one line when imported to a word-processor. Although glossing on several tiers is conceptually more appropriate, linguistic publications require a more condensed format.

Although to annotate manually is time consuming, it is the re-usability of the data that pays off. The ease with which already existing data can be exported from the system in order to be integrated into publications is one way to make this point.

In addition to export to Text Editors the system allows also from the graphical user interface the export of XML. The Akan sentence *àkyérɛw ǹhòmá nò* , meaning 'he has written the letter' (see Figure 1) is given as an XML structure in Figure 4. Notice that *Construction descriptions* and *Global tags* are exported together with the word- and morpheme annotations. Used for machine to machine communication, the XML rendering of interlinear glossses has interested the linguistic community (see for example (Bow et al., 2003)) as a means to find a generalised model for interlinear text.

2.2 Search

Data queries operate on phrases, which means that the result of a query is a phrase level representation. Each line (or block) of the search result represents an individual sentence.[7] Lists of sentences, as the result of a search, are more easily evaluated by human observers than lines of concordances. Search results come as either lines of sentences which allow a first quick scan of the data or as blocks of interlinear glosses. This latter search output gives the linguist access to the sentence internal annotations. Using general browser functionality search results can easily be scanned. The system allows for complex searches from the graphical interface where word or morpheme queries can relatively freely be combined with a search for specific glosses or com-

[7]or sentence fragment such as a noun phrase

Glossing tag	Tag description	Gloss class	GOLD Reference
ABES	abessive 'without'	Case	AbessiveCase
ABL	ablative 'from'	Case	AblativeCase
ABS	absolutive	Case	AbsolutiveCase
ACC	accusative	Case	AccusativeCase
ACTV	active voice	Voice	ActiveVoice
ADESS	adessive 'at', 'near'	Case	AdessiveCase
AGT	agent	Semantic Role	agent
ALL	allative	Case	AllativeCase
ANIM	animate	Animacy	AnimateGender
ACAUS	anti-causative	Diathesis	AntiCausativeVoice
APASS	anti-passive	Diathesis	AntiPassiveVoice
APPL	applicative	Diathesis	ApplicativeVoice
ASP	aspect - underspecified	Aspect	AspectProperty
BEN	benefactive	Case	BenefactiveCase
CASE	case marker - underspecified	Case	CaseProperty
CAUS	causative	Diathesis	CausativeVoice

Figure 3: Mapping between system-tags and GOLD concepts


```xml
<phrases>
  <phrase id="18659" valid="VALID">
    <original>ɔ̀ àkyérɛ́w ǹhómá nò</original>
    <translation>He has written the letter</translation>
    <description>Boadi states that the perfect morpheme has a low tone;
 the low tone on the pronoun seems contextual</description>
    <globaltags tagset="Default" id="1">
      <globaltag level="0">positive</globaltag>
      <globaltag level="5">active (direct)</globaltag>
      <globaltag level="6">achievement</globaltag>
      <globaltag level="1">declarative</globaltag>
      <globaltag level="7">ditransitiveVerb</globaltag>
    </globaltags>
    <word id="68409" text="ɔ̀">
      <pos>PRO</pos>
      <morpheme id="111636" text="ɔ̀" baseform="ɔ">
        <gloss>3SG</gloss>
      </morpheme>
    </word>
    <word id="68410" text="àkyérɛ́w" head="yes">
      <pos>V</pos>
      <morpheme id="111637" text="à" baseform="à">
        <gloss>PERF</gloss>
      </morpheme>
      <morpheme id="111638" text="kyérɛ́w" baseform="kyérɛ́w" meaning="write"/>
    </word>
    <word id="68411" text="ǹhómá">
      <pos>N</pos>
      <morpheme id="111639" text="ǹhómá" baseform="ǹhómá" meaning="letter"/>
    </word>
    <word id="68412" text="nò">
      <pos>DET</pos>
      <morpheme id="111640" text="nò" baseform="nò">
        <gloss>DEF</gloss>
      </morpheme>
    </word>
  </phrase>
</phrases>
```


Figure 4: XML export

binations of glosses. Search for portmanteau morphemes as well as for word-level co-occurrences of glosses is facilitated by allowing the user to determine the scope of gloss-co-occurrence which can either be the morph, the word or the phrase level. Queries are used to establish inter-annotator consistency, as well as to which degree an annotator is consistent in her annotations. For example, a search of 1154 Runyankore-Rukiga sentences, annotated by three different native-speakers in the context of different linguistic projects, shows that the annotators disagree on the meaning of the morpheme *-ire*. It is mainly annotated as PERF(ective) Aspect, but also as PAST, ANT(erior) and STAT(ive). However, when the same morpheme occurs in a negative context *-ire* is in 51 out of the 53 negative sentences annotated as expressing the perfective Aspect.[8] Although at present aggregate functions for the SQL queries can not be executed from the graphical user interface, the search offered by the system is already at this point a useful tool for linguistic data management.

3 Free data sharing and linguistic discovery

Collaborative databases where individual researchers or groups of researchers own portions of the data have their own dynamics and requirements for maintaining data sharing, recovery and integrity. They can be used with profit as an in-class tool or by research projects, and each of these uses requires a different set of rules for ensuring data quality and privacy. Annotations made by language specialists working on their own research reflect differences in interest and linguistic expertise.

Interesting data trends can be noticed by looking at the annotations made by annotators independently working on the same language. We will briefly illustrate this point with an example.

We have analysed the interlinear texts of four annotators working on individual linguistic projects in Akan, a Kwa language of Ghana. Together their work represents an annotated 3302 word corpus. We have analysed which glosses[9] were used and how frequently each of the glosses occurred. The most frequently used tags for Akan were SBJ and OBJ standing for subject and object, respectively. Comparing the Akan data with data coming from other users working on typologically distinct languages, we observe that the relative frequency in which the users annotate for the grammatical core relations 'subject' and 'object' differed from language to language.

As shown in Table 1 the absolute number of annotated morphemes and the relative frequency of SBJ and OBJ tags is highest for the two most configurational languages in our sample. This data has to be seen in the context of a possible use case not as the result of an empirical study. Other data tendencies indicative of annotator behaviour as much as of data properties can be observed too. Looking at Tense or Aspect within the same dataset shows that Akan which is a predominantly Aspect marking language (Boadi, 2008) (Osam, 2003) is by all four annotators mostly annotated for Aspect, with few tags for present tense. Between the Aspect tags we find HAB (habitual), as well as PRF and COMPL. The two latter glosses, referring to the *perfective* and the *completive* Aspect, where 'completive Aspect' means according to Bybee "to do something thoroughly and to completion", might have been used to refer to a completed event. In the nominal domain it is the frequent use of the DEF gloss, as opposed to the very few uses of the gloss INDEF, that highlights that Akan marks definiteness but not indefiniteness. Interesting is that deixis is hardly marked although the definite marker in Akan has been claimed to have a deictic interpretation (Appiah Amfo, 2007).

The success of real-time data sharing depends on the trust that data consumers have in the data quality. All public data can be traced back to the annotator through the system's Text search. As part of the first-time login procedure, each annotator is asked to contribute a small bio to her user page on the system's wiki. In this way 'data about the data' is created and can be used to judge the data's origin and authenticity. In addition an Advisory Board of senior linguists can be contacted for data review. Also, the list of Advisors can be viewed from the system's wiki.

However, the kernel of all efforts is to assure that the data quality conforms to established criteria and procedures in the field. One way to accomplish this

[8] Date of query 03-03-2011

[9] The present survey does not cover pos tags.

Language	SUBJ	OBJ	units	SBJ %	OBJ %
German	5	2	1680	0,29	0,12
Norwegian	328	144	1787	18,35	8,05
Akan	470	393	4700	10	8,36
Kistaninya	0	0	737	0	0
R.-Rukiga	25	5	5073	0,50	0,10

Table 1: Relative frequency of core relational tags for 5 languages

is to link annotations to an ontology of grammatical concepts that reflects our present knowledge of grammatical categories and their relations. While we can work towards data validity, data completeness for a collaborative database will always depend on the linguistic goals pursued by the individual annotators.

It has been suggested by the GOLD community that the creation of Language profiles (Farrar and Lewis, 2005) could be a way to account for the morpho-syntactic categories of a specific language by using concepts found in GOLD under annotation. Given our own experience with the present integration of GOLD a mapping from the system's gloss sets to the GOLD ontology could be equally interesting. As an exercise in Ontology Extraction the mapping of annotation profiles from the present system to GOLD could as a first step allow the filling of category gaps. For the category CASE the equative is not yet known to GOLD, likewise Deixis and its forms such as proximate, distal, medial and remote are not currently represented.[10] It would be interesting to develop an algorithm which would allow to (a) build a model that can predict the 'class' of a certain gloss tag and (b) let ontological categories inform data search in the system presented here.

4 Conclusion

Data annotation and real-time data sharing requires a tool that is suitable for work in the Humanities. The system discussed here represents linguistically annotated data in the form of interlinear glosses, a well established format within philology and the structural and generative fields of linguistics. The present system is novel in that is allows the exchange of research data within linguistics proper. The systems's design has a clear focus on real-time data sharing combined with simplicity of use and familiarity of representation. It allows its users to concentrate on the linguistic task at hand. The system is particularly suitable for the creation of corpora of less documented languages.

While linguistic software makes use of forums, blogs and other social software, the present system *IS* social software. It is a powerful tool, however, its real potential resides in a growing user community and the effect that the community approach might have on data quality and the use of standards. Standards are ignored if not disseminated through an attractive public site that makes it easy for annotators to use them.With its relative longevity, and its institutional support, the system has two of the main characteristics of a digital tool that can serve as part of the cyberinfrastructure which is needed to support e-Research for the humanities (Nguyen and Shilton, 2008).

[10]Gold 2010 Data of search: 03/29/2011

References

Nana Appiah Amfo. 2007. Akan demonstratives. In Doris L. Payne and Jaime Pea, editors, *Selected Proceedings of the 37th Annual Conference on African Linguistics*.

Chris Biemann, Uwe Quasthoff, and Christian Wolff. 2004. Linguistic corpus search. In *Proceedings Fourth International Conference on Language Resources and Evaluation*, Lissabon.

Steven Bird. 2009. Natural language processing and linguistic fieldwork. *Computational Linguistics*, 35(3):469–474.

Lawrence A. Boadi. 2008. Tense, aspect and mood in Akan. In Felix K. Ameka and Mary Esther Kropp Dakubu, editors, *Tense and Aspect in Kwa Languages*. John Benjamins.

Cathy Bow, Baden Hughes, and Steven Bird. 2003. Towards a general model of interlinear text. In *Proceedings of EMELD Workshop 2003: Digitizing & Annotating Texts & Field Recordings. Electronic Metastructure for Endangered Language Data.* (EMELD) Project, May.

Scott Farrar and Terence Langendoen. 2003. A linguistic ontology for the semantic web. *GLOT International*, 7(3):97–100.

Scott Farrar and William D. Lewis. 2005. The gold community of practice: An infrastructure for linguistic data on the web. In *Proceedings of the EMELD 2005 Workshop on Digital Language Documentation: Linguistic Ontologies and Data Categories for Language Resources*.

Nikolaus P. Himmelmann. 1998. Documentary and descriptive linguistics. *Linguistics*, 36.

Christian Lehmann. 2004. Data in linguistics. *The Linguistic Review*, 21(3-4):175–210.

Lilly Nguyen and Katie Shilton. 2008. Tools for Humanists. In D. Zorich, editor, *A Survey of Digital Humanities Centres in the United States*. Council on Library and Information Resources.

Emmanuel Kweku Osam. 2003. An Introduction to the Verbal and Multi-Verbal System of Akan. In Dorothee Beermann and Lars Hellan, editors, *Proceedings of the workshop on Multi-Verb Constructions Trondheim Summer School 2003*.

Keren. Rice. 1994. Language documentation: Whose ethics? In Lenore A. Grenobel and N. Louanna Furbee-Losee, editors, *Language Documentation: Practice and values*. John Benjamins.

Chris Rogers. 2010. Review of fieldworks language explorer (flex) 3.0. *Language Documentation & Conservation*, 04:78–84.

Thomas Schmidt. 2010. Linguistic tool development between community practices and technology standards. In *Proceedings of the LREC Workshop Language Resource and Language Technology Standards state of the art, emerging needs, and future developments*, Valletta, Malta, May. European Language Resources Association (ELRA).

Elena Tognini-Bonelli. 2001. *Corpus linguistics at work*. Amsterdam: Benjamins.

Automatic linguistic annotation of historical language: ToTrTaLe and XIX century Slovene

Tomaž Erjavec
Department of Knowledge Technologies,
Jožef Stefan Institute
Jamova cesta 39, 1000 Ljubljana
Slovenia
tomaz.erjavec@ijs.si

Abstract

The paper describes a tool developed to process historical (Slovene) text, which annotates words in a TEI encoded corpus with their modern-day equivalents, morphosyntactic tags and lemmas. Such a tool is useful for developing historical corpora of highly-inflecting languages, enabling full text search in digital libraries of historical texts, for modernising such texts for today's readers and making it simpler to correct OCR transcriptions.

1 Introduction

Basic processing of written language, in particular tokenisation, tagging and lemmatisation, is useful in a number of applications, such as enabling full-text search, corpus-linguistic studies, and adding further layers of annotation. Support for lemmatisation and morphosyntactic tagging is well-advanced for modern-day languages, however, the situation is very different for historical language varieties, where much less – if any – resources exist to train high-quality taggers and lemmatisers. Historical texts also bring with them a number of challenges not present with modern language:

- due to the low print quality, optical character recognition (OCR) produces much worse results than for modern day texts; currently, such texts must be hand-corrected to arrive at acceptable quality levels;
- full-text search is difficult, as the texts are not lemmatised and use different orthographic conventions and archaic spellings, typically not familiar to non-specialists;
- comprehension can also be limited, esp. when the text uses an alphabet different from the contemporary norm.

This paper describes a tool to help alleviate the above problems. The tool implements a pipeline, where it first tokenises the text and then attempts to transcribe the archaic words to their modern day equivalents. For here on, the text is tagged and lemmatised using the models for modern Slovene. Such an approach is not new, as it straightforwardly follows from a situation where good language models are available for contemporary language, but not for its historical variants.

The focus of the research in such cases is on the mapping from historical words to modern ones, and such approaches have already been attempted for other languages, e.g. for English (Rayson et al. 2007), German (Pilz et al. 2008), Spanish (Sánchez-Marco et al. 2010) and Icelandic (Rögnvaldsson and Helgadóttir, 2008). These studies have mostly concentrated on mapping historical variants to modern words or evaluating PoS tagging accuracy and have dealt with Germanic and Romance languages. This paper discusses the complete annotation process, including lemmatisation, and treats a Slavic language, which has substantially different morphology; in Slovene, words belong to complex inflectional paradigms, which makes tagging and lemmatisation models quite complex, esp. for unknown words.

The paper also discusses structural annotations supported by the tool, which takes as input a document encoded according to (a subset of) the Text Encoding Initiative Guidelines, TEI P5 (Burnard and Bauman, 2007) and also produces output in this format.

An example of the tool input fragment and the corresponding output is given in Figure 1.

2 The ToTrTaLe tool

The annotation tool implements a pipeline architecture and is essentially a wrapper program that calls a number of further processing modules. The tool is based on the ToTaLe tool (Erjavec et al., 2005), which performs Tokenisation, Tagging and Lemmatisation on modern text; as the present tool extends this with Transcription, it is called ToTrTaLe, and comprises the following modules:

1. extracting processing chunks from source TEI
2. tokenisation
3. extracting text to be annotated
4. transcription to modern word-forms
5. part-of-speech tagging
6. lemmatisation
7. TEI output

While the tool and its modules make some language specific assumption, they are rather broad, such as that text tokens are (typically) separated by space; otherwise, the tool relies on external language resources, so it could be made to work with most European languages, although it is especially suited for the highly-inflecting ones.

The tool is written in Perl and is reasonably fast, i.e. it processes about 100k words per minute on a Linux server. The greatest speed bottleneck is the tool start-up, mostly the result of the lemmatisation module, which for Slovene contains thousands of rules and exceptions. In the rest of this section we present the modules of ToTrTaLe, esp. as they relate to processing of historical language.

2.1 Extracting chunks

In the first step, the top-level elements of the TEI file that contain text to be processed in one chunk are identified and passed on for linguistic processing. This step serves two purposes. Certain TEI elements, in particular the <teiHeader>, which contains the meta-data of the document, should not be analysed but simply passed on to the output (except for recording the fact that the text has been linguistically annotated). Second, the processors in certain stages keep the text and annotations in memory. As a TEI document can be arbitrarily large the available physical memory can be exhausted, leading to severe slow-down or even out-of-memory errors. It is therefore possible to specify which elements (such as <body> or <div>) should be treated as chunks to be processed in one annotation run.

2.2 The tokenisation module

The multilingual tokenisation module `mlToken`[1] is written in Perl and in addition to splitting the input string into tokens has also the following features:

- assigns to each token its token type, e.g. XML tag, sentence final punctuation, digit, abbreviation, URL, etc.
- preserves (subject to a flag) white-space, so that the input can be reconstituted from the output.

The tokeniser can be fine-tuned by putting punctuation into various classes (e.g. word-breaking vs. non-breaking) and also uses several language-dependent resource files, in particular a list of abbreviations ("words" ending in period, which is a part of the token and does not necessarily end a sentence), list of multi-word units (tokens consisting of several space-separated "words") and a list of (right or left) clitics, i.e. cases where one "word" should be treated as several tokens. These resource files are esp. important in the context of processing historical language, as it often happens that words that used to be written apart and now written together or vice-versa. Such words are put in the appropriate resource file, so that their tokenisation is normalised. Examples of multi-word and split tokens are given in Figure 1.

2.3 Text extraction

A TEI encoded text can contain a fair amount of markup, which we, as much as possible, aim to preserve in the output. However, most of the markup should be ignored by the annotation modules, or, in certain cases, even the content of an element should be ignored; this goes esp. for markup found in text-critical editions of historical texts. For example, the top and bottom of the page can contain a running header, page number and catch-words (marked up in <fw> "forme work" elements), which should typically not be annotated as they are not linguistically interesting and would furthermore break the continuity of the text. The text might also contain editorial corrections (marked up as <choice> <sic>*mistyped text*</sic> <corr>*corrected text*</corr> </choice>), where, arguably, only the corrected text should be taken

[1] mlToken was written in 2005 by Camelia Ignat, then working at the EU Joint Research Centre in Ispra, Italy.

into account in the linguistic annotation. This module extracts the text that should be passed on to the annotation modules, where the elements to be ignored are specified in a resource file.

This solution does take care of most situations encountered so far in our corpora[2] but is not completely general. As discussed in Bennet et al. (2010), there are many cases where adding token (and sentence) tags to existing markup breaks XML well-formedness or TEI validity, such as sentences crossing structural boundaries or word-internal TEI markup.

A general "solution" to the problem is stand-off markup, where the annotated text is kept separate from the source TEI, but that merely postpones the problem of how to treat the two as a unit. And while TEI does offer solutions to such problems, implementing processing of arbitrary TEI in-place markup would, however, require much further research. So ToTrTaLe adds the linguistic mark-up in-place, but does so correctly only for a restricted, although still useful, set of TEI element configurations.

2.4 Transcription

The transcription of archaic word-forms to their modern day equivalents is the core module which distinguishes our processing of historical language as opposed to its contemporary form. The transcription process relies on three resources:

- a lexicon of modern-day word-forms;
- a lexicon of historical word-forms, with associated modern-day equivalent word-form(s);[3]
- a set of transcription patterns.

In processing historical texts, the word-form tokens are first normalised, i.e. de-capitalised and diacritic marks over vowels removed; the latter is most likely Slovene specific, as modern-day Slovene, unlike the language of the 19th century, does not use vowel diacritics.

To determine the modern-day word-form, the historical lexicon is checked first. If the normalized word-form is an entry of the historical lexicon, the equivalent modern-day word-form has also been identified; if not, it is checked against the modern-day lexicon. This order of searching the lexica is important, as the modern lexicon can contain word-forms which have an incorrect meaning in the context of historical texts, so the historical lexicon also serves to block such meanings.

If neither lexicon contains the word, the transcription patterns are tried. Many historical spelling variants can be traced to a set of rewrite rules or "patterns" that locally explain the difference between the contemporary and the historical spelling. For Slovene, a very prominent pattern is e.g. *r→er* as exemplified by the pair *brž→berž*, where the left side represents the modern and the right the historical spelling.

Such patterns are operationalized by the finite-state "Variant aware approximate matching" tool Vaam, (Gotscharek et al. 2009; Reffle, 2011), which takes as input a historical word-form, the set of patters, and a modern-day lexicon and efficiently returns the modern-day word-forms that can be computed from the archaic one by applying one or more patterns. The output list is ranked, preferring candidates where a small number of pattern applications is needed for the rewrite operation.[4]

It should be noted that the above process of transcription is non-deterministic. While this rarely happens in practice, the historical word-form can have several modern-day equivalents. More importantly, the Vaam module will typically return several possible alternative modernisations, of which only one is correct for the specific use of the word in context. We currently make use of frequency based heuristics to determine the "best" transcription, but more advanced models are possible, which would postpone the decision of the best candidate until the tagging and lemmatization has been performed.

We currently use a set of about 100 transcription patterns, which were obtained by corpus inspection, using a dedicated concordancer.

---

[2] The notable exception is <lb/>, line break, which, given the large font size and small pages, often occurs in the middle of a word in historical texts. We move such line breaks in the source documents to the start of the word and mark their displacement in lb/@n.

[3] The two lexica have in fact a somewhat more complicated structure. For example, many archaic words do not have a proper modern day equivalent; for these, the lexicon gives the word in its modern spelling but also its modern near synonyms.

[4] Vaam also supports approximate matching based on edit distance, useful for identifying (and correcting) OCR errors; we have, however, not yet made use of this functionality.

2.5 Tagging

For tagging words in the text with their context disambiguated morphosyntactic annotations we use TnT (Brants, 2000), a fast and robust tri-gram tagger. The tagger has been trained on jos1M, the 1 million word JOS corpus of contemporary Slovene (Erjavec and Krek, 2008), and is also given a large background lexicon extracted from the 600 million word FidaPLUS reference corpus of contemporary Slovene (Arhar and Gorjanc, 2007).

2.6 Lemmatisation

Automatic lemmatisation is a core application for many language processing tasks. In inflectionally rich languages assigning the correct lemma (base form) to each word in a running text is not trivial, as, for instance, Slovene adjectives inflect for gender, number and case (3x3x6) with a complex configuration of endings and stem modifications.

For our lemmatiser we use CLOG (Manandhar et al., 1998, Erjavec and Džeroski, 2004), which implements a machine learning approach to the automatic lemmatisation of (unknown) words. CLOG learns on the basis of input examples (pairs word-form/lemma, where each morphosyntactic tag is learnt separately) a first-order decision list, essentially a sequence of if-then-else clauses, where the defined operation is string concatenation. The learnt structures are Prolog programs but in order to minimise interface issues we made a converter from the Prolog program into one in Perl.

An interesting feature of CLOG is that it does not succeed in lemmatising just any word-form. With historical texts it almost invariably fails in lemmatising truly archaic words, making it a good selector for new entries in the historical lexicon.

The lemmatiser was trained on a lexicon extracted from the jos1M corpus, and the lemmatisation of contemporary language is quite accurate, with 92% on unknown words. However, as mentioned, the learnt model, given that there are 2,000 separate classes, is quite large: the Perl rules have about 2MB, which makes loading the lemmatiser slow.

2.7 TEI output

The final stage of processing is packing the original file with the added annotations into a valid TEI document. This is achieved by combining Perl processing with XSLT scripts. The last step in the processing is the validation of the resulting XML file against a TEI schema expressed in Relax NG. A validation failure indicates that the input document breaks some (possibly implicit) mark-up assumptions – in this case either the input document must be fixed, or, if the encoding choices were valid, the program should be extended to deal also with such cases.

3 Conclusions

The paper gave an overview of the ToTrTaLe tool, which performs basic linguistic annotation on TEI encoded historical texts. Some future work on the tool has already been mentioned, in particular exploring ways of flexibly connecting transcription to tagging and lemmatisation, as well as supporting more complex TEI encoded structures.

While the tool itself is largely language independent, it does need substantial language resources to operationalize it for a language. Specific for historical language processing are a corpus of transcribed historical texts, a lexicon of historical word forms and a pattern set. The paper did not discuss these language resources, although it is here that most work will be invested in the future.

The corpus we have used so far for Slovene lexicon building comes from the AHLib digital library (Prunč, 2007; Erjavec 2005), which contains 2 million words of 19th century texts; we now plan to extend this with older material, predominantly from the 18th century.

The on-going process of creating the Slovene historical lexicon is described in Erjavec et al., (2010), while the model of a TEI encoded lexicon containing not only historical word-forms, but also all the other lexical items needed to feed the tool (such as multi-word units) is presented in Erjavec et al. (2011). As we extend the corpus, we will also obtain new words, which will be automatically annotated with ToTrTaLe and then manually corrected, feeding into the lexicon building process.

For the patterns, the extension of the corpus will no doubt show the need to extend also the pattern set. Most likely this will be done by corpus inspection, via a dedicated concordancer, although alternative methods of pattern identification are possible. In particular, once when a substantial list of pairs historical word-form / contemporary word-form becomes available, automatic methods can be used to derive a list of patterns, ranked by how productive they are (Pilz et al., 2008; Oravecz et al. 2010).

Acknowledgements

The author thanks the anonymous reviewers for their useful comments and suggestions. The work presented in this paper has been supported by the EU IMPACT project “Improving Access to Text” and the Google Digital Humanities Research Award “Language models for historical Slovenian”.

References

Paul Bennett, Martin Durrell, Silke Scheible, and Richard J. Whitt, 2010. Annotating a historical corpus of German: A case study. *Proceedings of the LREC 2010 workshop on Language Resources and Language Technology Standards*. Valletta, Malta, 18 May 2010. 64-68.

Lou Burnard and Syd Bauman, 2007. *Guidelines for Electronic Text Encoding and Interchange (TEI P5)*. Text Encoding Initiative Consortium. Oxford, 2007. http://www.tei-c.org/release/doc/tei-p5-doc/

Tomaž Erjavec. 2007. Architecture for Editing Complex Digital Documents. Proceedings of the Conference on Digital Information and Heritage. Zagreb. pp. 105-114.

Tomaž Erjavec and Sašo Džeroski. 2004. Machine Learning of Language Structure: Lemmatising Unknown Slovene Words. *Applied Artificial Intelligence*, 18(1):17–41.

Tomaž Erjavec, Simon Krek, 2008. The JOS morphosyntactically tagged corpus of Slovene. In *Proceedings of the Sixth International Conference on Language Resources and Evaluation, LREC'08*, Paris, ELRA.

Tomaž Erjavec, Camelia Ignat, Bruno Pouliquen, and Ralf Steinberger. Massive Multi-Lingual Corpus Compilation: Acquis Communautaire and ToTaLe. In Proceedings of the 2nd Language & Technology Conference, April 21-23, 2005, Poznan, Poland. 2005, pp. 32-36.

Tomaž Erjavec, Christoph Ringlstetter, Maja Žorga, and Annette Gotscharek, 2010. Towards a Lexicon of XIXth Century Slovene. In Proceedings of the Seventh Language Technologies Conference, October 14th-15th, 2010, Ljubljana, Slovenia. Jožef Stefan Institute.

Tomaž Erjavec, Christoph Ringlstetter, Maja Žorga, and Annette Gotscharek, (submitted). A lexicon for processing archaic language: the case of XIXth century Slovene. ESSLLI Workshop on Lexical Resources workshop, WoLeR'11. Ljubljana, Slovenia.

Annette Gotscharek, Andreas Neumann, Ulrich Reffle, Christoph Ringlstetter and Klaus U. Schulz. 2009. Enabling Information Retrieval on Historical Document Collections - the Role of Matching Procedures and Special Lexica. Proceedings of the ACM SIGIR 2009 Workshop on Analytics for Noisy Unstructured Text Data (AND09), Barcelona.

Suresh Manandhar, Sašo Džeroski and Tomaž Erjavec 1998. Learning Multilingual Morphology with CLOG. In Proceedings of Inductive Logic Programming; 8th International Workshop ILP-98 (Lecture Notes in Artificial Intelligence 1446) (pp. 135-144). Springer-Verlag, Berlin.

Csaba Oravecz, Bálint Sass and Eszter Simon. 2010. Semi-automatic Normalization of Old Hungarian Codices. Proceedings of the ECAI 2010 Workshop on Language Technology for Cultural Heritage, Social Sciences, and Humanities (LaTeCH 2010), August 16, 2010, Lisbon, Portugal.

Thomas Pilz, Andrea Ernst-Gerlach, Sebastian Kempken, Paul Rayson and Dawn Archer, 2008. The Identification of Spelling Variants in English and German Historical Texts: Manual or Automatic? *Literary and Linguistic Computing*, 23/1, pp. 65-72.

Erich Prunč. 2007. Deutsch-slowenische/kroatische Übersetzung 1848-1918 [German-Slovene/Croatian translation, 1848-1918]. Ein Werkstättenbericht. Wiener Slavistisches Jahrbuch 53/2007. Austrian Academy of Sciences Press, Vienna. pp. 163-176.

Paul Rayson, Dawn Archer, Alistair Baron, Jonathan Culpeper, and Nicolas Smith, 2007. Tagging the Bard: Evaluating the accuracy of a modern POS tagger on Early Modern English corpora. In Proceedings of Corpus Linguistics 2007. University of Birmingham, UK.

Ulrich Reffle, Efficiently generating correction suggestions for garbled tokens of historical language, Journal of Natural Language Engineering, Special Issue on Finite State Methods and Models in Natural Language Processing, 2011.

Eiríkur Rögnvaldsson and Sigrún Helgadóttir, 2008. Morphological tagging of Old Norse texts and its use in studying syntactic variation and change. In Proceedings of the LREC 2008 Workshop on Language Technology for Cultural Heritage Data (LaTeCH 2008). ELRA, Paris.

Cristina Sánchez-Marco, Gemma Boleda, Josep Maria Fontana and Judith Domingo. 2010. Annotation and Representation of a Diachronic Corpus of Spanish. Proceedings of the Seventh conference on International Language Resources and Evaluation (LREC'10). ELRA, Paris.

TEI input fragment:

```
<p xml:id="p.401">Nekiga bogatiga kneza z nja <lb/>
  <pb n="93" facs="#FPG00012.097" xml:id="pb.97"/>
  družino, ki v mes nemore  <lb n="3"/>
  <gap/>
</p>
```

ToTrTaLe output:

```
<p xml:id="p.401">
  <s>
   <w subtype="lexicon" nform="nekiga" mform="nekega" lemma="nek" ctag="Pi-msg">Nekiga</w>
   <c> </c>
   <w subtype="pattern" pattern="[ega@←iga@]" mform="bogatega" lemma="bogat"
      ctag="Agpmsg">bogatiga</w>
   <c> </c>
   <w lemma="knez" ctag="Npmsg">kneza</w>
   <c> </c>
   <w lemma="z" ctag="Si">z</w>
   <c> </c>
   <w subtype="lexicon" mform="njegova" lemma="njegov" ctag="Ps3fsnsm">nja</w>
   <c> </c>
   <lb/>
   <pb n="93" facs="#FPG00012.097" xml:id="pb.97"/>
   <w lemma="družina" ctag="Ncfsa">družino</w>
   <pc ctag=",">,</pc>
   <c> </c>
   <w lemma="ki" ctag="Cs">ki</w>
   <c> </c>
   <w type="multiw" subtype="pattern" pattern="[@v←@v_]" mform="vmes" lemma="vmes" ctag="Rgp"
      n="mw_jeGx2">v</w>
   <c> </c>
   <w type="multiw" subtype="pattern" pattern="[@v←@v_]" mform="vmes" lemma="vmes" ctag="Rgp"
      n="mw_jeGx2">mes</w>
   <c> </c>
   <w type="split" mform="ne_more" lemma="ne_moči" ctag="Q_Vmpr3s">nemore</w>
   <c> </c>
   <lb n="3"/>
   <gap/>
  </s>
</p>
```

Figure 1. An example of ToTrTaLe input paragraph and the equivalent output.
Paragraphs, page and line breaks are preserved, and the program adds elements for words, punctuation symbols and white-space. Both punctuation and words are assigned a corpus tag and lemma, and, where different from the default, the type and subtype of the word, its normalised and modernised form, and possibly the used pattern(s). In cases of multi-words, each part is given its own word tag, which have identical analyses and are joined together by the unique value of @n; this approach allows also modelling discontinuous multi-word units, such as separable verbs in Germanic languages. Split words forms, on the other hand, are modelled by one word token, but with a portmanteau analysis.

Historical Event Extraction from Text

Agata Cybulska
VU University Amsterdam
De Boelelaan 1105
1081 HV Amsterdam
ak.cybulska@let.vu.nl

Piek Vossen
VU University Amsterdam
De Boelelaan 1105
1081 HV Amsterdam
p.vossen@let.vu.nl

Abstract

In this paper, we report on how historical events are extracted from text within the Semantics of History research project. The project aims at the creation of resources for a historical information retrieval system that can handle the time-based dynamics and varying perspectives of Dutch historical archives. The historical event extraction module will be used for museum collections, allowing users to search for exhibits related to particular historical events or actors within time periods and geographic areas, extracted from accompanying text. We present here the methodology and tools used for the purpose of historical event extraction alongside with the first evaluation results.

1 Introduction

The research project Semantics of History[1] is concerned with the development of a historical ontology and a lexicon that will be used in a new type of information retrieval system. In historical texts the reality changes over time (Ide & Woolner, 2007). Furthermore, historical realities can be seen differently depending on the subjective view of the writer. In the design of our search system, we will take into consideration the change of reality and the diverse attitudes of writers towards historical events so that they both can be used for the purpose of historical information retrieval.

In the first phase of the project we researched how descriptions of historical events are realized in different types of text and what the implications are for historical information retrieval. Different historical perspectives of writers correspond with genre distinctions and correlate with variation in language use. Texts, written shortly after an event happened, use more specific and uniquely occurring event descriptions than texts describing the same events but written from a longer time perspective. Statistical analysis performed within the first phase of the project confirmed this hypothesis[2]. To capture differences between event representations and to identify relations between historical events, we defined a historical event model which consists of 4 slots: a location slot, time, participant and an action slot (see also Van Hage et al 2011 for the formal SEM model).

After arriving at an understanding of how to model historical events, we moved on to actually extracting events from text. In this paper we report on our approach into historical event extraction from textual data about the Srebrenica Massacre from July 1995[3]. There are two problems that had to be tackled for the purpose of this task: 1) extraction of event actions with their participants, locations and time markers and 2) filtering of events lacking historical value from all events extracted by the system. We believe that event actions and their participants, locations and time markers can be extracted based on some syntactic clues, PoS, lemma and combinatory information together with semantic class definition and exclusion by means of Wordnet. Historical filtering can be performed through semantic classification of event actions.

[1] The Semantics of History is funded by the Interfaculty Research Institute CAMeRA at the Free University Amsterdam as a collaboration of the Faculties of Arts and Exact Science: http://www2.let.vu.nl/oz/cltl/semhis/index.html.

[2] For details see Cybulska, Vossen, LREC 2010.

[3] The Srebrenica corpus consists of 78 Dutch texts. For more information on the design of the corpus see Cybulska, Vossen (2010).

We tested this hypothesis within the KYOTO framework[4].

2 Related Work

Two other projects concerned with extraction of historical information are the FDR/Pearl Harbor project and the New Web Portal. The latter[5] aimed at creation of a digital archive of historical newspapers of the National Library of Finland[6]. Within the project a semantic search system for historical texts was created using a common ontology with semantically annotated cultural objects (Ahonen and Hyv¨onen, 2009). Related content is being linked through semantic annotation of historical texts based on ontology labels which presupposes that only high level historical events from text were annotated. The Pearl Harbor project aimed at facilitating enhanced search and retrieval from a set of documents from the FDRL library by utilizing a series of multiple temporally contextualized snapshot ontologies determined by the occurrence of key historical events (Ide & Woolner, 2007). We did not manage to find evaluation results for any of the two projects. Traditional approaches to event extraction that do report evaluation results use models that severely restrict the relations. They achieve high precision but poorly represent the text as a whole. E.g., Xu et. al. (2006) report over 80% precision for prize award extraction and Tanev et. al. (2008) 74% precision for violent events and disasters. Our approach models more events in a text and events of a broader scope, more comparable to Wunderwald (2011), who extracts participants and roles from news in general, reporting 50-60% precision. Wunderwald uses a machine-learning approach, while our method is knowledge-based. Furthermore, Wunderwald does not distinguish historical from non-historical events.

3 Historical Event Extraction

3.1 Generic Event Extraction by means of KYOTO

KYOTO tools were specifically designed to extract events from text. This pipeline-architecture of linguistic processors generates a uniform semantic representation of text in the so-called Kyoto Annotation Format (KAF)[7]. KAF is a stand-off format that distinguishes separate layers for text tokens, text terms, constituents and dependencies. It can be used to represent event actions with their participants, locations and time markers. For the purpose of this research, the Srebrenica corpus was processed by means of the KYOTO – architecture. First, the corpus was tagged with PoS- information; it was lemmatized and syntactically parsed by means of a dependency parser for Dutch - Alpino[8]. Next, word sense disambiguation was performed[9] and the corpus was semantically annotated with labels from the Dutch Wordnet[10] and ontological classes. Generic event information stored in the KAF – format can be extracted within KYOTO by means of Kybot-profiles which are stored in the XML format[11]. These profiles define patterns over different layers in KAF and create a semantic output layer for matches over these layers.

3.2 Semantic Tagging of Historical Events

To extract historical events we developed 'historical' Kybot-profiles which define appropriate constructions and semantic classes of historical actions and their participants, locations and time markers. In these profiles, the semantic action classes are used to distinguish historical from non-historical events. The semantic type specification was derived from manual tagging of historical event slots by means of the KAF-annotator[12] in 5 development texts from the Srebrenica corpus [13]. Manually tagged historical event actions as well as participants, locations and time markers were automatically mapped with corresponding Wordnet synsets. In case of multiple senses assigned per word the appropriate Wordnet ID was manually chosen.

Historical event tagging with Wordnet ID's revealed a few problematic issues. For a number of

[4] For more information about the KYOTO - project (www.kyoto-project.eu) see Vossen et al (2008a).
[5] The New Web Portal is part of the National Semantic Web 2.0 (FinnONTO 2.0) project.
[6] http://digi.lib.helsinki.fi/sanomalehti/secure/main.html

[7] Kyoto Annotation Format is described in Bosma et al (2009).
[8] http://www.let.rug.nl/vannoord/alp/Alpino/
[9] For word sense disambiguation the UKB system (http://ixa2.si.ehu.es/ukb/) was used. For more information the reader is referred to Agirre & Soroa (2009).
[10] For more information see Vossen et al (2008b).
[11] For more information see KYOTO deliverable 5.4 at http://www.kyoto-project.eu/.
[12] See tools at http://www.kyoto-project.eu/.
[13] The development set contains one Wikipedia entry, two educational texts and two newspaper articles written a few years after the Srebrenica massacre happened.

locations, time markers, participants and actions there were no Wordnet synsets automatically assigned. No WN-concepts were found for geographical names as *Srebrenica* or *Zagreb*. Also person and organization names (*Mladic*, *Dutchbat III*, *NIOD*) and dates would not get any synsets assigned. The same applies to compounds (*moslimmannen* 'Muslim men', *VN-militairen* 'UN soldiers'), pronoun participants and loanwords: (such as *safe haven* in a Dutch text). Furthermore there were some historical senses missing in the Dutch Wordnet (such as *vredesoperatie* 'peacekeeping operation', *oorlogspad* 'warpath'). To be able to handle proper names we used a named entity recognition module. By means of NER we added dates and geographical names to KAF so that we could further use them for the extraction of time markers and locations. In the future, we will look into compound splitting and we are also going to add the missing historical senses to the Wordnet database.

After identifying historical WN-synsets, we automatically determined the most informative hypernyms of the seed terms per historical label. Based on the chosen hypernyms (and their hyponyms), we manually selected a number of semantic classes to be able to identify event locations, time markers, participants and historical actions in historical texts. We defined six semantic classes denoting: human participants, time periods, moments in time, places, historical and motion actions. Furthermore we specified six more action classes to filter out non historical and potential events: actions indicating modality, polarity, intention, subjectivity, cognitive (also rarely of historical importance) and contentless actions. Next, we derived a table that assigns one of the ontological classes to every synset in Wordnet on the basis of the relations to the labeled hypernyms. All KAF-files were then annotated with the twelve semantic classes, on the basis of the Wordnet synsets assigned by the WSD module and this mapping table.

4 Kybot Profiles

Kyoto-Kybot extracts events from KAF by means of Kybot profiles. Based on event descriptions from the development set 402 profiles were defined, using semantic and constructional information and specifically PoS, lemma, compositional and semantic restrictions with regards to locations, time expressions, event actions and participants.

The current version of the system uses 22 profiles to extract historical actions, based on semantic tagging by means of Wordnet and the specification of some compositional properties. Historical actions are the most significant part of historical event extraction. They serve to distinguish historical actions from the non-historical ones and to identify parts of the same historical event. The profiles extract both, verbal actions (such as *deport, murder, occupy*) and nominal ones (such as *fight, war* and *offensive*) as well as actions with a syntactic object (*sign a treaty, start the offensive* etc). Next to the semantic class of historical actions also motion actions (often occurring with a goal or result phrase as *transport into* a location) are extracted as potential historical event actions. The action profiles exclude from the output the non-historical semantic action classes and by that the non historical events are filtered out.

For the extraction of historical participants we now use 314 profiles. The variation within historical participant descriptions of the development set was, as expected, much higher than the diversity of formulations denoting other event parts. Participant profiles specify noun phrases (also proper names) organized around the semantic class of human participants[14]. It is a relatively common phenomenon in historical event descriptions that geographical proper names are used for referral to participants. So we also created some profiles identifying country and city names occurring in the subject position of active sentences.

To extract historical event time we specified 43 temporal profiles. Thanks to the named entity recognition module of Kyoto we are able to retrieve dates and, based on Wordnet, the system can recognize temporal expressions which refer to weekdays or months and more general and relative time markers (such as *now* or *two weeks later*).

Furthermore, 23 location profiles are utilized to extract geographical proper names and other locative expressions based on the Wordnet class of places (as *street, city, country* etc).

[14] For now we focused on human animate participants and those referred to by personal pronouns. In the future we will also look into extracting participants indirectly named through word combinations consisting of geo adjectives preceding words denoting weapons and transportation vehicles (such as *Serbian tanks*).

5 Evaluation

For the evaluation purposes we used the KYOTO triplet representation of historical events, which is a generic event representation format. A triplet consists of a historical action, mapped with its nearby occurring participant, location or time expression together with a label indicating the event slot type. In the evaluation the gold standard triplets will be compared with triplets generated by the system. A set of five texts from the Srebrenica corpus, written some years after the massacre, was tagged manually with historical events by two independent annotators. We obtained a very high inter-annotator agreement of 94% (0.91 Kappa).

As a baseline, we generated triplets from all constituent heads in a sentence. Each constituent head is once treated as an action while all the others are seen as participants. Applying the default relation – historical participant – the baseline achieved an average of 66% recall and a (understandably) low precision of less than 0.01%. Tables 1 and 2 present the performance of the system on the evaluation set. The abbreviations in the tables stand for: T. Nr – Token Number, G. Trp – Gold Triplets, S. Trp – System Triplets, C.S. Trp – Correct System Triplets, R – Recall, P. – Precision, F – F-measure.

Counts / File	T. Nr	G. Trp	S. Trp	C.S. Trp	R. %	P. %	F
File 1	243	5	4	1	20	25	0.22
File 2	440	32	25	18	56	72	0.63
File 3	647	58	68	32	55	47	0.51
File 4	429	32	22	17	53	77	0.63
File 5	209	19	19	12	63	63	0.63
Micro Average	-	-	-	-	49	57	0.53

Table 1. Evaluation results per file (micro average).

Counts / Relation	G. Trp	S. Trp	C.S. Trp	R. %	P. %	F
Participants	98	95	57	58	60	0.59
Time	17	20	13	76	65	0.70
Location	31	23	10	32	43	0.37

Table 2. Evaluation results per relation (macro average)

The system reached an overall recall of 49% and a precision of 57%. The low scores for file 1 can be explained by the fact that in this text some so called 'political events' were described such as responsibility issues and an investigation w. r. t. events in Srebrenica that was performed in the Netherlands few years after the massacre. Currently the system is not prepared to handle any other events than the conflict related ones.

Historical actions, evaluated in a separate non triplet evaluation cycle, were extracted with a recall of 67.94% and a precision of 51.96%. We extracted time expressions with the highest precision of 65% and also the highest recall of 76%. The lower recall and precision measures reached for the extraction of participants and especially locations can be explained by the type shift of the semantic class of locations used for referral to event participants. As mentioned before, so far we only are able to identify these if occurring in subject position; in the future we will add deeper syntactic dependency information into KAF and by that we will improve the recognition of locations used as participants.

6 Conclusion and Future Work

In this paper we showed that historical events can successfully be extracted from text, based on constructional clues and semantic type specification. To extract events we used a generic fact mining system KYOTO; we specified language structures and Wordnet concepts denoting event actions, participants, locations and time markers and we identified the historical events through recognition of historical actions. The evaluation results confirm that historical events can be extracted from historical texts by means of this approach with a relatively high recall of almost 50% and a precision of 57%, (comparable to the results of Wunderwald, 2011). In our future work we are going to increase the performance of the system by utilizing in the profiles more specific syntactic information and the grammatical tense. We will also look into other possibilities of distinguishing between historical events and events lacking historical value, also in non historical genres. In the next stage of the project we will make an attempt to automatically determine relations between historical events over textual data. We will also apply the system to other historical descriptions that are connected to museum collections. Because of the generic design of the extraction module, we expect that the extraction of conflict events can be applied to other periods and events with little adaptation.

Acknowledgments

This research was funded by the interfaculty research institute CAMeRA (Center for Advanced Media Research) of the VU University of Amsterdam: http://camera.vu.nl.

References

Agirre, Eneko and Aitor Soroa, 2009, "Personalizing PageRank for Word Sense Disambiguation", in: Proceedings of the 12th conference of the European chapter of the Association for Computational Linguistics, (EACL-2009), Athens, Greece.

Ahonen, Eeva and Eero Hyv¨onen, 2009, "Publishing Historical Texts on the Semantic Web -A Case Study" [online] available: http://www.seco.tkk.fi/publications/2009/ahonen-hyvonen-historical-texts-2009.pdf

Bosma, Wauter, Vossen, Piek, Soroa, Aitor, Rigau, German, Tesconi, Maurizio, Marchetti, Andrea, Monachini, Monica, and Carlo Aliprandi, 2009 "KAF: a generic semantic annotation format.", in Proceedings of the GL2009 Workshop on Semantic Annotation, Pisa, Italy, Sept 17-19, 2009.

Bosma, Wauter and Piek Vossen, 2010, "Bootstrapping language neutral term extraction", in: Proceedings of the 7th international conference on Language Resources and Evaluation, (LREC2010), Valletta, Malta, May 17-23, 2010.

Cybulska, Agata and Piek Vossen, "Event models for Historical Perspectives: Determining Relations between High and Low Level Events in Text, Based on the Classification of Time, Location and Participants", in Proceedings of LREC 2010, Valletta, Malta, May 17-23, 2010

Ide, Nancy and David Woolner, 2007, "Historical Ontologies", in: Ahmad, Khurshid, Brewster, Christopher, and Mark Stevenson (eds.), Words and Intelligence II: Essays in Honor of Yorick Wilks, Springer, 137-152.

Tanev, Hristo, Piskorski, Jakub and Martin Atkinson, "Real-Time News Event Extraction for Global Crisis Monitoring", in NLDB 2008: Kapetanios, Epaminondas, Sugumaran, Vijayan, Spiliopoulou, Myra (eds.) Proceedings of the 13th International Conference on Applications of Natural Language to Information Systems, 2008, Springer: LNCS, vol. 5039, pp. 207-218.

Van Hage, Willem, Malaisé, Veronique, Segers, Roxane, Hollink, Laura (fc), Design and use of the Simple Event Model (SEM), the Journal of Web Semantics, Elsevier

Vossen, Piek, Agirre, Eneko, Calzolari, Nicoletta, Fellbaum, Christiane, Hsieh, Shu-kai, Huang, Chu-Ren, Isahara, Hitoshi, Kanzaki, Kyoko, Marchetti, Andrea, Monachini, Monica, Neri, Federico, Raffaelli, Remo, Rigau, German, Tescon, Maurizio, 2008a, "KYOTO: A system for Mining, Structuring and Distributing Knowledge Across Languages and Cultures", in: Proceedings of LREC 2008, Marrakech, Morocco, May 28-30, 2008.

Vossen, Piek, Bosma, Wauter, Agirre, Eneko, Rigau, German and Aitor Soroa, 2010, "A full Knowledge Cycle for Semantic Interoperability", in: Proceedings of the 5th Joint ISO-ACL/SIGSEM Workshop on Interoperable Semantic Annotation, in conjunction with the Second International Conference on Global Interoperability for Language Resources, (ICGL 2010), Hong Kong, January 15-17, 2010.

Wunderwald, Martin, 2011, "NewsX Event Extraction from News Articles", diploma thesis, Dresden University of Technology, Dresden, Germany, URL: http://www.rn.inf.tu-dresden.de/uploads/Studentische_Arbeiten/Diplomarbeit_Wunderwald_Martin.pdf

Xu, Feiyu, Uszkoreit, Hans, Li, Hong, 2006. "Automatic Event and Relation Detection with Seeds of Varying Complexity", in: Proceedings of the AAAI 2006 Workshop Event Extraction and Synthesis, Boston, 491-498.

Enrichment and Structuring of Archival Description Metadata

Kalliopi Zervanou[†], **Ioannis Korkontzelos**[‡], **Antal van den Bosch**[†] **and Sophia Ananiadou**[‡]

[†] Tilburg centre for Cognition and Communication (TiCC), University of Tilburg
Warandelaan 2 - PO Box 90153, 5000 LE Tilburg, The Netherlands
{K.Zervanou, Antal.vdnBosch}@uvt.nl

[‡] National Centre for Text Mining, University of Manchester
131 Princess Street, Manchester M1 7DN, UK
{Ioannis.Korkontzelos, Sophia.Ananiadou}@manchester.ac.uk

Abstract

Cultural heritage institutions are making their digital content available and searchable online. Digital metadata descriptions play an important role in this endeavour. This metadata is mostly manually created and often lacks detailed annotation, consistency and, most importantly, explicit semantic content descriptors which would facilitate online browsing and exploration of available information. This paper proposes the enrichment of existing cultural heritage metadata with automatically generated semantic content descriptors. In particular, it is concerned with metadata encoding archival descriptions (EAD) and proposes to use automatic term recognition and term clustering techniques for knowledge acquisition and content-based document classification purposes.

1 Introduction

The advent of the digital age has long changed the processes and the media which cultural heritage institutions (such as libraries, archives and museums) apply for describing and cataloguing their objects: electronic cataloguing systems support classification and search, while cultural heritage objects are associated to digital metadata content descriptions. The expansion of the web and the increasing engagement of web users throughout the world has brought about the need for cultural heritage institutions to make their content available and accessible to a wider audience online.

In this endeavour, cultural heritage institutions face numerous challenges. In terms of metadata, different metadata standards currently exist for describing various types of objects, both within the same institution and across different institutions. Moreover, metadata object descriptions have been typically both created by and addressed to librarian and archivist experts who have been expected to assist visitors in their search. For this reason, they primarily refer to bibliographic descriptions (e.g. author/creator, title, etc.), or physical descriptions (e.g. size, shape, material, etc.), and location. The lack of semantic descriptors in this type of metadata makes it difficult for potential online visitors to browse and explore available information based on more intuitive content criteria.

Work on metadata in cultural heritage institutions has been largely focused on the issue of metadata heterogeneity. There have been efforts towards the development and adoption of collection-specific metadata standards, such as *MARC 21* (Library of Congress, 2010) and *EAD* (Library of Congress, 2002), for library and archival material respectively, which are intended to standardise metadata descriptions across different institutions. To address the issue of heterogeneity across different types of object collections, generic metadata schemas have been proposed, such as the *Dublin Core Metadata Initiative* (DCMI, 2011). Moreover, current research has attempted to integrate diverse metadata schemas by mappings across existing schemas (Bountouri and Gergatsoulis, 2009), or mappings of existing metadata to ontologies, either based on ad-hoc manually developed ontologies (Liao et al., 2010), or on existing standard ontologies for cultural heritage purposes (Lourdi et al., 2009), such as the *CIDOC Con-*

ceptual Reference Model (CIDOC, 2006). Other approaches attempt to address the issue of metadata heterogeneity from a pure information retrieval perspective and discard the diverse metadata structures in favour of the respective text content descriptions for full text indexing (Koolen et al., 2007). Zhang and Kamps (2009) attempt to exploit the existing metadata XML structure for XML-based retrieval, thus targeting individual document components. Similarly to our approach, they investigate metadata describing archive collections.

The work presented in this paper focuses on metadata for textual objects, such as archive documents, and on the issue of explicit, semantic, content descriptors in this metadata, rather than heterogeneity. In particular, we are concerned with the lack of explicit content descriptors which would support exploratory information search. For this purpose, we attempt to automatically enrich manually created metadata with content information. We view the problem from an unsupervised, text mining perspective, whereby multi-word terms recognised in free text are assumed to indicate content. In turn, the respective inter-relationships among the recognised terms in the hierarchy are assumed to reveal the knowledge structure of the document collection.

In this paper, we start with a description of our EAD dataset and the challenges which our dataset poses in text processing. Subsequently, we discuss our approach to the enrichment and structuring of these archival descriptions and present our experiments. We conclude with a discussion on our results and our considerations for future work.

2 EAD and Challenges in Text Processing

The Encoded Archival Description (EAD) was conceived as *"a nonproprietary encoding standard for machine-readable finding aids such as inventories, registers, indexes, and other documents created by archives, libraries, museums, and manuscript repositories to support the use of their holdings"* (Library of Congress, 2002). It is intended to be a data communication format based on SGML/XML syntax, aiming at supporting the accessibility to archival resources across different institutions and focusing on the structural content of the archival description, rather than its presentation. For this reason, the EAD schema is characterised by a hierarchical informational structure, where the deepest levels in the schema may inherit descriptive information defined in the upper levels. The schema defines a total of 146 elements. The three highest level elements are `<eadheader>`, `<frontmatter>`, and `<archdesc>`. `<eadheader>` is an element containing bibliographic and descriptive information about the metadata document, while `<frontmatter>` is an optional element describing the creation, publication, or use of the metadata document (Library of Congress, 2002). Both these two upper level elements do not contain information about the archival material itself. The designated element for this purpose is `<archdesc>` which describes *"the content, context, and extent of a body of archival materials, including administrative and supplemental information that facilitates use of the materials"* (Library of Congress, 2002).

EAD metadata files can be lengthy and complex in structure, with deep nesting of the XML hierarchy elements. As Zhang and Kamps (2009) also observe, the EAD elements may be of three types:

i. atomic units (or text content elements) which contain only text and no XML elements;
ii. composite units (or nested elements) which contain as nested other XML elements;
iii. mixed elements which contain both atomic and composite units.

The EAD documents used in this study describe archival collections of the International Institute of Social History (IISH). They are of varying length and are often characterised by long spans of non-annotated, free text. The degree of annotation, especially within *mixed* element types is inconsistent. For example, some names may be annotated in one element and others not, while quite often repeated mentions of the same name may not be annotated. Moreover, the text within an annotated element may include annotator comments (e.g., translations, alternate names, questions, notes, etc.), either in square brackets or parentheses, again in an inconsistent manner. The multilingual text content poses another challenge. In particular, the languages used in the description text vary, not only within a single EAD document, but often also within an element (mixed or atomic). In our approach, the former is addressed by identifying the language at element level (cf. Section 3.2). However, the issue of mixed languages within an element is not addressed. This introduces errors, especially for multilingual elements of short text length.

3 Enrichment and Structuring Method

The overall rationale behind our method for the enrichment of EAD metadata with semantic content information is based on two hypotheses:

i. multi-word terms recognised in free text are valid indicators of content, and
ii. the respective term inter-relationships reflect the knowledge structure of the collection.

Thus, automatic term recognition and subsequent term clustering constitute the two core components of our EAD processing. In particular, as illustrated in Figure 1, we start with a pre-processing phase, where the EAD input SGML/XML files are first parsed, in order to retrieve the respective text content snippets, and then classified, based on language. Subsequently, terms are recognised automatically. The resulting terms are clustered as a hierarchy and, finally, the documents are classified according to the term hierarchy, based on the terms that they contain. To evaluate our term recognition process, we exploit knowledge from two sources: existing annotations in the EAD files, such as entity annotation residing in *mixed* elements (cf. Section 2) and entity and subject term information originating from the respective cultural heritage institution *Authority files*, namely the library files providing standard references for entities and terms that curators should use in their object descriptions. In this section, we discuss in more detail the methodology for each of the components of our approach.

3.1 EAD Text Element Extraction

In our processing of the EAD metadata XML, we focused on the free text content structured below the `<archdesc>` root element. As discussed in Section 2, it is the only top element which contains information about the archival material itself. In the *text element extraction* process, we parse the EAD XML and, from the hierarchically structured elements below `<archdesc>`, we select the text contained in `<abstract>`, `<bioghist>`, `<scopecontent>`, `<odd>`, `<note>` , `<dsc>` and `<descgrp>` and their nested elements.

Among these elements, the `<dsc>` (Description of Subordinate Components) provides information about the hierarchical groupings of the materials being described, whereas `<descgrp>` (DSC Group) defines nested encoded finding aids. They were selected because they may contain nested information of interest. The rest of the elements were selected because they contain important free text information related to the archive content:

- `<bioghist>`: describing the archive creator e.g. the life of the individual or family, or the administrative history of the organisation which created the archive;
- `<scopecontent>`: referring to the range and topical coverage of the described materials, often naming significant organisations, individuals, events, places, and subjects represented;
- `<odd>`: other descriptive data;
- `<note>`: referring to archivist comments and explanations;
- `<abstract>`: brief summaries of all the above information.

All other elements not referring to the archive semantic content, such as administrative information, storage arrangement, physical location, etc. were ignored. Moreover, atomic or composite elements without free text descriptions were not selected, because the descriptive information therein is assumed to be already fully structured.

3.2 Language Identification

As mentioned in Section 2, the languages used in the description text of the EAD documents vary, not only within a single EAD document, but often also within an EAD element. In our approach, the objective of the *language identification* process is to detect the language of the text content snippets, i.e. the output of the *text element extraction* process, and classify these snippets accordingly (cf. Figure 1).

Language identification is a text categorisation task, whereby identifiers attempt to learn the morphology of a language based on training text and, subsequently, use this information to classify unknown text accordingly. For this reason, training a language identification component requires a training corpus for each language of interest.

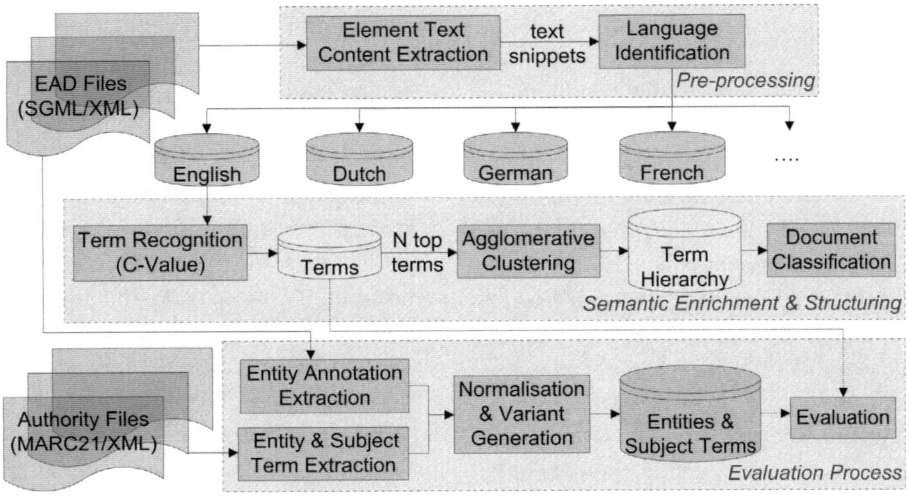

Figure 1: Block diagram of EAD metadata enrichment and structuring process

Computational approaches to language identification can be coarsely classified into information-theoretic, word-based, and N-gram-based. Information-theoretic approaches compare the compressibility of the input text to the compressibility of text in the known languages. Measuring compressibility employs mutual information measures (Poutsma, 2002). Word-based approaches consider the amount of common words or special characters between the input text and a known language. Finally, N-gram-based approaches construct language models beyond word boundaries, based on the occurrence statistics of N-grams up to some predefined length N (Dunning, 1994). The subsequent language identification in unknown text is based on the similarity of the unknown text N-gram model to each training language model.

As evidenced by these approaches, language identification relies on some form of comparison of the unknown text to known languages. For this reason, the respective text categorisation into a given language suffers when the input text is not long enough: the shorter the input text is, the fewer the available features for comparison against known language models. Moreover, errors in the categorisation process are also introduced, when the language models under comparison share the same word forms.

In our approach, we have opted for the most popular language identification method, the one based on N-grams. Nevertheless, any other language identification method could have been applied.

3.3 Term Recognition

The objective of *term recognition* is the identification of linguistic expressions denoting specialised concepts, namely domain or scientific terms. For information management and retrieval purposes, the automatic identification of terms is of particular importance because these specialised concept expressions reflect the respective document content.

Term recognition approaches largely rely on the identification of term formation patterns. Linguistic approaches use either syntactic (Justeson and Katz, 1995; Hearst, 1998), or morphological (Heid, 1998) rule patterns, often in combination with terminological or other lexical resources (Gaizauskas et al., 2000) and are typically language and domain specific.

Statistical approaches typically combine linguistic information with statistical measures. These measures can be coarsely classified into two categories: *unithood-based* and *termhood-based*. *Unithood-based* approaches measure the attachment strength among the constituents of a candidate term. For example, some unithood-based measures are frequency of co-occurrence, hypothesis testing statistics, log-likelihood ratios test (Dunning, 1993) and pointwise mutual information (Church and Hanks, 1990). *Termhood-based* approaches attempt to measure the degree up to which a candidate expression is a valid term, i.e. refers to a specialised concept. They attempt to measure this degree by considering *nestedness* information, namely the frequencies of candidate terms and their subsequences. Examples of such approaches are C-Value and NC-Value (Frantzi et al., 2000) and the statistical barrier method (Nakagawa, 2000).

It has been experimentally shown that *termhood-based* approaches to automatic term extraction outperform *unithood-based* ones and that *C-Value* (Frantzi et al., 2000) is among the best performing *termhood-based* approaches (Korkontzelos et al., 2008). For this reason, we choose to employ the *C-Value* measure in our pipeline. *C-Value* exploits nestedness and comes together with a computationally efficient algorithm, which scores candidate multi-word terms according to the measure, considering:

- the total frequency of occurrence of the candidate term;
- the frequency of the candidate term as part of longer candidate terms;
- the number of these **distinct** longer candidates;
- the length of the candidate term (in tokens).

These arguments are expressed in the following nestedness formula:

$$N(\alpha) = \begin{cases} f(\alpha), & \text{if } \alpha \text{ is not nested} \\ f(\alpha) - \frac{1}{|T_\alpha|} \sum_{b \in T_\alpha} f(b), & \text{otherwise} \end{cases} \quad (1)$$

where α is the candidate term, $f(\alpha)$ is its frequency, T_α is the set of candidate terms that contain α and $|T_\alpha|$ is the cardinality of T_α. In simple terms, the more frequently a candidate term appears as a substring of other candidates, the less likely it is to be a valid term. However, the greater the number of **distinct** term candidates in which the target term candidate occurs as nested, the more likely it is to be a valid term. The final *C-Value* score considers the length ($|\alpha|$) of each candidate term (α) as well:

$$C\text{-}value(\alpha) = \log_2 |\alpha| \times N(\alpha) \quad (2)$$

The C-Value method requires linguistic pre-processing in order to detect syntactic term formation patterns. In our approach, we used Lex-Tagger (Vasilakopoulos, 2003), which combines transformation-based learning with decision trees and we adapted its respective lexicon to our domain. We also included WordNet lemma information in our processing, for text normalisation purposes. Linguistic pre-processing is followed by the computation of C-Value on the candidate terms, in length order, longest first. Candidates that satisfy a C-Value threshold are sorted in decreasing C-Value order.

3.4 Hierarchical Agglomerative Clustering

In our approach, term recognition provides content indicators. In order to make explicit the knowledge structure of the EAD, our method requires some form of concept classification and structuring. The process of *hierarchical agglomerative clustering* serves this objective.

Agglomerative algorithms are very popular in the field of *unsupervised concept hierarchy induction* and are typically employed to produce unlabelled taxonomies (King, 1967; Sneath and Sokal, 1973). *Hierarchical clustering* algorithms are based on measuring the distance (dissimilarity) between pairs of objects. Given an object distance metric D, the similarity of two clusters, $\mathcal{A}$ and $\mathcal{B}$, can be defined as a function of the distance D between the objects that the clusters contain. According to this similarity, also called *linkage criterion*, the choice of which clusters to merge or split is made. In our approach, we have experimented with the three most popular criteria, namely:

Complete linkage (CL): The similarity of two clusters is the maximum distance between their elements

$$sim_{CL}(\mathcal{A}, \mathcal{B}) = \max_{x \in \mathcal{A}, y \in \mathcal{B}} D(x, y) \quad (3)$$

Single linkage (SL): The similarity of two clusters is the minimum distance between their elements

$$sim_{SL}(\mathcal{A}, \mathcal{B}) = \min_{x \in \mathcal{A}, y \in \mathcal{B}} D(x, y) \quad (4)$$

Average linkage (AL): The similarity of two clusters is the average distance between their elements

$$sim_{AL}(\mathcal{A}, \mathcal{B}) = \frac{1}{|\mathcal{A}| \times |\mathcal{B}|} \sum_{x \in \mathcal{A}} \sum_{y \in \mathcal{B}} D(x, y) \quad (5)$$

To estimate the distance metric D we use either the *document co-occurrence* or the *lexical similarity* metric. The chosen distance metric D and linkage criterion are employed to derive a hierarchy of terms by agglomerative clustering.

Our *document co-occurrence (DC)* metric is defined as the number of documents (d) in the collection (R) in which both terms (t_1 and t_2) co-occur:

$$DC = \frac{1}{|R|} |\{d : (d \in R) \wedge (t_1 \in d) \wedge (t_2 \in d)\}| \quad (6)$$

The above metric accepts that the distance between two terms is inversely proportional to the number of documents in which they co-occur.

Lexical Similarity (LS), as defined in Nenadić and Ananiadou (2006), is based on shared term constituents:

$$LS = \frac{|P(h_1) \cap P(h_2)|}{|P(h_1)| + |P(h_2)|} + \frac{|P(t_1) \cap P(t_2)|}{|P(t_1)| + |P(t_2)|} \qquad (7)$$

where t_1 and t_2 are two terms, h_1 and h_2 their heads, $P(h_1)$ and $P(h_2)$ their set of head words, and $P(t_1)$ and $P(t_2)$ their set of constituent words, respectively.

3.5 Document Classification

The term hierarchy is used in our approach for semantic classification of documents. In this process, we start by assigning to each leaf node of the term hierarchy the set of EAD documents in which the corresponding term occurs. Higher level nodes are assigned the union of the document sets of their daughters. The process is bottom-up and applied iteratively, until all hierarchy nodes are assigned a set of documents.

Document classification, i.e. the assignment of document sets to term hierarchy nodes, is useful, among others, for structured search and indexing purposes. Moreover, it provides a direct soft-clustering of documents based on semantics, given the number of desired clusters, C. C corresponds to a certain horizontal cut of the term hierarchy, so that C top nodes appear, instead of one. The document sets assigned to these C top nodes represent the C desired clusters. This document clustering approach is *soft*, since each document can occur in one or more clusters.

3.6 Evaluation Process

The automatic *evaluation process*, illustrated in Figure 1, serves the purpose of evaluating the *term recognition* accuracy. Since the objective of term recognition tools is the detection of linguistic expressions denoting specialised concepts, i.e. terms, the results evaluation would ideally require input from the respective domain experts. This is a laborious and time consuming process which also entails finding the experts willing to dedicate effort and time for this task. In response to this issue, we decided to exploit the available domain-specific knowledge resources and automate part of the evaluation process by comparing our results to this existing information. Thus, the automatic *evaluation process* is intended to give us an initial estimate of our performance and reduce the amount of results requiring manual evaluation. The available resources used are of two types:

i. entity annotations in the EAD documents (i.e. names of persons, organisations and geographical locations);
ii. entity and subject terms originating from the cultural heritage institution *Authority files*.

The entity annotations in the EAD documents were not considered during our *term recognition*. The entity and subject terms of the respective *Authority file* records are encoded in MARC21/XML format (Library of Congress, 2010). MARC (MAchine-Readable Cataloging) is a standard initiated by the US Library of Congress and concerns the representation of bibliographic information and related data elements used in library catalogues. The MARC21 Authority files resource used in our evaluation provides, among other information, the standard references for entities and the respective possible entity reference variations, such as alternate names or acronyms, etc., that curators should use in their object descriptions. The subject term Authority records provide mappings between a legacy subject term thesaurus which is no longer used for classification, and current library records.

In the *evaluation process* the EAD SGML/XML and the MARC21/XML Authority files are first parsed by the respective parsers in order to extract the XML elements of interest. Subsequently, the text-content of the elements is processed for normalisation and variant generation purposes. In this process, normalisation involves cleaning up the text from intercepted comments and various types of inconsistent notes, such as dates, aliases and alternate names, translations, clarifications, assumptions, questions, lists, etc. Variant generation involves detecting the acronyms, abbreviated names and aliases mentioned in the element text and creating the reversed variants for, e.g., `[Last_Name, First_Name]` sequences. The results of this process, from both EAD and Authority files, are merged into a single list for every respective category (or-

language	snippets	language	snippets
Dutch	50,363	Spanish	3,430
German	41,334	Danish	2,478
English	19,767	Italian	1,100
French	6,182	Swedish	699

Table 1: Number of snippets per identified language.

ganisations, persons, geographic locations and subject terms) and are compared to our term results list.

4 Experimental Setting

For training the *language identification* component, we used the European Parliament Proceedings Parallel Corpus (Europarl) which covers the proceedings of the European Parliament from 1996 to 2006 (Koehn, 2005). The corpus size is 40 million words per language and is translated in Danish, German, Greek, English, Spanish, Finnish, French, Italian, Dutch, Portuguese and Swedish. In our experiments, we take as input for subsequent term recognition only the snippets identified as English text.

In the experiments reported in this work, we accept as term candidates morpho-syntactic pattern sequences which consist of adjectives and nouns, and end with a noun. The *C-Value* algorithm (cf. Section 3.3) was implemented under two different settings:

i. one only considering as term candidates adjective and noun sequences that appear at least once as non-nested in other candidate terms; and
ii. one that considers all adjective and noun sequences, even if they never occur as non-nested.

Considering that part-of-speech taggers usually suffer high error rates when applied on specialty domains, the former setting is expected to increase precision, whereas the latter to increase recall (cf. Section 5).

We accepted as valid terms all term candidates whose *C-Value* score exceeds a threshold, which was set to 3.0 after experimentation. In the subsequent hierarchical agglomerative clustering process, we experimented with all six combinations of the three linkage criteria (i.e. *complete*, *single* and *average*) with the two distance metrics (i.e. *document co-occurrence* and *lexical similarity*) described in Section 3.4.

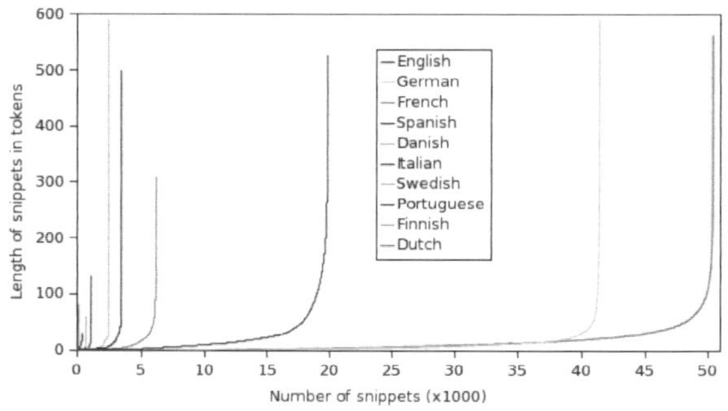

Figure 2: Length of snippets per identified language.

5 Results

The EAD document collection used for this study consisted of 3,093 SGML/XML files. As shown on Table 1, according to our language identifier, the majority of the text snippets of the selected EAD XML elements were in Dutch, followed by German and English. We selected for later processing 19,767 snippets classified as English text, corresponding to 419,857 tokens. A quantitative evaluation of the language identifier results has not been performed. However, our observation of the term recognition results showed that there were some phrases, mostly Dutch and German entity names (organisations and persons mostly) classified as English. This might be due to these entities appearing in their original language within English text, as it is often the case in our EAD files. Moreover, manual inspection of our results showed that other languages classified as English, e.g. Turkish and Czech, were not covered by Europarl.

As mentioned in Section 3.2, short text snippets may affect language identification performance. Figure 2 illustrates the snippet length per identified language. We observe that the majority of text snippets is below 10 tokens, few fall within an average length of 20 to 50 tokens approximately, and very few are above 100 tokens.

Figure 3 shows the results of our automatic evaluation for the term recognition process. In this graph, the upper, red curve shows the percentage of correct terms for the C-Value setting considering as term candidates adjective and noun sequences that appear at least once as non-nested in other candidate terms. The lower, blue curve shows the per-

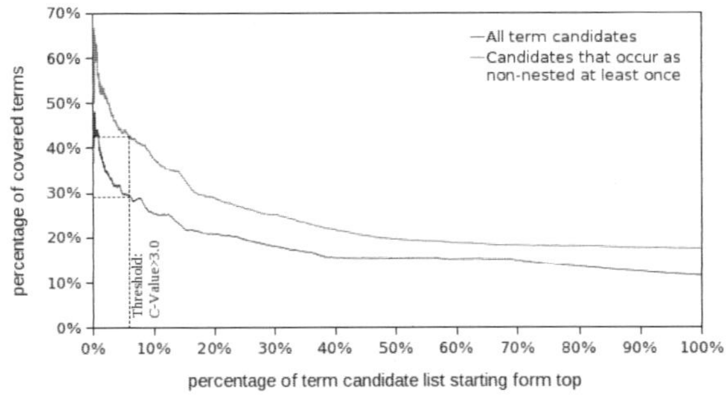

Figure 3: Term coverage for each C-Value setting based on EAD & Authority entity and subject term evaluation.

centage of correct terms for the C-Value setting considering all adjective and noun sequences, even if they never occur as non-nested. In this automatic evaluation, *correct* terms are, as presented in Section 3.6, those candidate terms matching the combined lists of entity and subject terms acquired by the respective EAD and MARC21 Authority files. We observe that the C-Value setting which considers only noun phrase patterns occurring at least once as non-nested, displays precision up to approximately 70% for the top terms in the ranked list, whereas the other setting considering all noun phrase sequences, reaches a maximum of 49%. The entire result set above the 3.0 C-Value threshold amounts to $1,345$ and $2,297$ terms for each setting, and reaches precision of 42.01% and 28.91% respectively. Thus, regarding precision, the selective setting clearly outperforms the one considering all noun phrases, but it also reaches a lower recall, as indicated by the actual terms within the threshold. We also observe that precision drops gradually below the threshold, an indication that the ranking of the C-Value measure is effective in promoting valid terms towards the top. This automatic evaluation considers as erroneous unknown terms which may be valid. Further manual evaluation by domain experts is required for a more complete picture of the results.

Figure 4 shows six dendrograms, each representing the term hierarchy produced by the respective combination of linkage criterion to distance metric. The input for these experiments consists of all terms exceeding the C-Value threshold, and by considering only noun phrase sequences appearing at least once as non-nested. Since the hierarchies contain $1,345$ terms, the dendrograms are very dense and difficult to inspect thoroughly. However, we include them based on the fact that the overall shape of the dendrogram can indicate how much narrow or broad the corresponding hierarchy is and indirectly its quality. Narrow here characterises hierarchies whose most non-terminal nodes are parents of one terminal and one non-terminal node. Narrow hierarchies are deep while broader hierarchies are shallower.

Broad and shallow hierarchies are, in our case, of higher quality, since terms are expected to be related to each other and form distinct groups. In this view, average linkage leads to richer hierarchies (Figures 4(c), 4(f)), followed by single linkage (Figures 4(b), 4(e)) and, finally, complete linkage (Figures 4(a), 4(d)). The hierarchy of higher quality seems to be the result of average linkage and *document co-occurrence* combination (Figure 4(c)), followed by the combination of average linkage and *lexical similarity* (Figure 4(f)). Clearly, these two hierarchies need to be investigated manually and closely to extract further conclusions. Moreover, an application-based evaluation could investigate whether different clustering settings suit different tasks.

6 Conclusion and Future Work

In this paper, we have presented a methodology for semantically enriching archival description metadata and structuring the metadata collection. We consider that terms are indicators of content semantics. In our approach, we perform term recognition and then hierarchically structure the recognised terms. Finally, we use the term hierarchy to classify the metadata documents. We also propose an automatic evaluation of the recognised terms, by comparing them to domain knowledge resources.

For term recognition, we used the C-Value algorithm and found that considering noun phrases which appear at least once independently, outperforms considering *all* noun phrases. Regarding hierarchical clustering, we observe that the average linkage criterion combined with a distance metric based on document co-occurrence produces a rich broad hierarchy. A more thorough evaluation of these results is required. This should include a manual evaluation of recognised terms by domain experts and an application-based evaluation of the resulting document classification.

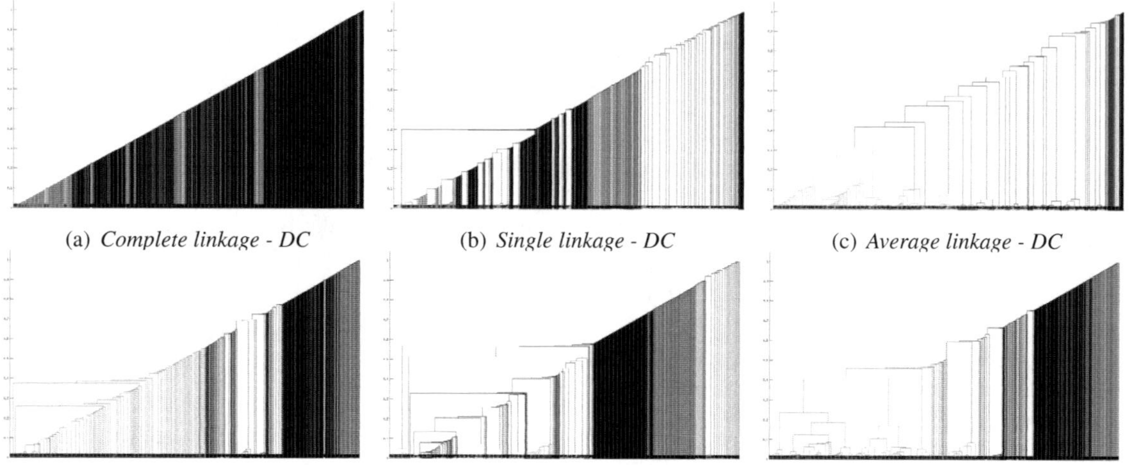

(a) *Complete linkage - DC* (b) *Single linkage - DC* (c) *Average linkage - DC*

(d) *Complete linkage - LS* (e) *Single linkage - LS* (f) *Average linkage - LS*

Figure 4: Dendrograms showing the results of agglomerative clustering for all linkage criteria and distance metrics, *document co-occurrence (DC)* and *Lexical Similarity (LS)*.

References

Lina Bountouri and Manolis Gergatsoulis. 2009. Interoperability between archival and bibliographic metadata: An EAD to MODS crosswalk. *Journal of Library Metadata*, 9(1-2):98–133.

Kenneth Church and Patrick Hanks. 1990. Word association norms, mutual information, and lexicography. *Computational Linguistics*, 16(1):22–29.

CIDOC. 2006. The CIDOC Conceptual Reference Model. CIDOC Documentation Standards Working Group, International Documentation Committee, International Council of Museums. `http://www.cidoc-crm.org/`.

DCMI. 2011. The Dublin Core Metadata Initiative. `http://dublincore.org/`.

Ted Dunning. 1993. Accurate methods for the statistics of surprise and coincidence. *Computational Linguistics*, 19(1):61–74.

Ted Dunning. 1994. Statistical identification of language. MCCS 94-273. Technical report, Computing Research Laboratory, New Mexico State University.

Katerina Frantzi, Sophia Ananiadou, and Hideki Mima. 2000. Automatic recognition of multi-word terms: the C-value/NC-value method. *International Journal on Digital Libraries*, 3(2):115–130.

Robert Gaizauskas, George Demetriou, and Kevin Humphreys. 2000. Term recognition in biological science journal articles. In *Proc. of the NLP 2000 Workshop on Computational Terminology for Medical and Biological Applications*, pages 37–44, Patras, Greece.

Marti Hearst. 1998. Automated discovery of WordNet relations. In Christiane Fellbaum, editor, *WordNet: An Electronic Lexical Database*, pages 131–153. MIT Press.

Ulrich Heid. 1998. A linguistic bootstrapping approach to the extraction of term candidates from german text. *Terminology*, 5(2):161–181.

John Justeson and Slava Katz. 1995. Technical terminology: some linguistic properties and an algorithm for identification in text. *Natural Language Engineering*, 1(1):9–27.

Benjamin King. 1967. Step-Wise clustering procedures. *Journal of the American Statistical Association*, 62(317):86–101.

Philipp Koehn. 2005. Europarl: A parallel corpus for statistical machine translation. In *Machine Translation Summit X*, pages 79–86, Phuket, Thailand.

Marijn Koolen, Avi Arampatzis, Jaap Kamps, Vincent de Keijzer, and Nir Nussbaum. 2007. Unified access to heterogeneous data in cultural heritage. In *Proc. of RIAO '07*, pages 108–122, Pittsburgh, PA, USA.

Ioannis Korkontzelos, Ioannis Klapaftis, and Suresh Manandhar. 2008. Reviewing and evaluating automatic term recognition techniques. In Bengt Nordström and Aarne Ranta, editors, *Proc. of GoTAL '08*, volume 5221 of *LNCS*, pages 248–259, Gothenburg, Sweden. Springer.

Shu-Hsien Liao, Hong-Chu Huang, and Ya-Ning Chen. 2010. A semantic web approach to heterogeneous metadata integration. In Jeng-Shyang Pan, Shyi-Ming Chen, and Ngoc Thanh Nguyen, editors, *Proc. of ICCCI '10*, volume 6421 of *LNCS*, pages 205–214, Kaohsiung, Taiwan. Springer.

Library of Congress. 2002. Encoded archival description (EAD), version 2002. Encoded Archival Description Working Group: Society of American Archivists,

Network Development and MARC Standards Office, Library of Congress. http://www.loc.gov/ead/.

Library of Congress. 2010. MARC standards. Network Development and MARC Standards Office, Library of Congress, USA. http://www.loc.gov/marc/index.html.

Irene Lourdi, Christos Papatheodorou, and Martin Doerr. 2009. Semantic integration of collection description: Combining CIDOC/CRM and Dublin Core collections application profile. *D-Lib Magazine*, 15(7/8).

Hiroshi Nakagawa. 2000. Automatic term recognition based on statistics of compound nouns. *Terminology*, 6(2):195–210.

Goran Nenadić and Sophia Ananiadou. 2006. Mining semantically related terms from biomedical literature. *ACM Transactions on Asian Language Information Processing (TALIP)*, 5(1):22–43.

Arjen Poutsma. 2002. Applying monte carlo techniques to language identification. *Language and Computers*, 45:179–189.

Peter Sneath and Robert Sokal. 1973. *Numerical taxonomy: the principles and practice of numerical classification*. Freeman, San Francisco, USA.

Argyris Vasilakopoulos. 2003. Improved unknown word guessing by decision tree induction for POS tagging with tbl. In *Proc. of CLUK '03*, Edinburgh, UK.

Junte Zhang and Jaap Kamps. 2009. Focused search in digital archives. In Gottfried Vossen, Darrell D. E. Long, and Jeffrey Xu Yu, editors, *Proc. of WISE '09*, volume 5802 of *LNCS*, pages 463–471, Poznan, Poland. Springer.

Structure-Preserving Pipelines for Digital Libraries

Massimo Poesio
University of Essex, UK and
Università di Trento, Italy

Eduard Barbu
Egon W. Stemle
Università di Trento, Italy

Christian Girardi
FBK-irst, Trento, Italy
cgirardi@fbk.eu

{massimo.poesio,eduard.barbu,egon.stemle}
@unitn.it

Abstract

Most existing HLT pipelines assume the input is pure text or, at most, HTML and either ignore (logical) document structure or remove it. We argue that identifying the structure of documents is essential in digital library and other types of applications, and show that it is relatively straightforward to extend existing pipelines to achieve ones in which the structure of a document is preserved.

1 Introduction

Many off-the-shelf Human Language Technology (HLT) pipelines are now freely available (examples include LingPipe,[1] OpenNLP,[2] GATE[3] (Cunningham et al., 2002), TextPro[4] (Pianta et al., 2008)), and although they support a variety of document formats as input, actual processing (mostly) takes no advantage of structural information, i.e. structural information is not used, or stripped off during preprocessing. Such processing can be considered safe, e.g. in case of news wire snippets, when processing does not need to be aware of sentence or paragraph boundaries, or of text being part of a table or a figure caption. However, when processing large documents, section or chapter boundaries may be considered an important segmentation to use, and when working with the type of data typically found in digital libraries or historical archives, such as whole books, exhibition catalogs, scientific articles, contracts we should keep the structure. At least three types of problems can be observed when trying to use a standard HLT pipeline for documents whose structure cannot be easily ignored:

- techniques for extracting content from plain text do not work on, say, bibliographic references, or lists;
- simply removing the parts of a document that do not contain plain text may not be the right thing to do for all applications, as sometimes the information contained in them may also be useful (e.g., keywords are often useful for classification, bibliographic references are useful in a variety of applications) or even the most important parts of a text (e.g., in topic classification information provided by titles and other types of document structure is often the most important part of a document);
- even for parts of a document that still can be considered as containing basically text—e.g., titles—knowing that we are dealing with what we will call here **non-paragraph** text can be useful to achieve good - or improve - performance as e.g., the syntactic conventions used in those type of document elements may be different - e.g., the syntax of NPs in titles can be pretty different from that in other sections of text.

In this paper we summarize several years of work on developing structure-preserving pipelines for different applications. We discuss the incorporation of

[1] `http://alias-i.com/lingpipe/`
[2] `http://incubator.apache.org/opennlp/`
[3] `http://http://gate.ac.uk/`
[4] `http://textpro.fbk.eu/`

document structure parsers both in pipelines which the information is passed in BOI format (Ramshaw and Marcus, 1995), such as the TEXTPRO pipeline (Pianta et al., 2008), and in pipelines based on a standoff XML (Ide, 1998). We also present several distinct applications that require preserving document structure.

The structure of the paper is as follows. We first discuss the notion of document structure and previous work in extracting it. We then introduce our architecture for a structure-preserving pipeline. Next, we discuss two pipelines based on this general architecture. A discussion follows.

2 The Logical Structure of a Document

Documents have at least two types of structure[5]. The term **geometrical**, or **layout**, structure, refers to the structuring of a document according to its visual appearance, its graphical representation (pages, columns, etc). The **logical** structure (Luong et al., 2011) refers instead to the content's organization to fulfill an intended overall communicative purpose (title, author list, chapter, section, bibliography, etc). Both of these structures can be represented as trees; however, these two tree structures may not be mutually compatible (i.e. representable within a single tree structure with non-overlapping structural elements): e.g. a single page may contain the end of one section and the beginning of the next, or a paragraph may just span part of a page or column. In this paper we will be exclusively concerned with logical structure.

2.1 Proposals concerning logical structure

Early on the separation of presentation and content, i.e. of layout and logical structure, was promoted by the early adopters of computers within the typesetting community; well-known, still widely used, systems include the LaTeXmeta-package for electronic typesetting. The importance of separating document logical structure from document content for electronic document processing and for the document creators lead to the ISO 8613-1:1989(E) specification where *logical structure* is defined as the result of dividing and subdividing the content of a document into increasingly smaller parts, on the basis of the human-perceptible meaning of the content, for example, into chapters, sections, subsections, and paragraphs. The influential ISO 8879:1986 Standard Generalized Markup Language (SGML) specification fostered document format definitions like the Open Document Architecture (ODA) and interchange format, CCITT T.411-T.424 / ISO 8613.

Even though the latter format never gained wide-spread support, its technological ideas influenced many of today's formats, like HTML and CSS as well as, the Extensible Markup Language (XML), today's successor of SGML. Today, the ISO 26300:2006 Open Document Format for Office Applications (ODF), and the ISO 29500:2008 Office Open XML (OOXML) format are the important XML-based document file formats.

For the work on digital libraries the Text Encoding Initiative (TEI)[6],most notably, developed guidelines specifying encoding methods for machine-readable texts. They have been widely used, e.g. by libraries, museums, and publishers.

The most common logical elements in such proposals—chapters, sections, paragraphs, footnotes, etc.—can all be found in HTML, LaTeX, or any other modern text processor. It should be pointed out however that many modern types of documents found on the Web do not fit this pattern: e.g. blog posts with comments, and the structure of reply threads and inner-linkings to other comments cannot be captured; or much of wikipedia's non-paragraph text. (For an in depth comparison and discussion of logical formats, and formal characterizations thereof we suggest (Power et al., 2003; Summers, 1998).)

2.2 Extracting logical structure

Two families of methods have been developed to extract document structure. Older systems tend to follow the **template-matching** paradigm. In this approach the assignment of the categories to parts of the string is done by matching a sequence of hand crafted templates against the input string S. An instance of this kind of systems is DeLos (Derivation of Logical Structure) (Niyogi and Srihari, 1995) which uses control rules, strategy rules and knowl-

[5]other structure types include e.g. (hyper)links, cross-references, citations, temporal and spatial relationships

[6]`http://www.tei-c.org`

edge rules to derive the logical document structure from a scanned image of the document. A more elaborate procedure for the same task is employed by Ishitani (Ishitani, 1999). He uses rules to classify the text lines derived from scanned document image and then employs a set of heuristics to assign the classified lines to logical document components. The template based approach is also used by the ParaTools, a set of Perl modules for parsing reference strings (Jewell, 2000). The drawback of the template based approaches is that they are usually not portable to new domains and are not flexible enough to accommodate errors. Domain adaptation requires the devising of new rules many of them from scratch. Further the scanned documents or the text content extracted from PDF have errors which are not easily dealt with by template based systems.

Newer systems use supervised machine learning techniques which are much more flexible but require training data. Extracting document structure is an instance of (hierarchical) **sequence labeling**, a well known problem which naturally arises in diverse fields like speech recognition, digital signal processing or bioinformatics. Two kinds of machine learning techniques are most commonly used for this problem: Hidden Markov Models (HMM) and Conditional Random Fields (CRF). A system for parsing reference strings based on HMMs was developed in (Hetzner, 2008) for the California Digital Library. The system implements a first order HMM where the set of states of the model are represented by the categories in C; the alphabet is hand built and tailored for the task and the probabilities in the probability matrix are derived empirically. The system obtains an average F_1 measure of 93 for the Cora dataset. A better performance for sequence labeling is obtained if CRF replaces the traditional HMM. The reason for this is that CRF systems better tolerate errors and they have good performance even when richer features are not available. A system which uses CRF and a series of post-processing rules for both document logical structure identification and reference string parsing is ParsCit (Councill et al., 2008). ParsCit comprises three sub-modules: SectLabel and ParseHead for document logical structure identification and ParsCit for reference string parsing. The system is built on top of the well known CRF++ package.

The linguistic surface level, i.e. the linear order of words, sentences, and paragraphs, and the hierarchical, tree-like, logical structure also lends itself to parsing-like methods for the structure analysis. However, the complexity of fostering, maintaining, and augmenting document structure grammars is challenging, and the notorious uncertainty of the input demands for the whole set of stochastic techniques the field has to offer – this comes at a high computing price; cf. e.g.,(Lee et al., 2003; Mao et al., 2003). It is therefore not surprising that high-throughput internet sites like CiteSeerX[7] use a flat text classifier (Day et al., 2007).[8]

3 Digital Libraries and Document Structure Preservation

Our first example of application in which document structure preservation is essential are digital libraries (Witten et al., 2003). In a digital library setting, HLT techniques can be used for a variety of purposes, ranging from indexing the documents in the library for search to classifying them to automatically extracting metadata. It is therefore becoming more and more common for HLT techniques to be incorporated in document management platforms and used to support a librarian when he / she enters a new document in the library. Clearly, it would be beneficial if such a pipeline could identify the logical structure of the documents being entered, and preserve it: this information could be used by the document management platform to, for instance, suggest the librarian the most important keywords, find the text to be indexed or even summarized, and produce citations lists, possibly to be compared with the digital library's list of citations to decide whether to add them.

We are in the process of developing a Portal for Research in the Humanities (Portale Ricerca Umanistica-PRU). This digital library will eventually include research articles about the Trentino region from Archeology, History, and History of Art. So far, the pipeline to be discussed next has been used to include in the library texts from the Italian archeology journal *Preistoria Alpina*. One of our goals was to develop a pipeline that could be used

[7] `http://citeseerx.ist.psu.edu/`

[8] Still, especially multimedia documents with their possible temporal and spatial relationships might need more sophisticated methods.

whenever a librarian uploads an article in this digital library, to identify title, authors, abstract, keywords, content, and bibliographic references from the article. The implemented portal already incorporates information extraction techniques that are used to identify in the 'content' part of the output of the pipeline temporal expressions, locations, and entities such as archeological sites, cultures, and artifacts. This information is used to allow spatial, temporal, and entity-based access to articles.

We are in the process of enriching the portal so that title and author information are also used to automatically produce a bibliographical card for the article that will be entered in the PRU Library Catalog, and bibliographical references are processed in order to link the article to related articles and to the catalog as well. The next step will be to modify the pipeline (in particular, to modify the Named Entity Recognition component) to include in the library articles from other areas of research in the Humanities, starting with History. There are also plans to make it possible for authors themselves to insert their research articles and books in the Portal, as done e.g., in the Semantics Archive.[9].

We believe the functionalities offered by this portal are or will become pretty standard in digital libraries, and therefore that the proposals discussed in this paper could find an application beyond the use in our Portal. We will also see below that a document structure-sensitive pipeline can find other applications.

4 Turning an Existing Pipeline into One that Extracts and Preserves Document Structure

Most freely available HLT pipelines simply eliminate markup during the initial phases of processing in order to eliminate parts of the document structure that cannot be easily processed by their modules (e.g., bibliographic references), but this is not appropriate for the Portal described in the previous section, where different parts of the output of the pipeline need to be processed in different ways. On the other end, it was not really feasible to develop a completely new pipeline from scratch. The approach we pursued in this work was to take an existing pipeline and turn it into one which extracts and outputs document structure. In this Section we discuss the approach we followed. In the next Section we discuss the first pipeline we developed according to this approach; then we discuss how the approach was adopted for other purposes, as well.

Incorporating a document structure extractor in a pipeline requires the solution of two basic problems: where to insert the module, and how to pass on document structure information. Concerning the first issue, we decided to insert the document structure parser after tokenization but before sentence processing. In regards to the second issue, there are at present three main formats for exchanging information between elements of an HLT pipeline:

- inline, where each module inserts information in a pre-defined fashion into the file received as input;
- tabular format as done in CONLL, where tokens occupy the first column and each new layer of information is annotated in a separate new column, using the so-called IOB format to represent bracketing (Ramshaw and Marcus, 1995);
- standoff format, where new layers of information are stored in separate files.

The two main formats used by modern HLT pipelines are tabular format, and inline or standoff XML format. Even though we will illustrate the problem of preserving document structure in a pipeline of the former type the PRU pipeline itself supports tabular format and inline XML (TEI compliant).

The solution we adopted, illustrated in Figure 1, involves using **sentence headers** to preserve document structure information. In most pipelines using a tabular interchange information, the output of a module consists of a number of sentences each of which consists of

- a **header**: a series of lines with a hash character # at the beginning;
- a set of tab-delimited lines representing tokens and token annotations;
- an empty EOF line.

[9] http://semanticsarchive.net/

```
# FILE: 11
# PART: id1
# SECTION: title
# FIELDS: token    tokenstart  sentence  pos   lemma        entity   nerType
Spondylus          0           -         SPN   Spondylus    O        B-SITE
gaederopus         10          -         YF    gaederopus   O        O
,                  20          -         XPW   ,            O        O
gioiello           22          -         SS    gioiello     O        O
dell'              31          -         E     dell'        O        O
Europa             36          -         SPN   europa       B-GPE    B-SITE
preistorica        43          -         AS    preistorico  O        O
.                  55          <eos>     XPS   full_stop    O        O
# FILE: 11
# PART: id2
# SECTION: author
# FIELDS: token    tokenstart  sentence  pos   lemma        entity   nerType
MARIA              0           -         SPN   maria        B-PER    O
A                  6           -         E     a            I-PER    O
BORRELLO           8           -         SPN   BORRELLO     I-PER    O
&                  17          -         XPO   &            O        O
.                  19          <eos>     XPS   full_stop    O        O

(TEI compliant inline XML snippet:)
<text>
  <body>
    <div type="section" xml:lang="it">
      [...]
      <p id="p2" type="author">
        <s id="p2s1"><name key="PER1" type="person">MARIA A BORRELLO</name>&.</s>
      </p>
    </div>
  </body>
</text>
```

Figure 1: Using sentence headers to preserve document structure information. For illustration, the TEI compliant inline XML snippet of the second sentence has been added.

The header in such pipelines normally specifies only the file id (constant through the file), the number of the sentence within the file, and the columns (see Figure 1). This format however can also be used to pass on document structure information provided that the pipeline modules ignore all lines beginning with a hash, as these lines can then be used to provide additional meta information. We introduce an additional tag, SECTION, with the following meaning: a line beginning with `# SECTION:` specifies the position in the document structure of the following sentence. Thus for instance, in Figure 1, the line

```
# SECTION: title
```

specifies that the following sentence is a title.

5 An Pipeline for Research Articles in Archeology

The pipeline currently in use in the PRU Portal we are developing is based on the strategy just discussed. In this Section We discuss the pipeline in more detail.

5.1 Modules

The pipeline for processing archaeological articles integrates three main modules: a module for recovering the logical structure of the documents, a module for Italian and English POS tagging and a general Name Entity Recognizer and finally, a Gazetteer Based Name Entity Recognizer. The architecture of the system is presented in figure 2. Each module except the first one takes as input the output of the previous module in the sequence.

1. **Text Extraction**. This module extracts the text from PDF documents. Text extraction from PDF is a notoriously challenging task. We experimented with many software packages and obtained the best results with *pdftotext*. This is a component of XPDF, an open source viewer for PDF documents. *pdftotext* allows the extraction of the text content of PDF documents in a variety of encodings. The main drawback of the text extractor is that it does not always preserve the original text order.

2. **Language Identification**. The archeology repository contains articles written in one of the two languages: Italian or English. This module uses the TextCat language guesser[10] for guessing the language of sentences. The language identification task is complicated by the fact that some articles contain text in both languages: for example, an article written in English may have an Italian abstract and/or an Italian conclusion.

3. **Logical Structure Identification**. This module extracts the logical structure of a document. For example, it identifies important parts like the title, the authors, the main headers, tables or figures. For this task we train the SectLabel component of ParsCit on the articles in the archeology repository. Details on the training process, the tag set and the performance of the module are provided in section 5.2.

4. **Linguistic Processing**. A set of modules in the pipeline then perform linguistic processing on specific parts of the document (the Bibliography Section is excluded for example). First English or Italian POS is carried out as appropriate, followed by English or Italian NER. NER adaptation techniques have been developed to identify non-standard types entities that are important in the domain, such as *Archeological Sites* and *Archeological Cultures*. (This work is discussed elsewhere.)

5. **Reference Parsing**. This module relies on the output of ParsCit software to update the Archeology Database Bibliography table with the parsed references for each article. First, each parsed reference is corrected in an automatic post processing step. Then, the module checks, using a simple heuristic, if the entry already exists in the table and updates the table, if appropriate, with the new record.

Finally, the documents processed by the pipeline are indexed using the Lucene search engine.

5.2 Training the Logical Document Structure Identifier

As mentioned in Section 5, we use ParsCit to find the logical structure of the documents in the archeology

[10] http://odur.let.rug.nl/~vannoord/TextCat/

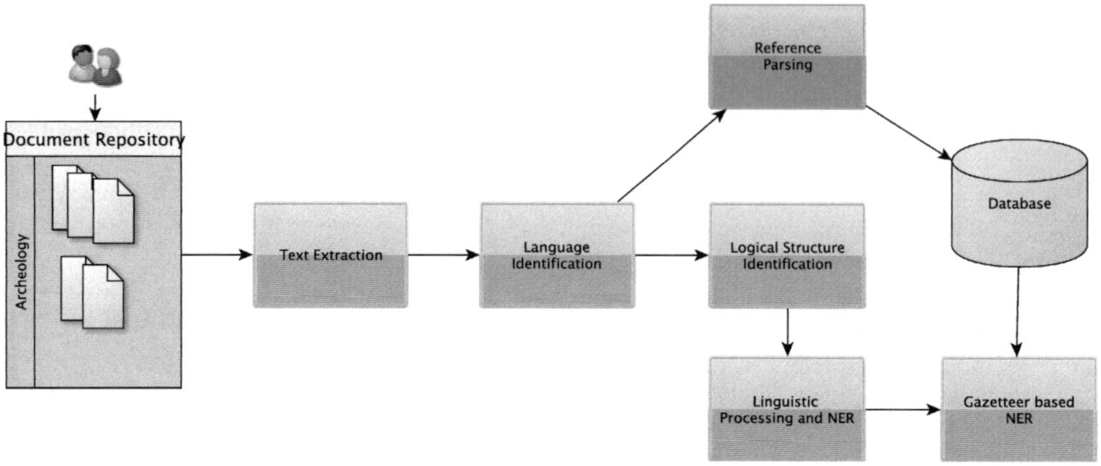

Figure 2: The pipeline of the system for PDF article processing in the Archeology Domain

domain. ParsCit comes with general CRF trained models; unfortunately, they do not perform well on archeology documents. There are some particularities of archeology repository articles that require the retraining of the models. First, as said before, the text extracted from PDF is not perfect. Second, the archeology articles contain many figures with bilingual captions. Third, the articles have portions of the texts in both languages: Italian and English. To improve the parsing performance two models are trained: the first model should capture the logical documents structure for those documents that have Italian as main language but might contain portions in English (like the abstract or summary). The second model is trained with documents that have English as main language but might contain fragments in Italian (like abstract or summary).

The document structure annotation was performed by a student in the archeology department, and was checked by one of the authors. In total 55 documents have been annotated (35 with Italian as main language, 20 with English as main Language). The tagset used for the annotation was specifically devised for archeology articles. However, as it can be seen below most of the devised tags can also be found in general scientific articles. In Table 1 we present the tag set used for annotation. The column "Tag Count" gives the number of each tag in the annotated documents.

In general the meaning of the tags is self-explanatory with the possible exception of the tag *VolumeInfo*, which reports information for volume the article is part of. An annotation example using this tag is: "<VolumeInfo> Preistoria Alpina v. 38 (2002) Trento 2002 ISSN 0393-0157 </VolumeInfo>". The volume information can be further processed by extracting the volume number, the year of the issue and the International Standard Serial Number (ISSN). To asses the performance of the trained models we performed a five fold cross-validation. The results are reported in the table 2 and are obtained for each tag using the F_1 measure (1):

$$F_1 = \frac{2 \times P \times R}{P + R} \quad (1)$$

The results obtained for the Archeology articles are in line with those obtained by the authors of ParsCit and reported in (Luong et al., 2011). The tag categories for which the performance of the system is bad are the multilingual tags (e.g. ItalianAbstract or Italian Summary in articles where the main language is English). We will address this issue in the future by adapting the language identifier to label multilingual documents. We also noticed that many mis-tagged titles, notes or section headers are split on multiple lines after the text extraction stage. The system performance might be further improved if a pre-processing step immediately after the text extraction is introduced.

Tag	Tag Count
ItalianFigureCaption	456
ItalianBodyText	347
EnglishFigureCaption	313
SectionHeader	248
EnglishTableCaption	58
ItalianTableCaption	58
Author	71
AuthorEmail	71
AuthorAddress	65
SubsectionHeader	50
VolumeInfo	57
Bibliography	55
English Summary	31
ItalianKeywords	35
EnglishKeywords	35
Title	55
ItalianSummary	29
ItalianAbstract	10
Table	25
EnglishAbstract	13
Note	18

Table 1: The tag set used for Archeology Article Annotation.

Tag	F_1
ItalianFigureCaption	70
ItalianBodyText	90
EnglishFigureCaption	71
SectionHeader	90
EnglishTableCaption	70
ItalianTableCaption	75
Author	72
AuthorEmail	75
AuthorAddress	73
SubsectionHeader	65
VolumeInfo	85
Bibliography	98
English Summary	40
ItalianKeywords	55
EnglishKeywords	56
Title	73
ItalianSummary	40
ItalianAbstract	50
Table	67
EnglishAbstract	50
Note	70

Table 2: The Precision and Recall for the trained models.

6 Additional Applications for Structure-Sensitive Pipelines

The pipeline discussed above can be used for a variety of other types of documents–archeology documents from other collections, or documents from other domains–by simply replacing the document structure extractor. We also found however that the pipeline is useful for a variety of other text-analysis tasks. We briefly discuss these in turn.

6.1 Blogs and Microblogging platforms

Content creation platforms like blogs, microblogs, community QA sites, forums, etc., contain user generated data. This data may be emotional, opinionated, personal, and sentimental, and as such, makes it interesting for sentiment analysis, opinion retrieval, and mood detection. In their survey on opinion mining and sentiment analysis Pang and Lee (2008) report that logical structure can be used to utilize the relationships between different units of content, in order to achieve a more accurate labeling; e.g. the relationships between discourse participants in discussions on controversial topics when responding are more likely to be antagonistic than to be reinforcing, or the way of quoting–a user can refer to another post by quoting part of it or by addressing the other user by name or user ID–in posts on political debates hints at the perceived opposite end of the political spectrum of the quoted user.

We are in the process of creating an annotated corpus of blogs; the pipeline discussed in this paper was easily adapted to pre-process this type of data as well.

6.2 HTML pages

In the IR literature it has often been observed that certain parts of document structure contain information that is particularly useful for document retrieval. For instance, Kruschwitz (2003) automatically builds domain models – simple trees of related terms – from documents marked up in HTML to assist users during search tasks by performing automatic query refinements, and improves users' experience for browsing the document collection. He uses term counts in different **markup contexts** like non-paragraph text and running text, and markups like bold, italic, underline to identify concepts and the corresponding shallow trees. However, this domain-independent method is suited for all types of data with logical structure annotation and similar data sources can be found in many places, e.g. corporate intranets, electronic archives, etc.

6.3 Processing Wikipedia pages

Wikipedia, as a publicly available web knowledge base, has been leveraged for semantic information in much work, including from our lab. Wikipedia articles consist mostly of free text, but also contain different types of structured information, e.g. infoboxes, categorization and geo information, links to other articles, to other wiki projects, and to external Web pages. Preserving this information is therefore useful for a variety of projects.

7 Discussion and Conclusions

The main point of this paper is to argue that the field should switch to structure-sensitive pipelines. These are particularly crucial in digital library applications, but novel type of documents require them as well. We showed that such extension can be achieved rather painlessly even in tabular-based pipelines provided they allow for meta-lines.

References

Isaac G. Councill, C. Lee Giles, and Min-Yen Kan. 2008. Parscit: An open-source crf reference string parsing package. In *Proceedings of the Language Resources and Evaluation Conference (LREC 08)*, May.

Hamish Cunningham, Diana Maynard, Kalina Bontcheva, and Valentin Tablan. 2002. GATE: A framework and graphical development environment for robust NLP tools and applications. In *Proceedings of the 40th Anniversary Meeting of the Association for Computational Linguistics*.

Min-Yuh Day, Richard Tzong-Han Tsai, Cheng-Lung Sung, Chiu-Chen Hsieh, Cheng-Wei Lee, Shih-Hung Wu, Kun-Pin Wu, Chorng-Shyong Ong, and Wen-Lian Hsu. 2007. Reference metadata extraction using a hierarchical knowledge representation framework. *Decision Support Systems*, 43(1):152–167, February.

Erik Hetzner. 2008. A simple method for citation metadata extraction using hidden markov models. In *Proceedings of the 8th ACM/IEEE-CS joint conference on Digital libraries*, JCDL '08, pages 280–284, New York, NY, USA. ACM.

Nancy Ide. 1998. Corpus encoding standard: SGML guidelines for encoding linguistic corpora. In *Proceedings of LREC*, pages 463–70, Granada.

Yasuto Ishitani. 1999. Logical structure analysis of document images based on emergent computation. In *Proceedings of International Conference on Document Analysis and Recognition*.

Michael Jewell. 2000. Paracite: An overview.

Udo Kruschwitz. 2003. An Adaptable Search System for Collections of Partially Structured Documents. *IEEE Intelligent Systems*, 18(4):44–52, July.

Kyong-Ho Lee, Yoon-Chul Choy, and Sung-Bae Cho. 2003. Logical structure analysis and generation for structured documents: a syntactic approach. *IEEE transactions on knowledge and data engineering*, 15(5):1277–1294, September.

Minh-Thang Luong, Thuy Dung Nguyen, and Min-Yen Kan. 2011. Logical structure recovery in scholarly articles with rich document feature. *Journal of Digital Library Systems. Forthcoming*.

Song Mao, Azriel Rosenfeld, and Tapas Kanungo. 2003. Document Structure Analysis Algorithms: A Literature Survey.

Debashish Niyogi and Sargur N. Srihari. 1995. Knowledge-based derivation of document logical structure. In *Proceedings of International Conference on Document Analysis and Recognition*, pages 472–475.

Bo Pang and Lillian Lee. 2008. Opinion Mining and Sentiment Analysis. *Foundations and Trends in Information Retrieval*, 2(1-2):1–135, January.

Emanuele Pianta, Christian Girardi, and Roberto Zanoli. 2008. The TextPro tool suite. In *LREC, 6th edition of the Language Resources and Evaluation Conference*, Marrakech (Marocco).

Richard Power, Donia Scott, and Nadjet Bouayad-Agha. 2003. Document Structure. *Computational Linguistics*, 29(2):211–260, June.

Lance A. Ramshaw and Mitchell P. Marcus. 1995. Text chunking using tranformation-based learning. In *Proceedings of Third ACL Workshop on Very Large Corpora*, pages 82–94.

Kristen M. Summers. 1998. *Automatic discovery of logical document structure*. Ph.D. thesis, Cornell University.

Ian H. Witten, David Bainbridge, and David M. Nichols. 2003. *How to build a digital library*. Morgan Kaufmann.

The ARC Project: Creating logical models of Gothic cathedrals using natural language processing

Charles Hollingsworth
Inst. for Artificial Intelligence
The University of Georgia
Athens, GA 30602
`cholling@uga.edu`

Stefaan Van Liefferinge
Rebecca A. Smith
Lamar Dodd School of Art
The University of Georgia
Athens, GA 30602

Michael A. Covington
Walter D. Potter
Inst. for Artificial Intelligence
The University of Georgia
Athens, GA 30602

Abstract

The ARC project (for **A**rchitecture **R**epresented **C**omputationally) is an attempt to reproduce in computer form the architectural historian's mental model of the Gothic cathedral. This model includes the background information necessary to understand a natural language architectural description. Our first task is to formalize the description of Gothic cathedrals in a logical language, and provide a means for translating into this language from natural language. Such a system could then be used by architectural historians and others to facilitate the task of gathering and using information from architectural descriptions. We believe the ARC Project will represent an important contribution to the preservation of cultural heritage, because it will offer a logical framework for understanding the description of landmark monuments of the past. This paper presents an outline of our plan for the ARC system, and examines some of the issues we face in implementing it.

1 Introduction

The ARC project is designed to assist architectural historians and others with the task of gathering and using information from architectural descriptions.[1] The architectural historian is confronted with an overwhelming amount of information. Even if we restrict ourselves to Gothic architecture (our primary area of interest), any given building has probably been described dozens, if not hundreds, of times. These descriptions may have been written in different time periods, using different vocabularies, and may describe the same building during different stages of construction or renovation. Descriptions may be incomplete or even contradictory. An architectural historian should be able to extract necessary information about a building without encountering anything contradictory or unclear.

To facilitate information gathering, we propose a logic-based knowledge representation for architectural descriptions. Our approach is similar to that used by Liu et al. (2010), but while their representation took the form of a set of production rules for an L-system, ours is more closely tied to the semantics of natural language. Descriptions of various cathedrals would then be translated into this representation. The resulting knowledge base would be used to give intelligent responses to queries, identify conflicts among various descriptions, and highlight relationships among features that a human reader might have missed.

2 Why Gothic?

In addition to being major monuments of cultural heritage, Gothic cathedrals are particularly well-suited for logical analysis. The structure of Gothic follows a logical form. Despite variations, Gothic cathedrals present a number of typical features, such as pointed arches, flying buttresses, and a plan on a Latin cross (Figure 1). The repetition of elements

[1]This research benefited from the generous support of a Digital Humanities Start-Up Level I Grant from the National Endowment for the Humanities (Grant Number HD5110110), a University of Georgia Research Foundation Grant, and from The University of Georgia President's Venture Fund.

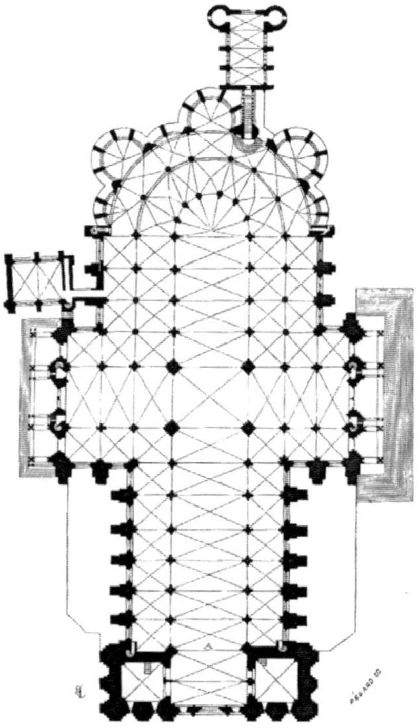

Figure 1: Example of a cathedral ground plan (Chartres, France), from Viollet-le-Duc (1854-68)

Figure 2: Nave of Notre Dame de Paris, showing the repetition of elements. (Photograph by S. Van Liefferinge)

like columns and vaulting units allows for more succinct logical descriptions (Figure 2). And the historical importance of Gothic means that a wealth of detailed descriptions exist from which we can build our knowledge base.

The study of Gothic cathedrals is also important for cultural preservation. Some cathedrals have been modified or renovated over the years, and their original forms exist only in descriptions. And tragedies such as the 1976 earthquake which destroyed the cathedral in Venzone underscore the importance of architectural information. A usable and versatile architectural knowledge base would greatly facilitate the task of restoring damaged buildings.

3 Outline of the ARC system

The outline of the ARC system is the result of close collaboration between architectural historians and artificial intelligence researchers. While the system is still in its infancy, the complete ARC system will have three distinct modes of interaction, to be used by three different types of user. We will refer to these modes as superuser mode, administrator mode, and user mode. The superuser mode will be used to write and edit a generic model for Gothic architecture that will serve as background information prior to dealing with any specific descriptions. The administrator mode will be used to enter the details of particular buildings. The purpose of the user mode will be to allow end users to submit queries to the knowledge base.

3.1 Superuser mode

A small set of superusers will be able to create and edit the generic model of a Gothic cathedral. This will consist of information about features generally considered typical of Gothic (such as the cruciform ground plan and use of pointed arches) as well as more common-sense information (such as the fact that the ceiling is above the floor). These are facts that are unlikely to be explicitly stated in an architectural description because the reader is assumed to know them already. Individual descriptions need only describe how a particular building differs from this generic model. The generic model will be underdetermined, in that it will remain silent about features that vary considerably across buildings (such as the number of vaulting units in the nave).

The generic description will be written in a domain-specific architectural description language (ADL) modeled on English, and translated into a logical programming language such as Prolog. The

A column is a type of support. Every column has a base, a shaft, and a capital. Most columns have a plinth. The base is above the plinth, the shaft is above the base, and the capital is above the shaft. Some columns have a necking. The necking is between the shaft and the capital.

Figure 3: Sample ADL listing.

general task of rendering the semantics of natural language into logic programming is addressed extensively by Blackburn and Bos (2005), and an architecture-specific treatment is given by Mitchell (1990). However, our goal is not a complete implementation of English semantics. Rather, our task is more like natural language programming, in which the computer is able to extract its instructions from human language. (For treatments of natural language programming systems in other domains, see Nelson (2006) and Lieberman and Liu (2005).) In particular, historical details, asides, and other language not pertaining to architecture would be treated as comments and safely ignored. A syntactic parser can extract those sentences and phrases of interest to the system and pass over the rest. The ADL should allow anyone reasonably familiar with architectural terminology to work on the description without the steep learning curve of a programming language. It should be able to understand multiple wordings for the same instruction, perhaps even learning new ones over time. As our eventual goal is to be able to understand real-world architectural texts, grammatical English sentences should not produce errors. Any such misunderstanding should be seen as an opportunity to improve the system rather than a failure on the part of the user. As an example of how a portion of a column description in an ADL might look, see Figure 3. In order to implement this ADL, a number of interesting problems must be solved. The following section describes a few we have dealt with so far.

Referring to unnamed entities

The simple statement "Every column has a base" does not have a straightforward rendering in a logical language like Prolog. In order to render it, we must be able to say that for each column, there exists some (unnamed) base belonging to that column. To do this, we use *Skolemization* (after Skolem (1928)), a technique for replacing existential quantifiers with unique identifiers (Skolem functions). Blackburn and Bos (2005) demonstrate the use of Skolem functions in capturing natural language semantics, and a contemporary application is demonstrated by Cua et al. (2010). Our implementation is a modified version of that described by Covington et al. (1988).

To say "Every column has a base", we insert two rules into the knowledge base. The first declares the existence of a base for each column:

```
base(base_inst(X, 1)) :- column(X).
```

The second tells us that the base belongs to the column:

```
has(X, base_inst(X, 1)) :- column(X).
```

Here `base_inst(X, 1)` is a Skolem function for an instance of `base`, where `X` is the name of the object to which it belongs, and `1` is its index. (In the case of a base, there is only one per column.) Thus a column named `column1` would have a base named `base_inst(column1, 1)`, and so forth.

Context sensitivity

Sentences are not isolated semantic units, but must be understood in terms of information provided by previous sentences. In the listing in Figure 3, the statement "the base is above the plinth" is interpreted to mean "each column's base is above that column's plinth". In order to make the correct interpretation, the system must know that the present topic is columns, and recognize that "base" and "plinth" are among the listed components of columns.

We assume the superuser's description constitutes a single discourse, divided into topics by paragraph. Accessibility domains correspond to paragraphs. When the description mentions "the base", it is assumed to refer to the base mentioned earlier in the paragraph as a component of the column. That the column is the paragraph's topic is indicated in the first sentence. Our treatment of discourse referents and accessibility domains is similar to that of discourse representation theory (Kamp and Reyle, 1993).

Default reasoning

We must have a way to dismiss facts from the knowledge base on the basis of new evidence. Our model describes the "typical" Gothic cathedral, not *every* Gothic cathedral. There is usually an exception to an apparent rule. To handle this, we make use of defeasible or nonmonotonic reasoning, as described by Reiter (1987) and Antoniou (1997). (Several variants of defeasible reasoning are also described by Billington et al. (2010).)

The ADL accommodates exceptions through the use of modifiers. Words like "all" and "every" indicate a rule that holds without exception. Words like "most" or "usually" indicate that a rule is present by default in the model, but can be altered or removed by future assertions. Finally, the word "some" indicates that a rule is not present by default, but can be added. The system's internal logical representation can keep track of which rules are defeasible and which are not. Attempts to make an assertion that conflicts with a non-defeasible rule will fail, whereas assertions contradicting a defeasible rule will modify the knowledge base. Conclusions derivable from the defeated rule will no longer be derivable. Our implementation is a somewhat simplified version of the system presented by Nute (2003).

Partial ordering

Defeasible reasoning can help us resolve a particular type of ambiguity found in natural language. Architectural descriptions contain many partial ordering relations, such as "above" or "behind". These relations are irreflexive, antisymmetric, and transitive. When such relations are described in natural language, as in the description in Figure 3, they are typically underspecified. We say that an item is "above" another, without making explicit whether it is immediately above. We also do not specify which is the first (e.g. lowest) element in the series. In our generic model, if it is simply stated that one item is above another, we insert a non-defeasible rule in the knowledge base, such as

above(capital, shaft)

The further assertion

immediately(above(capital, shaft))

is also made, but is defeasible. Should another item be introduced that is above the shaft but below the capital, the immediately relation no longer holds. We can also deal with underspecificity by recognizing when more than one state of affairs might correspond to the description. For example, if it has been asserted that item A is above item C, and that item B is above item C, we have no way of knowing the positions of A and B relative to each other. A query Is A above B? must then return the result maybe.

3.2 Administrator mode

The administrator mode is used to input information about particular buildings, as opposed to Gothic cathedrals in general. When an administrator begins an interactive session, the generic model designed by the superuser is first read into the knowledge base. The administrator simply describes how the particular cathedral in question differs from the generic model, using the same architectural description language. We would also like for the administrator mode to accept real-world cathedral descriptions in natural language rather than ADL. This is a nontrivial task, and complete understanding is likely a long way away. In the short term, the system should be able to scan a description, identify certain salient bits of information, and allow the administrator to fill in the gaps as needed. To illustrate the problem of understanding real-world descriptions, we present the following excerpt from a description of the Church of Saint-Maclou:

> The nave arcade piers, chapel opening piers, transept crossing piers, and choir hemicycle piers are all composed of combinations of five sizes of individual plinths, bases, and moldings that rise from complex socles designed around polygons defined by concave scoops and flat faces. All the piers, attached and freestanding on the north side of the church, are complemented by an identical pier on the opposite side. However, no two piers on the same side of the church are identical. (Neagley, 1998) p. 29.

There are important similarities between this description and our own architectural description language. We see many key entities identified (*nave arcade piers, chapel opening piers, etc.*), as well as words indicating relationships between them (*composed, identical,* etc.) Even if complete understanding is not currently feasible, we could still use techniques such as named entity extraction to add details to our model.

3.3 User mode

The user mode will consist of a simple query answering system. Users will input queries such as "How many vaulting units are in the nave at Saint-Denis?" or "Show me all cathedrals with a four-story elevation." The system will respond with the most specific answer possible, but no more, so that yes/no questions might be answered with "maybe," and quantitative questions with "between four and six", depending on the current state of the knowledge base. Unlike web search engines, which only attempt to match particular character strings, our system will have the advantage of understanding. Since descriptions are stored as a logical knowledge base rather than a string of words, we can ensure that more relevant answers are given.

4 Conclusion

The ARC project is a great undertaking, and presents us with a number of problems that do not have ready solutions. We have presented just a few of these problems, and the techniques we have developed for solving them. There is still much work to be done in implementing the architectural description language, and processing real-world descriptions. In addition, there are some capabilities we would like to add to the system, such as producing graphical renderings from descriptions.

It is our hope that the ARC system, when completed, will be of great benefit to architectural historians, or anyone interested in Gothic cathedrals. Having a knowledge base of cathedral designs that can respond to queries will make the historian's task easier. The system's ability to identify vague or contradictory statements allows us to see how historical descriptions differ from one another. And the process of rendering architectural descriptions in a logical form could provide new insights into the design and structure of cathedrals.

References

Grigoris Antoniou. 1997. *Nonmonotonic Reasoning.* The MIT Press, Cambridge, MA.

David Billington, Grigoris Antoniou, Guido Governatori and Michael Maher. 2010. An Inclusion Theorem for Defeasible Logics. *ACM Transactions on Computational Logic* Vol. 12, No.1, Article 6, October 2010.

Patrick Blackburn and Johan Bos. 2005. *Representation and Inference for Natural Language: A First Course in Computational Semantics.* CSLI Publications, Stanford, California.

Michael A. Covington, Donald Nute, Nora Schmitz and David Goodman. 1988. From English to Prolog via Discourse Representation Theory. ACMC Research Report 01-0024, The University of Georgia. URL (viewed May 5, 2011): `http://www.ai.uga.edu/ftplib/ai-reports/ai010024.pdf`

Jeffrey Cua, Ruli Manurung, Ethel Ong and Adam Pease. 2010. Representing Story Plans in SUMO. In *Proceedings of the NAACL HLT 2010 Second Workshop on Computational Approaches to Linguistic Creativity.* Association for Computational Linguistics, Los Angeles, California, June 2010, 40-48.

Hans Kamp and Uwe Reyle. 1993. *From Discourse to Logic.* Kluwer, Dordrecht.

Henry Lieberman and Hugo Liu. 2005. Feasibility Studies for Programming in Natural Language. *End-User Development. H. Lieberman, F. Paterno, V. Wulf, eds.* Kluwer, Dordrecht.

Yong Liu, Yunliang Jiang and Lican Huang. 2010. Modeling Complex Architectures Based on Granular Computing on Ontology. *IEEE Transactions on Fuzzy Systems,* vol. 18, no. 3, 585-598.

William J. Mitchell. 1990. *The Logic of Architecture: Design, Computation, and Cognition.* The MIT Press, Cambridge, MA.

Linda Elaine Neagley. 1998. *Disciplined Exuberance: The Parish Church of Saint-Maclou and Late Gothic Architecture in Rouen.* The Pennsylvania State University Press, University Park, PA.

Graham Nelson. 2006. Natural Language, Semantic Analysis and Interactive Fiction. URL (viewed May 5, 2011): `http://www.inform-fiction.org/I7Dowloads/Documents/WhitePaper.pdf`

Donald Nute. 2003. Defeasible Logic. In *Proceedings of the Applications of Prolog 14th International Conference on Web Knowledge Management And Decision Support* (INAP'01), Oskar Bartenstein, Ulrich Geske, Markus Hannebauer, and Osamu Yoshie (Eds.). Springer-Verlag, Berlin, Heidelberg, 151-169.

Raymond Reiter. 1987. Nonmonotonic Reasoning. *Ann. Rev. Comput. Sci.* 1987.2: 147-86.

Thoralf Skolem. 1928. Über die mathematische Logik (Nach einem Vortrag gehalten im Norwegischen Mathematischen Verein am 22. Oktober 1928). In *Selected Works in Logic*. Jens Erik Fenstad, ed. Universitetsforlaget, Oslo - Bergen - Tromsö, 1970, 189-206.

Eugène-Emmanuel Viollet-le-Duc. 1854-68. *Dictionnaire raisonné de l'architecture française du XIe au XVIe siècle.* vol. 2. Libraries-Imprimeries Réunies, Paris. Image URL (viewed May 5, 2011): `http://fr.wikisource.org/wiki/Fichier:Plan.cathedrale.Chartres.png`

Crowdsourcing syntactic relatedness judgements for opinion mining in the study of information technology adoption

Asad B. Sayeed, Bryan Rusk, Martin Petrov, Hieu C. Nguyen, Timothy J. Meyer
Department of Computer Science
University of Maryland
College Park, MD 20742 USA
asayeed@cs.umd.edu, brusk@umd.edu, martin@martinpetrov.com, {hcnguyen88, tmeyer88}@gmail.com

Amy Weinberg
Center for the Advanced Study of Language and Department of Linguistics
University of Maryland
College Park, MD 20742 USA
aweinberg@casl.umd.edu

Abstract

We present an end-to-end pipeline including a user interface for the production of word-level annotations for an opinion-mining task in the information technology (IT) domain. Our pre-annotation pipeline selects candidate sentences for annotation using results from a small amount of trained annotation to bias the random selection over a large corpus. Our user interface reduces the need for the user to understand the "meaning" of opinion in our domain context, which is related to community reaction. It acts as a preliminary buffer against low-quality annotators. Finally, our post-annotation pipeline aggregates responses and applies a more aggressive quality filter.

We present positive results using two different evaluation philosophies and discuss how our design decisions enabled the collection of high-quality annotations under subjective and fine-grained conditions.

1 Introduction

Crowdsourcing permits us to use a bank of anonymous workers with unknown skill levels to perform complex tasks given a simple breakdown of these tasks with user interface design that hides the full task complexity. Use of these techniques is growing in the areas of computational linguistics and information retrieval, particularly since these fields now rely on the collection of large datasets for use in machine learning. Considering the variety of applications, a variety of datasets is needed, but trained, known workers are an expense in principle that must be furnished for each one. Consequently, crowdsourcing offers a way to collect this data cheaply and quickly (Snow et al., 2008; Sayeed et al., 2010a).

We applied crowdsourcing to perform the fine-grained annotation of a domain-specific corpus. Our user interface design and our annotator quality control process allows these anonymous workers to perform a highly subjective task in a manner that correlates their collective understanding of the task to our own expert judgements about it. The path to success provides some illustration of the pitfalls inherent in opinion annotation. Our task is: domain and application-specific sentiment classification at the sub-sentence level—at the word level.

1.1 Opinions

For our purposes, we define opinion mining (sometimes known as sentiment analysis) to be the retrieval of a triple {*source, target, opinion*} (Sayeed et al., 2010b; Pang and Lee, 2008; Kim and Hovy, 2006) in which the *source* is the entity that originated the opinionated language, the *target* is a mention of the entity or concept that is the opinion's topic, and the *opinion* is a value (possibly a structure) that reflects some kind of emotional orientation expressed by the source towards the target.

In much of the recent literature on automatic opinion mining, *opinion* is at best a gradient between positive and negative or a binary classification thereof; further complexity affects the reliability of machine-learning techniques (Koppel and Schler, 2006).

We call opinion mining "fine-grained" when we are attempting to retrieve potentially many different {*source, target, opinion*} triples per document. This is particularly challenging when there are multiple triples even at a sentence level.

1.2 Corpus-based social science

Our work is part of a larger collaboration with social scientists to study the diffusion of information technology (IT) innovations through society by identifying opinion leaders and IT-relevant opinionated language (Rogers, 2003). A key hypothesis is that the language used by opinion leaders causes groups of others to encourage the spread of the given IT concept in the market.

Since the goal of our exercise is to ascertain the correlation between the source's behaviour and that of others, then it may be more appropriate to look at opinion analysis with the view that what we are attempting to discover are the views of an aggregate reader who may otherwise have an interest in the IT concept in question. We thus define an expression of opinion in the following manner:

> A expresses opinion about B if an interested third party C's actions towards B may be affected by A's textually recorded actions, in a context where actions have positive or negative weight.

This perspective runs counter to a widespread view (Ruppenhofer et al., 2008) which has assumed a treatment of opinionated language as an observation of a latent "private state" held by the source. This definition reflects the relationship of sentiment and opinion with the study of social impact and market prediction. We return to the question of how to define opinion in section 6.2.

1.3 Crowdsourcing in sentiment analysis

Paid crowdsourcing is a relatively new trend in computational linguistics. Work exists at the paragraph and document level, and it exists for the Twitter and blog genres (Hsueh et al., 2009).

A key problem in crowdsourcing sentiment analysis is the matter of quality control. A crowdsourced opinion mining task is an attempt to use untrained annotators over a task that is inherently very subjective. It is doubly difficult for specialized domains, since crowdsourcing platforms have no way of directly recruiting domain experts.

Hsueh et al. (2009) present results in quality control over snippets of political blog posts in a task classifying them by sentiment and political alignment. They find that they can use a measurement of annotator noise to eliminate low-quality annotations at this coarse level by reweighting snippet ambiguity scores with noise scores. We demonstrate that we can use a similar annotator quality measure alone to eliminate low-quality annotations on a much finer-grained task.

1.4 Syntactic relatedness

We have a downstream application for this annotation task which involves acquiring patterns in the distribution of opinion-bearing words and targets using machine learning (ML) techniques. In particular, we want to acquire the syntactic relationships between opinion-bearing words and within-sentence targets. Supervised ML techniques require gold standard data annotated in advance.

The Multi-Perspective Question-Answering (MPQA) newswire corpus (Wilson and Wiebe, 2005) and the J. D. Power & Associates (JDPA) automotive review blog post (Kessler et al., 2010) corpus are appropriate because both contain sub-sentence annotations of sentiment-bearing language as text spans. In some cases, they also include links to within-sentence targets. This is an example of an MPQA annotation:

> That was the moment at which the fabric of compassion tore, and worlds cracked apart; when **the contrast and conflict of civilisational values** became so great as to *remove any sense of common ground* - even on which to do battle.

The italicized portion is intended to reflect a negative sentiment about the bolded portion. However, while it is the case that the whole italicized phrase represents a negative sentiment, "remove" appears to represent far more of the negativity than "common" and "ground". While there are techniques that depend on access to entire phrases, our project is to identify sentiment spans at the length of a single word.

2 Data source

Our corpus for this task is a collection of articles from the IT professional magazine, *Information*

Week, from the years 1991 to 2008. This consists of 33K articles of varying lengths including news bulletins, full-length magazine features, and opinion columns. We obtained the articles via an institutional subscription, and reformatted them in XML[1].

Certain IT concepts are particularly significant in the context of the social science application. Our target list consists of 59 IT innovations and concepts. The list includes plurals, common variations, and abbreviations. Examples of IT concepts include "enterprise resource planning" and "customer relationship management". To avoid introducing confounding factors into our results, we only include explicit mentions and omit pronominal coreference.

3 User interface

Our user interface (figure 1) uses a drag-and-drop process through which workers make decisions about whether particular highlighted words within a given sentence reflect an opinion about a particular mentioned IT concept or innovation. The user is presented with a sentence from the corpus surrounded by some before and after context. Underneath the text are four boxes: "No effect on opinion" (none), "Affects opinion positively" (postive), "Affects opinion negatively" (negative), and "Can't tell" (ambiguous).

The worker must drag each highlighted word in the sentence into one of the boxes, as appropriate. If the worker cannot determine the appropriate box for a particular word, she is expected to drag this to the ambiguous box. The worker is presented with detailed instructions which also remind her that most of words in the sentence are not actually likely to be involved in the expression of an opinion about the relevant IT concept[2]. The worker is not permitted to submit the task without dragging all of the highlighted words to one of the boxes. When a word is dragged to a box, the word in context changes colour; the worker can change her mind by clicking an X next to the word in the box.

[1]We will likely be able to provide a sample of sentence data annotated by our process as a resource once we work out documentation and distribution issues.

[2]We discovered when testing the interface that workers can feel obliged to find a opinion about the selected IT concept. We reduced it by explicitly reminding them that most words do not express a relevant opinion and by placing the none box first.

We used CrowdFlower to manage the task with Amazon Mechanical Turk as its distribution channel. We set CrowdFlower to present three sentences at a time to users. Only users with USA-based IP addresses were permitted to perform the final task.

4 Procedure

In this section, we discuss the data processing pipeline (figure 3) through which we select candidates for annotations and the crowdsourcing interface we present to the end user for classifying individual words into categories that reflect the effect of the word on the worker.

4.1 Data preparation

4.1.1 Initial annotation

Two social science undergraduate students were hired to do annotations on *Information Week* with the original intention of doing all the annotations this way. There was a training period where they annotated about 60 documents in sets of 20 in iterative consultation with one of the authors. Then they were given 142 documents to annotate simultaneously in order to assess their agreement after training.

Annotation was performed in Atlas.ti, an annotation tool popular with social science researchers. It was chosen for its familiarity to the social scientists involved in our project and because of their stated preference for using tools that would allow them to share annotations with colleagues. Atlas.ti has limitations, including the inability to create hierarchical annotations. We overcame these limitations using a special notation to connect related annotations. An annotator highlights a sentence that she believes contains an opinion about a mentioned target on one of the lists. She then highlights the mention of the target and, furthermore, highlights the individual words that express the opinion about the target, using the notation to connect related highlights.

4.1.2 Candidate selection

While the use of trained annotators did not produce reliable results (section 6.2) in acceptable time frames, we decided to use the annotations in a process for selecting candidate sentences for crowdsourcing. All 219 sentences that the annotators selected as having opinions about within-sentence IT

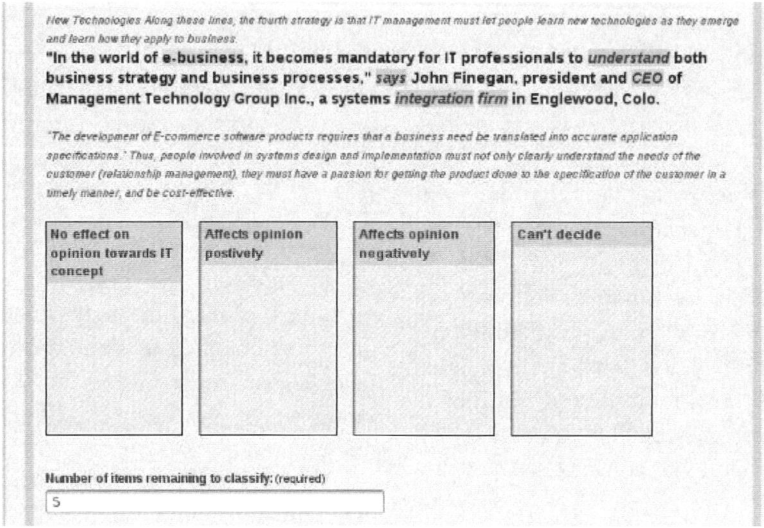

Figure 1: A work unit presented in grayscale. "E-business" is the IT concept and would be highlighted in blue. The words in question are highlighted in gray background and turn red after they are dragged to the boxes.

concepts were concatenated into a single string and converted into a TFIDF unit vector.

We then selected all the sentences that contain IT concept mentions from the entire Information Week corpus using an OpenNLP 1.4.3 model as our sentence-splitter. This produced approximately 77K sentences. Every sentence was converted into a TFIDF unit vector, and we took the cosine similarity of each sentence with the TFIDF vector. We then ranked the sentences by cosine similarity.

4.1.3 Selecting highlighted words

We ran every sentence through the Stanford part-of-speech tagger. Words that belonged to open classes such as adjectives and verbs were selected along with certain closed-class words such as modals and negation words. These candidate words were highlighted in the worker interface.

We did not want to force workers to classify every single word in a sentence, because this would be too tedious. So we instead randomly grouped the highlighted words into non-overlapping sets of six. (Remainders less than five were dropped from the task.) We call these combinations of sentence, six words, and target IT concept a "highlight group" (figure 2).

Each highlight group represents a task unit which we present to the worker in our crowdsourcing application. We generated 1000 highlight groups from the top-ranked sentences.

> The amount of industry attention *paid* to this *new class* of integration software *speaks* volumes about the *need* to extend the *reach* of **ERP** systems.
>
> The *amount* of industry attention paid to this new class of integration *software* speaks *volumes* about the need to *extend* the reach of **ERP** *systems*.

Figure 2: Two highlight groups consisting of the same sentence and concept (ERP) but different non-overlapping sets of candidate words.

4.2 Crowdsourced annotation

4.2.1 Training gold

We used CrowdFlower partly because of its automated quality control process. The bedrock of this process is the annotation of a small amount of gold standard data by the task designers. CrowdFlower randomly selects gold-annotated tasks and presents them to workers amidst other unannotated tasks. Workers are evaluated by the percentage of gold-annotated tasks they perform correctly. The result of a worker performing a task unit is called a "judgement."

Workers are initially presented their gold-annotated tasks without knowing that they are answering a test question. If they get the question wrong, CrowdFlower presents the correct answer to them along with a reason why their answer was an error. They are permitted to write back to the task designer if they disagree with the gold judgement.

This process functions in a manner analogous to the training of a machine-learning system. Furthermore, it permits CrowdFlower to exclude or reject low-quality results. Judgements from a worker who slips below 65% correctness are rated as untrustworthy and not included in the CrowdFlower's results.

We created training gold in the manner recommended by CrowdFlower. We randomly selected 50 highlight groups from the 1000 mentioned in the previous section. We ran these examples through CrowdFlower using the interface we discuss in the next section. Then we used the CrowdFlower gold editor to select 30 highlight groups that contained clear classification decisions where it appeared that the workers were in relative consensus and where we agreed with their decision. Of these, we designated only the clearest-cut classifications as gold, leaving more ambiguous-seeming ones up to the users. For example, in the second highlight group in 2, we would designate *software* and *systems* as none and *extend* as positive in the training gold and the remainder as up to the workers. That would be a "minimum effort" to indicate that the worker understands the task the way we do.

Unfortunately, CrowdFlower has some limitations in the way it processes the responses to gold—it is not possible to define a minimum effort precisely. CrowdFlower's setting either allow us to pass workers based on getting at least one item in each class correct or by placing all items in their correct classes. The latter is too strict a criterion for an inherently subjective task. So we accepted the former. We instead applied our minimum effort criterion in some of our experiments as described in section 4.3.

4.2.2 Full run

We randomly selected another 200 highlight groups and posted them at 12 US cents for each set of three highlight groups, with at least three Mechanical Turk workers seeing each highlight group. The 30 training gold highlight groups were posted along with them. Including CrowdFlower and Amazon fees, the total cost was approximately 60 USD. We permitted only USA-based workers to access the task. Once initiated, the entire task took approximately 24 hours to complete.

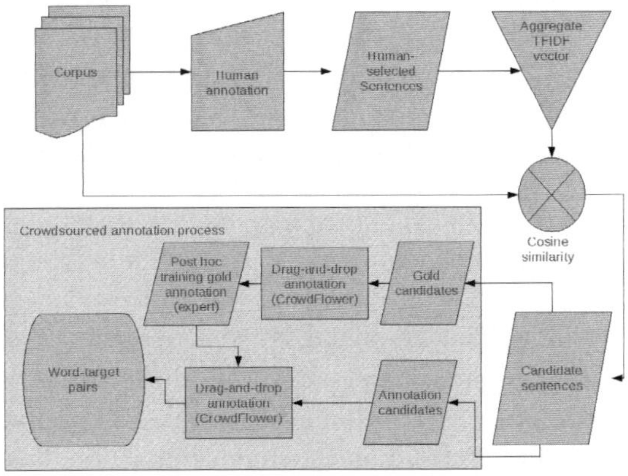

Figure 3: Schematic view of pipeline.

4.3 Post-processing

4.3.1 Aggregation

Each individual worker's ambiguous annotations are converted to none annotations, as the ambiguous box is intended as an outlet for a worker's uncertainty, but we choose to interpret anything that a worker considers too uncertain to be classified as positive or negative as something that is not strongly opinionated under our definitions.

Aggregation is performed by majority vote of the annotators on each word in each highlight group. If no classification obtains more than 50% for a given word, the word is dropped as too ambiguous to be accepted either way as a result. This aggregation has the effect of smoothing out individual annotator differences.

4.3.2 Extended quality control

While CrowdFlower provides a first-pass quality control system for selecting annotators who are doing the task in good faith and with some understanding of the instructions, we wanted particularly to select annotators who would be more likely to be consistent on the most obvious cases without overly constraining them. Even with the same general idea of our intentions, some amount of variation among the annotators is unavoidable; how do we then reject annotations from those workers who pass CrowdFlower's liberal criteria but still do not have an idea of annotation close enough to ours?

Our solution was to score the annotators *post hoc* by their accuracy on our minimum-effort training gold data. Then we progressively dropped the worst n annotators starting from $n = 0$ and measured the quality of the aggregated annotations as per the following section.

5 Results

This task can be interpreted in two different ways: as an annotation task and as a retrieval system. Annotator reliability is an issue insofar as it is important that the annotations themselves conform to a predetermined standard. However, for the machine learning task that is downstream in our processing pipeline, obtaining a consistent pattern is more important than conformance to an explicit definition. We can thus interpret the results as being the output of a system whose computational hardware happens to be a crowd of humans rather than silicon, considering that the time of the "run" is comparable to many automated systems; Amazon Mechanical Turk's slogan is "artificial artificial intelligence" for a reason.

Nevertheless, we evaluated our procedure under both interpretations by comparing against our own annotations in order to assess the quality of our collection, aggregation, and filtering process:

1. **As an annotation task**: we use Cohen's κ between the aggregated and filtered data vs. our annotations in the belief that higher above-chance agreement would imply that the aggregate annotation reflected collective understanding of our definition of sentiment. Considering the inherently subjective nature of this task and the interdependencies inherent in within-sentence judgements, Cohen's κ is not a definitive proof of success or failure.

2. **As a retrieval task**: Relative to our own annotations, we use the standard information retrieval measures of precision, recall, and F-measure (harmonic mean) as well as accuracy. We merge positive and negative annotations into a single opinion-bearing class and measure whether we can retrieve opinion-bearing words while minimizing words that are, in context, not opinion-bearing relative to the given target. (We do not merge the classes for agreement-based evaluation as there was not much overlap between positive and negative classifications.) The particular relative difference between precision and recall will suggest whether the workers had a consistent collective understanding of the task.

It should be noted that the MPQA and the JDPA do not report Cohen's κ for subjective text spans partly for the reason we suggest above: the difficulty of assessing objective agreement on a task in which subjectivity is inherent and desirable. There is also a large class imbalance problem. Both these efforts substitute retrieval-based measures into their assessment of agreement.

We annotated a randomly-selected 30 of the 200 highlight groups on our own. Those 30 had 169 annotated words of which 117 were annotated as none, 35 as positive, and 17 as negative. The results of our process are summarized in table 1.

In the 30 highlight groups, there were 155 total words for which a majority consensus (>50%) was reached. 48 words were determined by us in our own annotation to have opinion weight (positive or negative). There are only 22 annotators who passed CrowdFlower's quality control.

The stringent filter on workers based on their accuracy on our minimum-effort gold annotations has a remarkable effect on the results. As we exclude workers, the F-measure and the Cohen's κ appear to rise, up to a point. By definition, each exclusion raises the threshold score for acceptance. As we cross the 80% threshold, the performance of the system drops noticeably, as the smoothing effect of voting is lost. Opinion-bearing words also reduce in number as the threshold rises as some highlight groups simply have no one voting for them. We achieve our best result in terms of Cohen's κ on dropping the 7 lowest workers. We achieve our highest precision and accuracy after dropping the 10 lowest workers.

Between the 7th and 10th underperforming annotator, we find that precision starts to exceed recall, possibly due to the loss of retrievable words as some highlight groups lose all their annotators. Lost words can be recovered in another round of annotation.

Workers excluded	No. of words lost (of 48)	Prec/Rec/F	Acc	Cohen's κ	Score threshold
(prior polarity)	N/A	0.87 / 0.38 / 0.53	0.79	*-0.26*	N/A
0	0	0.64 / 0.71 / 0.67	0.79	0.48	0.333
1	0	0.64 / 0.71 / 0.67	0.79	0.48	0.476
3	0	0.66 / 0.73 / 0.69	0.80	0.51	0.560
5	0	0.69 / 0.73 / 0.71	0.81	0.53	0.674
7	2	0.81 / 0.76 / **0.79**	0.86	**0.65**	0.714
10	9	**0.85** / 0.74 / **0.79**	**0.88**	0.54	0.776
12	11	0.68 / 0.68 / 0.68	0.82	0.20	0.820

Table 1: Results by number of workers excluded from the task. The prior polarity baseline comes from a lexicon by Wilson et al. (2005) that is not specific to the IT domain.

6 Discussion

We have been able to show that crowdsourcing a very fine-grained, domain-specific sentiment analysis task with a nonstandard, application-specific definition of sentiment is possible with careful user interface design and mutliple layers of quality control. Our techniques succeed on two different interpretations of the evaluation measure, and we can reclaim any lost words by re-running the task. We used an elaborate processing pipeline before and after annotation in order to accomplish this. In this section, we discuss some aspects of the pipeline that led to the success of this technique.

6.1 Quality

There are three major aspects of our procedure that directly affect the quality of our results: the first-pass quality control in CrowdFlower, the majority-vote aggregation, and the stringent *post hoc* filtering of workers. These interact in particular ways.

The first-pass quality control interacts with the stringent filter in that even if it were possible to have run the stringent filter on CrowdFlower itself, it would probably not have been a good idea. Although we intended the stringent filter to be a minimum effort, it would have rejected workers too quickly. It is technically possible to implement the stringent filtering directly without the CrowdFlower built-in control, but that would have entailed spending an unpredictable amount more money paying for additional unwanted annotations from workers.

Furthermore, the majority-vote aggregation requires that there not be too few annotators; our results show that filtering the workers too aggressively harms the aggregation's smoothing effect. The lesson we take from this is that it can be beneficial to accept some amount of "bad" with the "good" in implementing a very subjective crowdsourcing task.

6.2 Design decisions

Our successful technique for identifying opinionated words was developed after multiple iterations using other approaches which did not succeed in themselves but produced outputs that were amenable to refinement, and so these techniques became part of a larger pipeline. However, the reasons why they did not succeed on their own are illustrative of some of the challenges in both fine-grained domain-specific opinion annotation and in annotation via crowdsourcing under highly subjective conditions.

6.2.1 Direct annotation

We originally intended to stop with the trained annotation we described in 4.1.1, but collecting opinionated sentences in this corpus turned out to be very slow. Despite repeated training rounds, the annotators had a tendency to miss a large number of sentences that the authors found to be relevant. On discussion with the annotators, it turned out that the variable length of the articles made it easy to miss relevant sentences, particularly in the long feature articles likely to contain opinionated language—a kind of "needle-in-a-haystack" problem.

Even worse, however, the annotators were variably conservative about what constituted an opinion. One annotator produced far fewer annotations than the other one—but the majority of her annotations were also annotated by the other one. Discussion with the annotators revealed that one of them simply had a tighter definition of what constituted an opinion. Attempts to define opinion explicitly for them still led to a situations in which one was far more conservative than the other.

6.2.2 Cascaded crowdsourcing technique

Insofar as we were looking for training data for use in downstream machine learning techniques, getting uniform sentence-by-sentence coverage of the corpus was not necessary. There are 77K sentences in this corpus which mention the relevant IT concepts; even if only a fraction of them mention the IT concepts with opinionated language, we would still have a potentially rich source of training data.

Nevertheless the direct annotation with trained annotators provided data for selecting candidate sentences for a more rapid annotation. We used the process in section 4.1.2 and chose the top-ranked sentences. Then we constructed a task design that divided the annotation into two phases. In the first phase, for each candidate sentence, we ask the annotator whether or not the sentence contains opinionated language about the mentioned IT concept. (We permit "unsure" answers.)

In the second phase, for each candidate sentence for which a majority vote of annotators decided that the sentence contained a relevant opinion, we run a second task asking whether particular words (selected as per section 4.1.3) were words directly involved in the expression of the opinion.

We tested this process with the 90 top-ranked sentences. Four individuals in our laboratory answered the "yes/no/unsure" question of the first phase. However, when we took their pairwise Cohen's κ score, no two got more than approximately 0.4. We also took majority votes of each subset of three annotators and found the Cohen's κ between them and the fourth. The highest score was 0.7, but the score was not stable, and we could not trust the results enough to move onto the second phase.

We also ran this first phase through Amazon Mechanical Turk. It turned out that it was far too easy to cheat on this yes/no question, and some workers simply answered "yes" or "no" all the time. Agreement scores of a Turker majority vote vs. one of the authors turned out to yield a Cohen's κ of 0.05—completely unacceptable.

Discussion with the in-laboratory annotators suggested the roots of the problem: it was the same problem as with the direct Atlas.ti annotation we reported in the previous section. It was very difficult for them to agree on what it meant for a sentence to contain an opinion expressed about a particular concept. Opinions about the nature of opinion ranged from very "conservative" to very "liberal." Even explicit definition with examples led annotators to reach very different conclusions. Furthermore, the longer the annotators thought about it, the more confused and uncertain they were about the criterion.

What is an opinion can itself be a matter of opinion. It became clear that without very tight review of annotation and careful task design, asking users an explicit yes/no question about whether a particular concept has a particular opinion mentioned in a particular sentence has the potential to induce overthinking by annotators, despite our variations on the task. The difficulty may also lead to a tendency to cheat. Crowdsourcing allows us to make use of non-expert labour on difficult tasks if we can break the tasks down into simple questions and aggregate non-expert responses, but we needed a somewhat more complex task design in order to eliminate the difficulty of the task and the tendency to cheat.

7 Future work

Foremost among the avenues for future work is experimentation with other vote aggregration and *post hoc* filtering schemes. For example, one type of experiment could be the reweighting of votes by annotator quality rather than the wholesale dropping of annotators. Another could involve the use of general-purpose sentiment analysis lexica to bias the vote aggregation in the manner of work in sentiment domain transfer (Tan et al., 2007).

This work also points to the potential for crowdsourcing in computational linguistics applications beyond opinion mining. Our task is a sentiment-specific instance of a large class of syntactic relatedness problems that may suitable for crowdsourcing. One practical application would be in obtaining training data for coreference detection. Another one may be in the establishment of empirical support for theories about syntactic structure.

Acknowledgements

This paper is based on work supported by the National Science Foundation under grant IIS-0729459.

References

Pei-Yun Hsueh, Prem Melville, and Vikas Sindhwani. 2009. Data quality from crowdsourcing: a study of annotation selection criteria. In *Proceedings of the NAACL HLT 2009 Workshop on Active Learning for Natural Language Processing*, HLT '09, Stroudsburg, PA, USA. Association for Computational Linguistics.

Jason S. Kessler, Miriam Eckert, Lyndsay Clark, and Nicolas Nicolov. 2010. The 2010 ICWSM JDPA sentment corpus for the automotive domain. In *4th Int'l AAAI Conference on Weblogs and Social Media Data Workshop Challenge (ICWSM-DWC 2010)*.

Soo-Min Kim and Eduard Hovy. 2006. Extracting opinions, opinion holders, and topics expressed in online news media text. In *SST '06: Proceedings of the Workshop on Sentiment and Subjectivity in Text*, pages 1–8, Morristown, NJ, USA. Association for Computational Linguistics.

Moshe Koppel and Jonathan Schler. 2006. The importance of neutral examples for learning sentiment. *Computational Intelligence*, 22(2).

Bo Pang and Lillian Lee. 2008. Opinion mining and sentiment analysis. *Found. Trends Inf. Retr.*, 2(1-2).

Everett M. Rogers. 2003. *Diffusion of Innovations, 5th Edition*. Free Press.

Josef Ruppenhofer, Swapna Somasundaran, and Janyce Wiebe. 2008. Finding the sources and targets of subjective expressions. In Nicoletta Calzolari, Khalid Choukri, Bente Maegaard, Joseph Mariani, Jan Odjik, Stelios Piperidis, and Daniel Tapias, editors, *Proceedings of the Sixth International Language Resources and Evaluation (LREC'08)*, Marrakech, Morocco. European Language Resources Association (ELRA).

Asad B. Sayeed, Timothy J. Meyer, Hieu C. Nguyen, Olivia Buzek, and Amy Weinberg. 2010a. Crowdsourcing the evaluation of a domain-adapted named entity recognition system. In *Human Language Technologies: The 2010 Annual Conference of the North American Chapter of the Association for Computational Linguistics*. Association for Computational Linguistics.

Asad B. Sayeed, Hieu C. Nguyen, Timothy J. Meyer, and Amy Weinberg. 2010b. Expresses-an-opinion-about: using corpus statistics in an information extraction approach to opinion mining. In *Proceedings of the 23rd International Conference on Computational Linguistics*, COLING '10.

Rion Snow, Brendan O'Connor, Daniel Jurafsky, and Andrew Y. Ng. 2008. Cheap and fast—but is it good?: evaluating non-expert annotations for natural language tasks. In *EMNLP 2008*.

Songbo Tan, Gaowei Wu, Huifeng Tang, and Xueqi Cheng. 2007. A novel scheme for domain-transfer problem in the context of sentiment analysis. In *Proceedings of the sixteenth ACM conference on Conference on information and knowledge management*, CIKM '07, New York, NY, USA.

Theresa Wilson and Janyce Wiebe. 2005. Annotating attributions and private states. In *CorpusAnno '05: Proceedings of the Workshop on Frontiers in Corpus Annotations II*, Morristown, NJ, USA. Association for Computational Linguistics.

Theresa Wilson, Janyce Wiebe, and Paul Hoffmann. 2005. Recognizing contextual polarity in phrase-level sentiment analysis. In *HLT/EMNLP*.

What We Know About The Voynich Manuscript

Sravana Reddy*
Department of Computer Science
The University of Chicago
Chicago, IL 60637
sravana@cs.uchicago.edu

Kevin Knight
Information Sciences Institute
University of Southern California
Marina del Rey, CA 90292
knight@isi.edu

Abstract

The Voynich Manuscript is an undeciphered document from medieval Europe. We present current knowledge about the manuscript's text through a series of questions about its linguistic properties.

1 Introduction

The Voynich manuscript, also referred to as the VMS, is an illustrated medieval folio written in an undeciphered script.

There are several reasons why the study of the manuscript is of interest to the natural language processing community, besides its appeal as a long-enduring unsolved mystery. Since even the basic structure of the text is unknown, it provides a perfect opportunity for the application of unsupervised learning algorithms. Furthermore, while the manuscript has been examined by various scholars, it has much to benefit from attention by a community with the right tools and knowledge of linguistics, text analysis, and machine learning.

This paper presents a review of what is currently known about the VMS, as well as some original observations. Although the manuscript raises several questions about its origin, authorship, the illustrations, etc., we focus on the *text* through questions about its properties. These range from the level of the letter (for example, *are there vowels and consonants?*) to the page (*do pages have topics?*) to the document as a whole (*are the pages in order?*).

2 Background

2.1 History

From the illustrations – hairstyles and features of the human figures – as well as the shapes of the glyphs, the manuscript is posited to have been created in Europe. Carbon-dating at the University of Arizona has found that the vellum was created in the 15th century, and the McCrone Research Institute has asserted that the ink was added shortly afterwards[1].

The exact history of the VMS is not established. According to Zandbergen (2010), the earliest owner that it can be traced to is Jacobus de Tepenec in Prague in the early 1600s. It is speculated that it was given to him by Emperor Rudolf II, but it is unclear how and from where the manuscript entered Prague.

The VMS appears to have circulated in Prague for some time, before being sent to Athanasius Kircher in Italy in 1665. It remained in Italy until 1912, when it was sold to Wilfrid Voynich, who brought it to America. It was then sold to the bookdealer Kraus, who later donated it to the Yale University library[2], where it is currently housed.

2.2 Overview

The manuscript is divided into *quires* – sections made out of folded parchment, each of which consists of *folios*, with writing on both sides of each folio (Reeds, 2002). Including blank pages and pages with no text, there are 240 pages, although it is believed that some are missing (Pelling, 2006). 225

* This work was completed while the author was visiting the Information Sciences Institute.

[1]These results are as yet unpublished. A paper about the carbon-dating experiments is forthcoming in 2011.

[2]High-resolution scans are available at http://beinecke.library.yale.edu/digitallibrary/voynich.html

pages include text, and most are illustrated. The text was probably added after the illustrations, and shows no evidence of scratching or correction.

The text is written left to right in paragraphs that are left-aligned, justified, and divided by whitespace into words. Paragraphs do not span multiple pages.

A few glyphs are ambiguous, since they can be interpreted as a distinct character, or a ligature of two or more other characters. Different transcriptions of the manuscript have been created, depending on various interpretations of the glyphs. We use a machine-readable transcription based on the alphabet proposed by Currier (1976), edited by D'Imperio (1980) and others, made available by the members of the Voynich Manuscript Mailing List (Gillogly and Reeds, 2005) at http://www.voynich.net/reeds/gillogly/voynich.now. The Currier transcription maps the characters to the ASCII symbols A-Z, 0-9, and *. Under this transcription, the VMS is comprised of 225 pages, 8114 word types, and 37919 word tokens. Figure 1 shows a sample VMS page and its Currier transcription.

2.3 Manuscript sections

Based on the illustrations, the manuscript has traditionally been divided into six sections: (1) *herbal*, containing drawings of plants; (2) *Astronomical*, containing zodiac-like illustrations; (3) *Biological*, mainly containing drawings of female human figures; (4) *Cosmological*, consisting of circular illustrations; (5) *Pharmaceutical*, containing drawing of small containers and parts of plants, and (6) *Stars* (sometimes referred to as *Recipes*), containing very dense text with drawings of stars in the margins.

Currier (1976) observed from letter and substring frequencies that the text is comprised of two distinct 'languages', A and B. Interestingly, the Biological and Stars sections are mainly written in the B language, and the rest mainly in A.

Using a two-state bigram HMM over the entire text, we find that the two word classes induced by EM more or less correspond to the same division – words in pages classified as being in the A language tend to be tagged as one class, and words in B language pages as the other, indicating that the manuscript does indeed contain two different vocabularies (which may be related languages, dialects, or simply different textual domains). In Figure 2, we

Figure 1: Page *f81v* (from the Biological section).

(a) Scan of page

```
BAR ZC9 FCC89 ZCFAE 8AE 8AR OE BSC89 ZCF 8AN
OVAE ZCF9 4OFC89 OFAM FAT OFAE 2AR OE FAN
OEFAN AE OE ROE 8E 2AM 8AM OEFCC89 OFC89 89FAN
ZCF S89 8AEAE OE89 4OFAM OFAN SCCF9 89 OE FAM
8AN 89 8AM SX9 OFAM 8AM OPAN SX9 OFCC89 4OF9
FAR 8AM OFAR 4OFAN OFAM OE SC89 SCOE EF9 E2
AM OFAN 8AE89 OEOR OE ZCXAE 8AM 4OFCC8AE 8AM
SX9 2SC89 4OE 9FOE OR ZC89 ZCC89 4OE FCC89 8AM
8FAN WC89 OE89 9AR OESC9 FAM OFCC9 8AM OEOR
SCX9 8AII89

BOEZ9 OZ9PCC8 4OB OFCC89 OPC89 OFZC89 4OP9
8ATAJ OZC9 4OFCC9 OFCC9 OF9 9FCC9 4OF9 OF9EF9
OES9 F9 8ZOE98 4OE OE S89 ZC89 4OFC89 9PC89
SCPC89 EFC8C9 9PC89 9FCC2C9 8SC8 9PC89 9PC89
8AR 9FC8A IB*9 4OP9 9FC89 OFAE 8ZC89 9FCC89
C2CCF9 8AM OFC89 4OFCC8 4OFC89 ESBS89 4OFAE
SC89 OE ZCC9 2AEZQ89 4OVSC89 R SC89 EPAR9
EOR ZC89 4OCC89 OE S9 RZ89 EZC89 8AR S89
BS89 2ZFS89 SC89 OE ZC89 4OESC89 4OFAN ZX9 8E
RAE 4OFS89 SC9 OE SCF9 OE ZC89 4OFC89 4OFC89
SX9 4OF9 2OEFCC9 OE ZC89 4OFAR ZCX9 8C2C89
4OFAR 4OFAE 8OE S9 4OQC9 SCFAE SO89 4OFC89
EZCP9 4OE89 EPC89 4OPAN EZO 4OFC9 EZC89 EZC89
SC89 4OEF9 ESC8AE 4OE OPAR 4OFAE 4OE OM SCC9
8AE EO*C89 ZC89 2AE SPC89PAR ZOE 4CFS9 9FAM
OEFAN ZC89 4OF9 8SC89 ROE OE Q89 9PC9 OFSC89
4OFAE OFCC9 4OE SCC89 2AE PCOE 8S89 E9 OZC89
4OPC89 ZOE SC89 9ZSC9 OE SC9 4OE SC89 PS8 OF9
OE SCSOE PAR OM OFC89 8AE ZC9 OEFCOE OEFCC89
OFCOE 8ZCOE O3 OEFCC89 PC89 SCF9 ZXC89 SAE

OPON OEFOE
```

(b) Transcription in the Currier alphabet. Paragraph (but not line) breaks are indicated.

illustrate the division of the manuscript pages into the six sections, and show the proportion of words in each page that are classified as the B language.

For coherence, all our experimental results in the rest of this paper are on the B language (which we denote by VMS B) – specifically, the Biological and Stars sections – unless otherwise specified. These sections together contain 43 pages, with 3920 word types, 17597 word tokens, and 35 characters. We compare the VMS's statistical properties with three natural language texts of similar size: the first 28551 words from the English Wall Street Journal Corpus, 19327 words from the Arabic Quran (in Buckwalter transcription), and 18791 words from the Chinese Sinica Treebank.

3 The Letter

3.1 Are vowels and consonants represented?

If a script is alphabetic, i.e., it uses approximately one character per phoneme, vowel and consonant characters can be separated in a fully unsupervised way. Guy (1991) applies the vowel-consonant separation algorithm of (Sukhotin, 1962) on two pages of the Biological section, and finds that four characters (`O`, `A`, `C`, `G`) separate out as vowels. However, the separation is not very strong, and several words do not contain these characters.

Another method is to use a two-state bigram HMM (Knight et al., 2006; Goldsmith and Xanthos, 2009) over letters, and induce two clusters of letters with EM. In alphabetic languages like English, the clusters correspond almost perfectly to vowels and consonants. We find that a curious phenomenon occurs with the VMS – the last character of every word is generated by one of the HMM states, and all other characters by another; i.e., the word grammar is a^*b.

There are a few possible interpretations of this. It is possible that the vowels from every word are removed and placed at the end of the word, but this means that even long words have only one vowel, which is unlikely. Further, the number of vowel types would be nearly half the alphabet size. If the script is a syllabary or a logograph, a similar clustering will surface, but given that there are only 35 characters, it is unlikely that each of them represents a syllable or word. A more likely explanation is that the script is an abjad, like the scripts of Semitic languages, where all or most vowels are omitted. Indeed, we find that a 2-state HMM on Arabic without diacritics and English without vowels learns a similar grammar, a^*b^+.

3.2 Do letters have cases?

Some characters (`F`, `B`, `P`, `V`) that appear mainly at paragraphs beginnings are referred to 'gallows' – glyphs that are taller and more ornate than others. Among the glyphs, these least resemble Latin, leading to the belief that they are null symbols, which Morningstar (2001) refutes.

Another hypothesis is that gallows are uppercase versions of other characters. We define $\text{BESTSUB}(c)$ to be the character x that produces the highest decrease in unigram word entropy when x is substituted for all instances of c. For English uppercase characters c, $\text{BESTSUB}(c)$ is the lowercase version. However, BESTSUB of the VMS gallows is one of the other gallows! This demonstrates that they are not uppercase versions of other letters, and also that they are contextually similar to one another.

3.3 Is there punctuation?

We define punctuation as symbols that occur only at word edges, whose removal from the word results in an existing word. There are two characters that are only found at the ends of words (Currier `K` and `L`), but most of the words produced by removing `K` and `L` are not in the vocabulary. Therefore, there is most likely no punctuation, at least in the traditional sense.

4 The Word

4.1 What are the word frequency and length distributions?

The word frequency distribution follows Zipf's law, which is a necessary (though not sufficient) test of linguistic plausibility. We also find that the unigram word entropy is comparable to the baseline texts (Table 1).

Table 1: Unigram word entropy in bits.

VMS B	English	Arabic	Chinese
9.666	10.07	9.645	10.31

Several works have noted the narrow binomial distribution of word lengths, and contrasted it with

Figure 2: VMS sections, and percentage of word tokens in each page that are tagged as language B by the HMM.

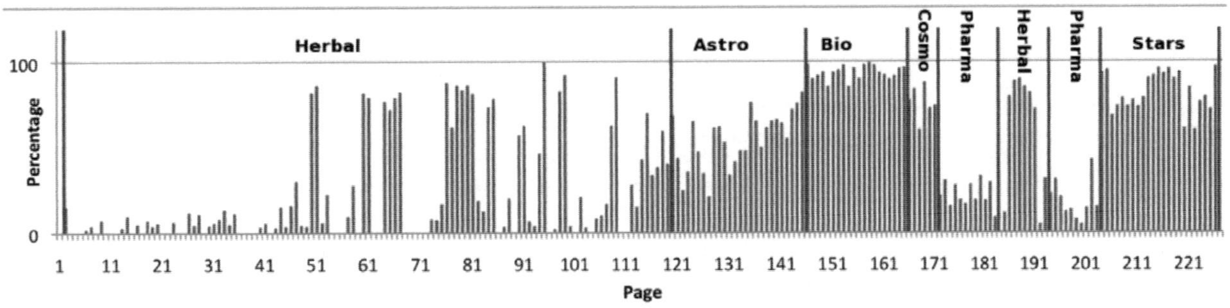

the wide asymmetric distribution of English, Latin, and other European languages. This contributed to speculation that the VMS is not a natural language, but a code or generated by some other stochastic process. However, Stolfi (2005) show that Pinyin Chinese, Tibetan, and Vietnamese word lengths follow a binomial distribution, and we found (Figure 3) that certain scripts that do not contain vowels, like Buckwalter Arabic and devoweled English, have a binomial distribution as well.[3] The similarity with devoweled scripts, especially Arabic, reinforces the hypothesis that the VMS script may be an abjad.

Figure 3: Word length distributions (word types).

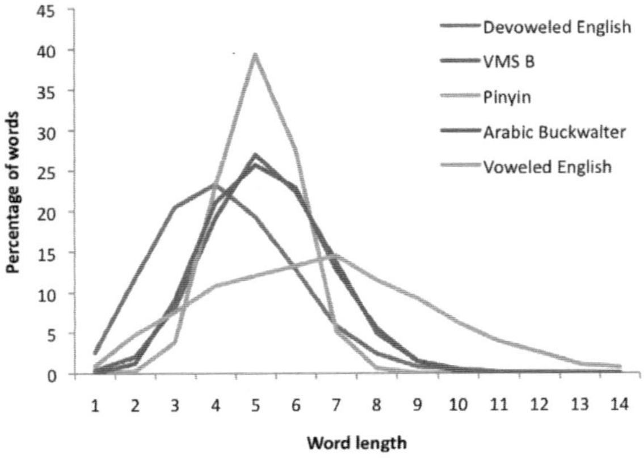

Landini (2001) found that the VMS follows Zipf's law of word lengths: there is an inverse relationship between the frequency and length of a word.

[3]This is an example of why comparison with a range of languages is required before making conclusions about the language-like nature of a text.

4.2 How predictable are letters within a word?

Bennett (1976) notes that the second-order entropy of VMS letters is lower than most European languages. Stolfi (2005) computes the entropy of each character given the left and right contexts and finds that it is low for most of the VMS text, particularly the Biological section, compared to texts in other languages. He also ascertains that spaces between words have extremely low entropy.

We measure the *predictability* of letters, and compare it to English, Arabic, and Pinyin Chinese. Predictability is measured by finding the probabilities over a training set of word types, guessing the most likely letter (the one with the highest probability) at each position in a word in the held-out test set, and counting the proportion of times a guess is correct. Table 2 shows the predictability of letters as unigrams, and given the preceding letter in a word (bigrams). VMS letters are more predictable than other languages, with the predictability increasing sharply given the preceding contexts, similarly to Pinyin.

Table 2: Predictability of letters, averaged over 10-fold cross-validation runs.

	VMS B	English	Arabic	Pinyin
Bigram	40.02%	22.62%	24.78%	38.92%
Unigram	14.65%	11.09%	13.29%	11.20%

Zandbergen (2010) computes the entropies of characters at different positions in words in the Stars section, and finds that the 1st and 2nd characters of a word are more predictable than in Latin or Vulgate, but the 3rd and 4th characters are less predictable.

It has also been observed that word-final characters have much lower entropy compared to most other languages – some characters appear almost exclusively at the ends of words.

4.3 Is there morphological structure?

The above observations suggest that words are made up of morpheme-like chunks. Several hypotheses about VMS word structure have been proposed. Tiltman (1967) proposed a template consisting of roots and suffixes. Stolfi (2005) breaks down the morphology into 'prefix-midfix-suffix', where the letters in the midfixes are more or less disjoint from the letters in the suffixes and prefixes. Stolfi later modified this to a 'core-mantel-crust' model, where words are composed of three nested layers.

To determine whether VMS words have affixal morphology, we run an unsupervised morphological segmentation algorithm, Linguistica (Goldsmith, 2001), on the VMS text. The MDL-based algorithm segments words into prefix+stem+suffix, and extracts 'signatures', sets of affixes that attach to the same set of stems. Table 3 lists a few sample signatures, showing that stems in the same signature tend to have some structural similarities.

Table 3: Some morphological signatures.

Affixes	Stems
OE+, OP+, null+	A3 AD AE AE9 AEOR AJ AM AN AR AT E O O2 OE OJ OM ON OR SAJ SAR SCC9 SCCO SCO2 SO
OE+	BSC28 BSC9 CCC8 COC8CR FAEOE FAK FAU FC8 FC8AM FCC FCC2 FCC9R FCCAE FCCC2 FCCCAR9 FCO9 FCS9 FCZAR FCZC9 OEAR9 OESC9 OF9 OR8 SC29 SC89O SC8R SCX9 SQ9
+89, +9, + C89	4OFCS 4OFCZ 4OFZ 4OPZ 8AES 8AEZ 9FS 9PS EFCS FCS PS PZ OEFS OF OFAES OFCS OFS OFZ

5 Syntax

5.1 Is there word order?

One of the most puzzling features of the VMS is its weak word order. Notably, the text has very few repeated word bigrams or trigrams, which is surprising given that the unigram word entropy is comparable to other languages. Furthermore, there are sequences of two or more repeated words, or repetitions of very similar words. For example, the first page of the Biological section contains the line `4OFCC89 4OFCC89 4OFC89 4OFC89 4OFCC89 E89`.

We compute the predictability of a word given the previous word (Table 4). Bigram contexts only provide marginal improvement in predictability for the VMS, compared to the other texts. For comparison with a language that has 'weak word order', we also compute the same numbers for the first 22766 word tokens of the Hungarian Bible, and find that the *empirical* word order is not that weak after all.

Table 4: Predictability of words (over 10-fold cross-validation) with bigram contexts, compared to unigrams.

	Unigram	Bigram	Improvement
VMS B	2.30%	2.50%	8.85%
English	4.72%	11.9%	151%
Arabic	3.81%	14.2%	252%
Chinese	16.5%	19.8%	19.7%
Hungarian	5.84%	13.0%	123%

5.2 Are there latent word classes?

While there are very few repeated word bigrams, perhaps there are latent classes of words that govern word order. We induce ten word classes using a bigram HMM trained with EM (Figure 4). As with the stems in the morphological signatures, the words in each class show some regularities – although it is hard to quantify the similarities – suggesting that these latent classes are meaningful.

Currier (1976) found that some word-initial characters are affected by the word-final characters of the immediately preceding word. He concludes that the 'words' being syllables or digits would explain this phenomenon, although that is unlikely given the rarity of repeated sequences.

We redo the predictability experiments of the previous section, using the last m letters of the previous word to predict the first n letters of the current word. When $n > 2$, improvement in predictability remains low. However, when n is 1 or 2, there is a noticeable improvement when using the last few characters of the previous word as contexts (Table 5).

5.3 Are there long-distance word correlations?

Weak bigram word order can arise if the text is scrambled or is generated by a unigram process. Alternately, the text might have been created by inter-

Figure 4: Some of the induced latent classes.

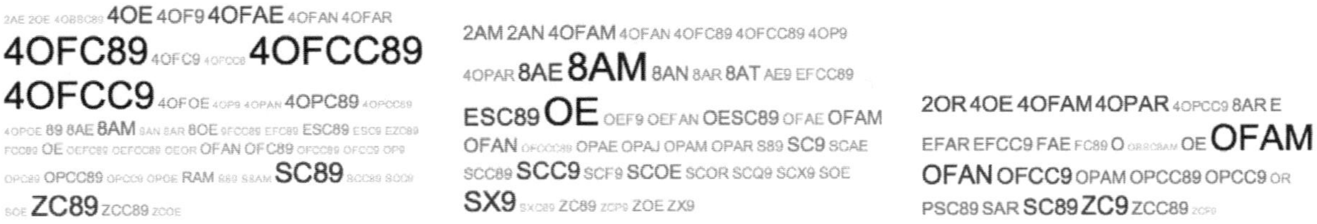

(a) (b) (c)

Table 5: Relative improvement in predictability of first n word-characters using last m characters of previous word, over using no contextual information.

		VMS B	English	Arabic
Whole words		8.85%	**151%**	**252%**
$n = 1$	$m = 1$	**31.8%**	31.1%	26.8%
	$m = 2$	30.7%	45.8%	61.5%
	$m = 3$	29.9%	60.3%	92.4%
$n = 2$	$m = 1$	16.0%	42.8%	0.0736%
	$m = 2$	12.4%	67.5%	14.1%
	$m = 3$	10.9%	94.6%	33.2%

leaving the words of two or more texts, in which case there will be long-distance correlations.

Schinner (2007) shows that the probability of *similar* words repeating in the text at a given distance from each other follows a geometric distribution.

Figure 5 illustrates the 'collocationness' at distance d, measured as the average pointwise mutual information over all pairs of words w_1, w_2 that occur more than once at distance d apart. VMS words do not show significant long-distance correlations.

Figure 5: Long-range collocationness. Arabic shows stronger levels of long-distance correlation compared to English and Chinese. VMS B shows almost no correlations for distance $d > 1$.

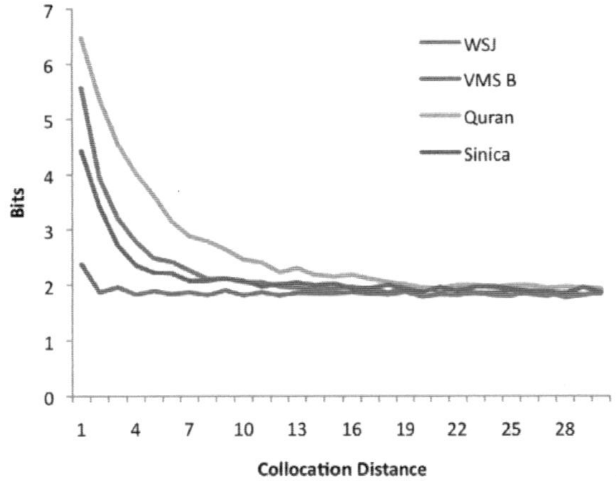

6 The Page

6.1 Do pages have topics?

That is, do certain words 'burst' with a high frequency within a page, or are words randomly distributed across the manuscript? Figure 6 shows a visualization of the TF-IDF values of words in a VMS B page, where the 'documents' are pages, indicating the relevance of each word to the page. Also shown is the same page in a version of the document created by scrambling the words of the original manuscript, and repaginating to the same page lengths. This simulates a document where words are generated independent of the page, i.e., the pages have no topics.

To quantify the degree to which a page contains topics, we measure the entropy of words within the page, and denote the overall 'topicality' T of a document as the average entropy over all the pages. As a control, we compute the topicality T_{rand} of the scrambled version of the document. $1 - T/T_{rand}$ indicates the extent to which the pages of the document contain topics. Table 6 shows that by this measure, the VMS's strength of page topics is less than the English texts, but more than the Quran[4], signifying that the pages probably do have topics, but are not independent of one another.

6.2 Is the text prose?

Visually, the text looks like prose written in paragraphs. However, Currier (1976) stated that "the line

[4]We demarcate a 'page' to be approximately 25 verses for the Quran, a chapter for the Genesis, and an article for the WSJ.

Figure 6: TF-IDF visualization of page *f108v* in the Stars section.

(a) Original document, showing bursts

(b) Scrambled version – flatter distribution

Table 6: Strength of page topics in VMS and other texts, cropped to be of comparable length to the VMS.

	VMS B	English WSJ	English Genesis	Arabic Quran
T	7.5	6.3	6.6	7.7
T_{rand}	7.7	6.5	7.1	7.9
$1 - T/T_{rand}$	0.033	0.037	0.069	0.025

is a functional entity" – that is, there are patterns to lines on the page that are uncharacteristic of prose. In particular, certain characters or sequences appear almost exclusively at the beginnings or ends of lines.

Figure 7 shows the distribution of characters at line-edges, relative to their occurrences at word beginnings or endings,confirming Currier's observation. It is particularly interesting that lower-frequency characters occur more at line-ends, and higher-frequency ones at the beginnings of lines.

Schinner (2007) found that characters show long-range correlations at distances over 72 characters, which is a little over the average line length.

7 The Document

7.1 Are the pages in order?

We measure the similarity between two pages as the cosine similarity over bags of words, and count the proportion of pages P_i where the page P_{i-1} or P_{i+1} is the most similar page to P_i. We denote this measure by ADJPAGESIM. If ADJPAGESIM is high, it indicates that (1) the pages are not independent of each other and (2) the pages are in order.

Table 7 shows ADJPAGESIM for the VMS and other texts. As expected, ADJPAGESIM is close to zero for the VMS with pages scrambled, as well as the WSJ, where each page is an independent article, and is highest for the VMS, particularly the B pages.

Table 7: ADJPAGESIM for VMS and other texts.

VMS B	38.8%
VMS All	15.6%
VMS B pages scrambled	0%
VMS All pages scrambled	0.444%
WSJ	1.34%
English Genesis	25.0%
Arabic Quran	27.5%

This is a convincing argument for the pages being mostly in order. However, the non-contiguity of the herbal and pharmaceutical sections and the interleaving of the A and B languages indicates that larger chunks of pages were probably re-ordered. In addition, details involving illustrations and ink-transfer across pages point to a few local re-orderings (Pelling, 2006).

7.2 How many authors were involved?

Currier (1976) observed that the distinction between the A and B languages corresponds to two different types of handwriting, implying at least two authors. He claimed that based on finer handwriting analysis, there may have been as many as eight scribes.

8 Latin, Cipher, or Hoax?

Claims of decipherment of the VMS script have been surfacing for several years, none of which are convincing. Newbold (1928) believed that microscopic irregularities of glyph edges correspond to anagrammed Latin. Feely in 1943 proposed that the script is a code for abbreviated Latin (D'Imperio, 1980). Sherwood (2008) believes that the words are coded anagrams of Italian. Others have hypoth-

Figure 7: Proportion of word-edge characters at line-edges for lines that span the width of the page. Characters are in ascending order of their total frequencies.

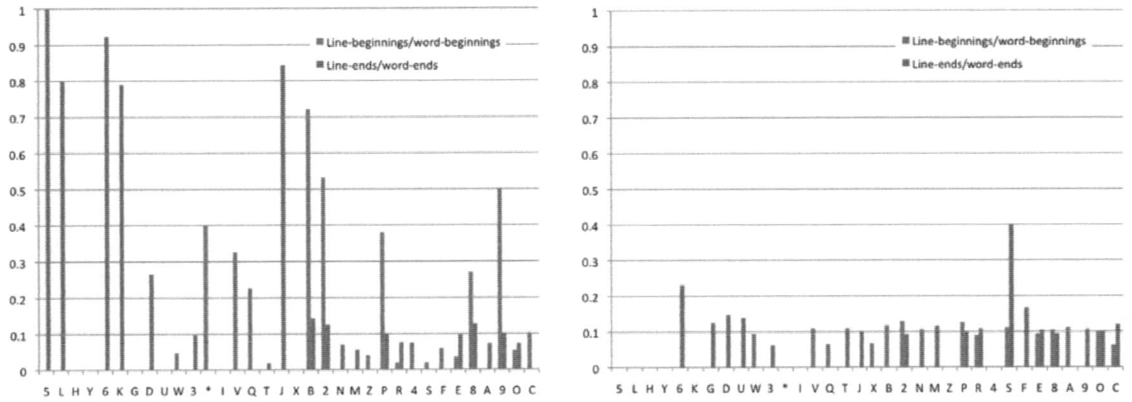

(a) Original document, showing biased distribution.

(b) Flat distribution when words within lines are scrambled.

esized that the script is an encoding of Ukrainian (Stojko, 1978), English (Strong, 1945; Brumbaugh, 1976), or a Flemish Creole (Levitov, 1987). The word length distribution and other properties have invoked decodings into East Asian languages like Manchu (Banasik, 2004). These theories tend to rely on arbitrary anagramming and substitutions, and are not falsifiable or well-defined.

The mysterious properties of the text and its resistance to decoding have led some to conclude that it is a hoax – a nonsensical string made to look vaguely language-like. Rugg (2004) claims that words might have been generated using a 'Cardan Grille' – a way to deterministically generate words from a table of morphemes. However, it seems that the Grille emulates a restricted finite state grammar of words over prefixes, midfixes, and suffixes. Such a grammar underlies many affixal languages, including English. Martin (2008) proposes a method of generating VMS text from anagrams of number sequences. Like the previous paper, it only shows that this method *can* create VMS-like words – not that it is the most plausible way of generating the manuscript. It is also likely that the proposed scheme can be used to generate any natural language text.

Schinner (2007) votes for the hoax hypothesis based on his observations about characters showing long-range correlations, and the geometric distribution of the probability of similar words repeating at a fixed distance. These observations only confirm that the VMS has some properties unlike natural language, but not that it is necessarily a hoax.

9 Conclusion

We have detailed various known properties of the Voynich manuscript text. Some features – the lack of repeated bigrams and the distributions of letters at line-edges – are linguistically aberrant, which others – the word length and frequency distributions, the apparent presence of morphology, and most notably, the presence of page-level topics – conform to natural language-like text.

It is our hope that this paper will motivate research into understanding the manuscript by scholars in computational linguistics. The questions presented here are obviously not exhaustive; a deeper examination of the statistical features of the text in comparison to a number of scripts and languages is needed before any definite conclusions can be made. Such studies may also inspire a quantitative interest in linguistic and textual typologies, and be applicable to the decipherment of other historical scripts.

Acknowledgments

We would like to thank the anonymous reviewers and our colleagues at ISI and Chicago for their helpful suggestions. This work was supported in part by NSF Grant 0904684.

References

Zbigniew Banasik. 2004. http://www.ic.unicamp.br/ stolfi/voynich/04-05-20-manchu-theo/alphabet.html.

William Ralph Bennett. 1976. *Scientific and engineering problem solving with a computer*. Prentice-Hall.

Robert Brumbaugh. 1976. The Voynich 'Roger Bacon' cipher manuscript: deciphered maps of stars. *Journal of the Warburg and Courtauld Institutes*.

Prescott Currier. 1976. New research on the Voynich Manuscript: Proceedings of a seminar. Unpublished communication, available from http://www.voynich.nu/extra/curr_pdfs.html.

Mary D'Imperio. 1980. *The Voynich Manuscript: An Elegant Enigma*. Aegean Park Press.

Jim Gillogly and Jim Reeds. 2005. Voynich Manuscript mailing list. http://voynich.net/.

John Goldsmith and Aris Xanthos. 2009. Learning phonological categories. *Language*, 85:4–38.

John Goldsmith. 2001. Unsupervised learning of the morphology of a natural language. *Computational Linguistics*.

Jacques Guy. 1991. Statistical properties of two folios of the Voynich Manuscript. *Cryptologia*.

Kevin Knight, Anish Nair, Nishit Rathod, and Kenji Yamada. 2006. Unsupervised analysis for decipherment problems. In *Proceedings of COLING*.

Gabriel Landini. 2001. Evidence of linguistic structure in the Voynich Manuscript using spectral analysis. *Cryptologia*.

Leo Levitov. 1987. *Solution of the Voynich Manuscript: A Liturgical Manual for the Endura Rite of the Cathari Heresy, the Cult of Isis*. Aegean Park Press.

Claude Martin. 2008. Voynich, the game is over. http://www.voynich.info/.

Jason Morningstar. 2001. Gallows variants as null characters in the Voynich Manuscript. Master's thesis, University of North Carolina.

William Newbold. 1928. *The Cipher of Roger Bacon*. University of Pennsylvania Press.

Nicholas John Pelling. 2006. *The Curse of the Voynich: The Secret History of the World's Most Mysterious Manuscript*. Compelling Press.

Jim Reeds. 2002. Voynich Manuscript. http://www.ic.unicamp.br/ stolfi/voynich/mirror/reeds.

Gordon Rugg. 2004. The mystery of the Voynich Manuscript. *Scientific American Magazine*.

Andreas Schinner. 2007. The Voynich Manuscript: Evidence of the hoax hypothesis. *Cryptologia*.

Edith Sherwood. 2008. The Voynich Manuscript decoded? http://www.edithsherwood.com/voynich_decoded/.

John Stojko. 1978. *Letters to God's Eye: The Voynich Manuscript for the first time deciphered and translated into English*. Vantage Press.

Jorge Stolfi. 2005. Voynich Manuscript stuff. http://www.dcc.unicamp.br/ stolfi/voynich/.

Leonell Strong. 1945. Anthony Ashkam, the author of the Voynich Manuscript. *Science*.

Boris Sukhotin. 1962. Eksperimental'noe vydelenie klassov bukv s pomoscju evm. *Problemy strukturnoj lingvistiki*.

John Tiltman. 1967. The Voynich Manuscript, the most mysterious manuscript in the world. *NSA Technical Journal*.

René Zandbergen. 2010. Voynich MS. http://www.voynich.nu/index.html.

Automatic Verb Extraction from Historical Swedish Texts

Eva Pettersson
Department of Linguistics and Philology
Uppsala University
Swedish National Graduate School
of Language Technology
eva.pettersson@lingfil.uu.se

Joakim Nivre
Department of Linguistics and Philology
Uppsala University
joakim.nivre@lingfil.uu.se

Abstract

Even though historical texts reveal a lot of interesting information on culture and social structure in the past, information access is limited and in most cases the only way to find the information you are looking for is to manually go through large volumes of text, searching for interesting text segments. In this paper we will explore the idea of facilitating this time-consuming manual effort, using existing natural language processing techniques. Attention is focused on automatically identifying verbs in early modern Swedish texts (1550–1800). The results indicate that it is possible to identify linguistic categories such as verbs in texts from this period with a high level of precision and recall, using morphological tools developed for present-day Swedish, if the text is normalised into a more modern spelling before the morphological tools are applied.

1 Introduction

Historical texts constitute a rich source of data for researchers interested in for example culture and social structure over time. It is however a very time-consuming task to manually search for relevant passages in the texts available. It is likely that language technology could substantially reduce the manual effort involved and thus the time needed to access this information, by automatically suggesting sections that may be of interest to the task at hand. The interesting text segments could be identified using for example semantic features or morphological and syntactic cues in the text.

This would however require natural language processing tools capable of handling historical texts, which are in many respects different from contemporary written language, concerning both spelling and syntax. Ideally, one would of course like to have tools developed specifically for the time period of interest, and emerging efforts to develop resources and tools for historical languages are therefore welcome. Despite these efforts, however, it is unlikely that we will have anything close to complete coverage of different time periods even for a single language within the foreseeable future.

In this paper, we will therefore instead examine the possibility of improving information access in historical texts by adapting language technology tools developed for contemporary written language. The work has been carried out in close cooperation with historians who are interested in what men and women did for a living in the early modern Swedish society (1550–1800). We will hence focus on identifying linguistic categories in Swedish texts from this period. The encouraging results show that you may successfully analyse historical texts using NLP tools developed for contemporary language, if analysis is preceded by an orthographic normalisation step.

Section 2 presents related work and characteristics of historical Swedish texts. The extraction method is defined in section 3. In section 4 the experiments are described, while the results are presented in section 5. Section 6 describes how the verb extraction tool is used in ongoing historical research. Finally, conclusions are drawn in section 7.

2 Background

2.1 Related Work

There are still not many studies performed on natural language processing of historical texts. Pennacchiotti and Zanzotto (2008) used contemporary dictionaries and analysis tools to analyse Italian texts from the period 1200–1881. The results showed that the dictionary only covered approximately 27% of the words in the oldest text, as compared to 62.5% of the words in a contemporary Italian newspaper text. The morphological analyser used in the study reached an accuracy of 0.48 (as compared to 0.91 for modern text), while the part-of-speech tagger yielded an accuracy of 0.54 (as compared to 0.97 for modern text).

Rocio et al. (1999) used a grammar of contemporary Portuguese to syntactically annotate medieval Portuguese texts. To adapt the parser to the medieval language, a lexical analyser was added including a dictionary and inflectional rules for medieval Portuguese. This combination proved to be successful for partial parsing of medieval Portuguese texts, even though there were some problems with grammar limitations, dictionary incompleteness and insufficient part-of-speech tagging.

Oravecz et al. (2010) tried a semi-automatic approach to create an annotated corpus of texts from the Old Hungarian period. The annotation was performed in three steps: 1) sentence segmentation and tokenisation, 2) standardisation/normalisation, and 3) morphological analysis and disambiguation. They concluded that normalisation is of vital importance to the performance of the morphological analyser.

For the Swedish language, Borin et al. (2007) proposed a named-entity recognition system adapted to Swedish literature from the 19th century. The system recognises Person Names, Locations, Organisations, Artifacts (food/wine products, vehicles etc), Work&Art (names of novels, sculptures etc), Events (religious, cultural etc), Measure/Numerical expressions and Temporal expressions. The named entity recognition system was evaluated on texts from the Swedish Literature Bank without any adaptation, showing problems with spelling variation, inflectional differences, unknown names and structural issues (such as hyphens splitting a single name into several entities).[1] Normalising the texts before applying the named entity recognition system made the f-score figures increase from 78.1% to 89.5%.

All the results presented in this section indicate that existing natural language processing tools are not applicable to historical texts without adaptation of the tools, or the source text.

2.2 Characteristics of Historical Swedish Texts

Texts from the early modern Swedish period (1550–1800) differ from present-day Swedish texts both concerning orthography and syntax. Inflectional differences include a richer verb paradigm in historical texts as compared to contemporary Swedish. The Swedish language was also strongly influenced by other languages. Evidence of this is the placement of the finite verb at the end of relative clauses in a German-like fashion not usually found in Swedish texts, as in *...om man i hächtelse sitter* as compared to *om man sitter i häkte* (*"...if you in custody are"* vs *"...if you are in custody"*).

Examples of the various orthographic differences are the duplication of long vowels in words such as *saak* (*sak* "thing") and *stoor* (*stor* "big/large"), the use of of *fv* instead of *v*, as in *öfver* (*över* "over"), and *gh* and *dh* instead of the present-day *g* and *d*, as in *någhon* (*någon* "somebody") and *fadhren* (*fadern* "the father") (Bergman, 1995).

Furthermore, the lack of spelling conventions causes the spelling to vary highly between different writers and text genres, and even within the same text. There is also great language variation in texts from different parts of the period.

3 Verb Extraction

In the following we will focus on identifying verbs in historical Swedish texts from the period 1550–1800. The study has been carried out in cooperation with historians who are interested in finding out what men and women did for a living in the early modern Swedish society. One way to do this would be to search for occupational titles occurring in the text. This is however not sufficient since many people, especially women, had no occupational title. Occupational titles are also vague, and may include several subcategories of work. In the material

[1] http://litteraturbanken.se/

already (manually) analysed by the historians, occupation is often described as a verb with a direct object. Hence, automatically extracting and displaying the verbs in a text could help the historians in the process of finding relevant text segments. The verb extraction process developed for this purpose is performed in maximally five steps, as illustrated in figure 1.

The first step is tokenisation. Each token is then optionally matched against dictionaries covering historical Swedish. Words not found in the historical dictionaries are normalised to a more modern spelling before being processed by the morphological analyser. Finally, the tagger disambiguates words with several interpretations, yielding a list of all the verb candidates in the text. In the experiments, we will examine what steps are essential, and how they are combined to yield the best results.

3.1 Tokenisation

Tokenisation is performed using an in-house standard tokeniser. The result of the tokenisation is a text segmented into one token per line, with a blank line marking the start of a new sentence.

3.2 Historical Dictionaries

After tokenisation, the tokens are optionally matched against two historical dictionaries distributed by *The Swedish Language Bank*:[2]

- **The Medieval Lexical Database**
  A dictionary describing Medieval Swedish, containing approximately 54 000 entries from the following three books:
  - K.F. Söderwalls *Ordbok Öfver svenska medeltids-språket, vol I-III* (Söderwall, 1918)
  - K.F. Söderwalls *Ordbok Öfver svenska medeltids-språket, vol IV-V* (Söderwall, 1973)
  - C.J. Schlyters *Ordbok till Samlingen af Sweriges Gamla Lagar* (Schlyter, 1877)
- **Dalin's Dictionary**
  A dictionary covering 19th Century Swedish, created from the printed version of *Ordbok Öfver svenska språket, vol I–II* by Dalin (1855). The dictionary contains approximately 64 000 entries.

[2]http://spraakbanken.gu.se/

The dictionaries cover medieval Swedish and 19th century Swedish respectively. We are actually interested in the time period in between these two periods, but it is assumed that these dictionaries are close enough to cover words found in the early modern period as well. It should further be noticed that the electronically available versions of the dictionaries are still in an early stage of development. This means that coverage varies between different word classes, and verbs are not covered to the same extent as for example nouns. Words with an irregular inflection (which is often the case for frequently occurring verbs) also pose a problem in the current dictionaries.

3.3 Normalisation Rules

Since both the morphological analyser and the tagger used in the experiments are developed for handling modern Swedish written language, running a text with the old Swedish spelling preserved presumably means that these tools will fail to assign correct analyses in many cases. Therefore, the text is optionally transformed into a more modern spelling, before running the document through the analysis tools.

The normalisation procedure differs slightly for morphological analysis as compared to tagging. There are mainly two reasons why the same set of normalisation rules may not be optimally used both for the morphological analyser and for the tagger. First, since the tagger (unlike the morphological analyser) is context sensitive, the normalisation rules developed for the tagger need to be designed to also normalise words surrounding verbs, such as nouns, determiners, etc. For the morphological analyser, the main focus in formulating the rules has been on handling verb forms. Secondly, to avoid being limited to a small set of rules, an incremental normalisation procedure has been used for the morphological analyser in order to maximise recall without sacrificing precision. In this incremental process, normalisation rules are applied one by one, and the less confident rules are only applied to words not identified by the morphological analyser in the previous

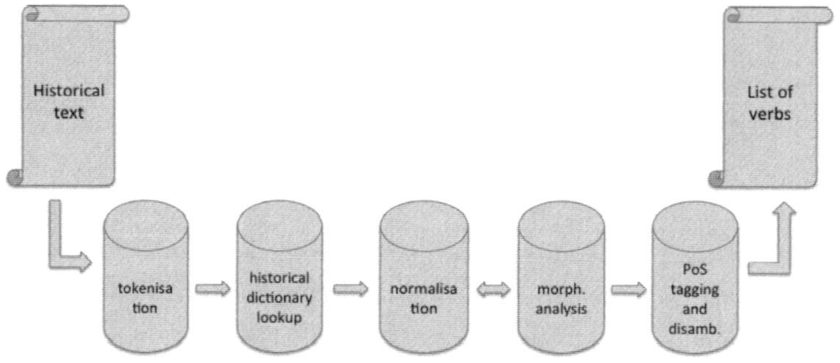

Figure 1: Overview of the verb extraction experiment

normalisation step. The tagger on the other hand is robust, always yielding a tag for each token, even in cases where the word form is not present in the dictionary. Thus, the idea of running the normalisation rules in an incremental manner is not an option for the tagger.

The total set of normalisation rules used for the morphological analyser is 39 rules, while 29 rules were defined for the tagger. The rules are inspired by (but not limited to) some of the changes in the reformed Swedish spelling introduced in 1906 (Bergman, 1995). As a complement to the rules based on the spelling reform, a number of empirically designed rules were formulated, based on the development corpus described in section 4.1. The empirical rules include the rewriting of verbal endings (e.g. *begärade* – *begärde* "requested" and *utviste* – *utvisade* "deported"), transforming double consonants into a single consonant (*vetta* – *veta* "know", *prövass* – *prövas* "be tried") and vice versa (*upsteg* – *uppsteg* "rose/ascended", *viste* – *visste* "knew").

3.4 Morphological Analysis and Tagging

SALDO is an electronically available lexical resource developed for present-day written Swedish. It is based on *Svenskt AssociationsLexikon* (SAL), a semantic dictionary compiled by Lönngren (1992). The first version of the SALDO dictionary was released in 2008 and comprises 72 396 lexemes. Inflectional information conforms to the definitions in Nationalencyklopedins ordbok (1995), Svenska Akademiens ordlista över svenska språket (2006) and Svenska Akademiens grammatik (1999). Apart from single word entries, the SALDO dictionary also contains approximately 2 000 multi-word units, including 1 100 verbs, mainly particle verbs (Borin et al., 2008). In the experiments we will use SALDO version 2.0, released in 2010 with a number of words added, resulting in a dictionary comprising approximately 100 000 entries.

When running the SALDO morphological analyser alone, a token is always considered to be a verb if there is a verb interpretation present in the dictionary, regardless of context. For example, the word *för* will always be analysed both as a verb (*bring*) and as a preposition (*for*), even though in most cases the prepositional interpretation is the correct one.

When running the maximum five steps in the verb extraction procedure, the tagger will disambiguate in cases where the morphological analyser has produced both a verb interpretation and a non-verb interpretation. The tagger used in this study is HunPOS (Halácsy et al., 2007), a free and open source reimplementation of the HMM-based TnT-tagger by Brants (2000). Megyesi (2008) showed that the HunPOS tagger trained on the Stockholm-Umeå Corpus (Gustafson-Capková and Hartmann, 2006) is one of the best performing taggers for Swedish texts.

4 Experiments

This section describes the experimental setup including data preparation and experiments.

4.1 Data Preparation

A subset of *Per Larssons dombok*, a selection of court records from 1638, was used as a basis for developing the automatic verb extraction tool. This text consists of 11 439 tokens in total, and was printed by Edling (1937). The initial 984 tokens of the text were used as development data, i.e. words used when formulating the normalisation rules, whereas the rest of the text was used solely for evaluation.

A gold standard for evaluation was created, by manually annotating all the verbs in the text. For the verb annotation to be as accurate as possible, the same text was annotated by two persons independently, and the results analysed and compared until consensus was reached. The resulting gold standard includes 2 093 verbs in total.

4.2 Experiment 1: Normalisation Rules

In the first experiment we will compare morphological analysis results before and after applying normalisation rules. To investigate what results could optimally be expected from the morphological analysis, SALDO was also run on present-day Swedish text, i.e. the Stockholm-Umeå Corpus (SUC). SUC is a balanced corpus consisting of a number of different text types representative of the Swedish language in the 1990s. The corpus consists of approximately one million tokens, distributed among 500 texts with approximately 2 000 tokens in each text. Each word in the corpus is manually annotated with part of speech, lemma and a number of morphological features (Gustafson-Capková and Hartmann, 2006).

4.3 Experiment 2: Morphological Analysis and Tagging

In the second experiment we will focus on the combination of morphological analysis and tagging, based on the following settings:

morph A token is always considered to be a verb if the morphological analysis contains a verb interpretation.

tag A token is always considered to be a verb if it has been analysed as a verb by the tagger.

morph *or* **tag** A token is considered to be a verb if there is a morphological verb analysis **or** if it has been analysed as a verb by the tagger.

morph *and* **tag** A token is considered to be a verb if there is a morphological verb analysis **and** it has been tagged as a verb.

To further refine the combination of morphological analysis and tagging, a more fine-grained disambiguation method was introduced, where the tagger is only used in contexts where the morphological analyser has failed to provide an unambiguous interpretation:

morph + tag A token is considered to be a verb if it has been unambiguously analysed as a verb by SALDO. Likewise a token is considered not to be a verb, if it has been given one or more analyses from SALDO, where none of the analyses is a verb interpretation. If the token has been given both a verb analysis and a non-verb analysis by SALDO, the tagger gets to decide. The tagger also decides for words not found in SALDO.

4.4 Experiment 3: Historical Dictionaries

In the third experiment, the historical dictionaries are added, using the following combinations:

medieval A token is considered to be a verb if it has been unambiguously analysed as a verb by the medieval dictionary. Likewise a token is considered not to be a verb, if it has been given one or more analyses from the medieval dictionary, where none of the analyses is a verb interpretation. If the token has been given both a verb analysis and a non-verb analysis by the medieval dictionary, or if the token is not found in the dictionary, the token is processed by the morphological analyser and the tagger as described in setting *morph + tag*.

19c A token is considered to be a verb if it has been unambiguously analysed as a verb by the 19th century dictionary. Likewise a token is considered not to be a verb, if it has been given one or more analyses from the 19th century dictionary, where none of the analyses is a verb interpretation. If the token has been given both a verb analysis and a non-verb analysis by the 19th century dictionary, or if the token is not found in the dictionary, the token is processed by the morphological analyser and the tagger as described in setting *morph + tag*.

medieval + 19c A token is considered to be a verb if it has been unambiguously analysed as a verb by the medieval dictionary. Likewise a token is considered not to be a verb, if it has been given one or more analyses from the medieval dictionary, where none of the analyses is a verb interpretation. If the token has been given both a verb analysis and a non-verb analysis by the medieval dictionary, or if the token is not found in the dictionary, the token is matched against the 19th century dictionary before being processed by the morphological analyser and the tagger as described in setting *morph + tag*.

19c + medieval A token is considered to be a verb if it has been unambiguously analysed as a verb by the 19th century dictionary. Likewise a token is considered not to be a verb, if it has been given one or more analyses from the 19th century dictionary, where none of the analyses is a verb interpretation. If the token has been given both a verb analysis and a non-verb analysis by the 19th century dictionary, or if the token is not found in the dictionary, the token is matched against the medieval dictionary before being processed by the morphological analyser and the tagger as described in setting *morph + tag*.

5 Results

5.1 Normalisation Rules

Running the SALDO morphological analyser on the test text with the old Swedish spelling preserved, meant that only 30% of the words were analysed at all. Applying the normalisation rules before the morphological analysis is performed, drastically increases recall. After only 5 rules have been applied, recall is increased by 11 percentage units, and adding another 5 rules increases recall by another 26 percentage units. All in all, recall increases from 30% for unnormalised text to 83% after all normalisation rules have been applied, whereas precision increases from 54% to 66%, as illustrated in table 1.

Recall is still significantly higher for contemporary Swedish texts than for the historical text (99% as compared to 83% with the best normalisation settings). Nevertheless, the rapid increase in recall when applying the normalisation rules is very promising, and it is yet to be explored how good results it is possible to reach if including more normalisation rules.

	Precision	**Recall**	**f-score**
raw data	0.54	0.30	0.39
5 rules	0.61	0.41	0.49
10 rules	0.66	0.67	0.66
15 rules	0.66	0.68	0.67
20 rules	0.67	0.73	0.70
25 rules	0.66	0.78	0.72
30 rules	0.66	0.79	0.72
35 rules	0.66	0.82	0.73
39 rules	0.66	0.83	0.74
SUC corpus	0.53	0.99	0.69

Table 1: Morphological analysis results using SALDO version 2.0, before and after incremental application of normalisation rules, and compared to the Stockholm-Umeå corpus of contemporary Swedish written language.

5.2 Morphological Analysis and Tagging

Table 2 presents the results of combining the SALDO morphological analyser and the HunPOS tagger, using the settings described in section 4.3.

	Precision	**Recall**	**f-score**
morph	0.66	0.83	0.74
tag	0.81	0.86	0.83
morph *or* **tag**	0.61	0.92	0.74
morph *and* **tag**	0.92	0.80	0.85
morph + tag	0.82	0.88	0.85

Table 2: Results for normalised text, combining morphological analysis and tagging. morph = morphological analysis using SALDO. tag = tagging using HunPOS.

As could be expected, the tagger yields higher precision than the morphological anlayser, due to the fact that the morphological analyser renders all analyses for a word form given in the dictionary, regardless of context. The results of combining the morphological analyser and the tagger are also quite expected. In the case where a token is considered to be a verb if there is a morphological verb analysis *or* it has been analysed as a verb by the tagger, a very high level of recall (92%) is achieved at the expense of low precision, whereas the opposite is true for the case where a token is considered to be a verb if there is a morphological verb analysis *and* it has been tagged as a verb. Using the tagger for disambiguation only in ambiguous cases yields the best results. It should be noted that using the morph-and-tag setting results in the same f-score as the disambiguation setting. However, the disambiguation setting performs better in terms of recall, which is of importance to the historians in the project at hand. Another advantage of using the disambiguation setting is that the difference between precision and recall is less.

5.3 Historical Dictionaries

The results of using the historical dictionaries are presented in table 3.

	Precision	Recall	f-score
morph + tag	0.82	0.88	0.85
medieval	0.82	0.81	0.81
19c	0.82	0.86	0.84
medieval + 19c	0.81	0.79	0.80
19c + medieval	0.81	0.79	0.80

Table 3: Results for normalised text, combining historical dictionaries and contemporary analysis tools. medieval = *Medieval Lexical Database*. 19c = *Dalin's Dictionary*. morph = morphological analysis using SALDO. tag = tagging using HunPOS.

Adding the historical dictionaries did not improve the verb analysis results; actually the opposite is true. Studying the results of the analyses from the medieval dictionary, one may notice that only two verb analyses have been found when applied to the test text, and both of them are erroneous in this context (in both cases the word *lass* "load" as in the phrase *6 lass höö* "6 loads of hay"). Furthermore, the medieval dictionary produces quite a lot of non-verb analyses for commonly occurring verbs, for example *skola* (noun: "shool", verb: "should/shall"), *kunna* ("can/could"), *kom* ("come"), *finna* ("find") and *vara* (noun: "goods", verb: "be"). Another reason for the less encouraging results seems to be that most of the words actually found and analysed correctly are words that are correctly analysed by the contemporary tools as well, such as *i* ("in"), *man* ("man/you"), *sin* ("his/her/its"), *honom* ("him") and *in* ("into").

As for the 19th century dictionary, the same problems apply. For example, a number of frequent verb forms are analysed as non-verbs (e.g. *skall* "should/shall" and *ligger* "lies"). There are also non-verbs repeatedly analysed as verbs, such as *stadgar* ("regulations") and *egne* ("own"). As was the case for the medieval dictionary, most of the words analysed correctly by the 19th century dictionary are commonly occuring words that would have been correctly analysed by the morphological analyser and/or the tagger as well, for example *och* ("and"), *men* ("but") and *när* ("when").

6 Support for Historical Research

In the ongoing *Gender and Work* project at the Department of History, Uppsala University, historians are interested in what men and women did for a living in the early modern Swedish Society.[3] Information on this is registered and made available for research in a database, most often in the form of a verb and its object(s). The automatic verb extraction tool was developed in close cooperation with the Gender and Work participants, with the aim of reducing the manual effort involved in finding the relevant information to enter into the database.

The verb extraction tool was integrated in a prototypical graphical user interface, enabling the historians to run the system on historical texts of their choice. The interface provides facilities for uploading files, generating a list of all the verbs in the file, displaying verb concordances for interesting verbs, and displaying the verb in a larger context. Figure 2 illustrates the graphical user interface, displaying concordances for the verb *anklaga* ("accuse"). The historians found the interface useful and are interested in integrating the tool in the Gender and Work database. Further development of the verb extraction tool is now partly funded by the Gender and Work project.

[3] http://gaw.hist.uu.se/

Tillbaka till Start : Verblista

Söksida för excerpering av verb

Förekomster av verbet *anklaga* i filen **PL_dombok_hand.txt**.
Klicka på respektive konkordans för större kontext.

1. : kom för Rätten Olof Ramunder , och Ratione officij **ahnklagadhe** Bönderne på Gränöön , som Eek huggidt haffva till therass
2. D : kom för Rätten Olof Ramundher , och **ahnklagadhe** Erich Erichsson i Lindrijss på huilkenss äghor några Eeker förbrändhe
3. : D : framkom Peer i Stridzby , och **ahnklagade** Olof i Lervijken , som effter sinss Sonss dödz affall
4. lag begångidt hafuer , och förthenskull af befallningzmannen Ratione officij **ahnklagadess** , Thetta vedherstyggeligha åhrendet hafuer sigh såleedess med sine omstendigheeter
5. Chatarinæ Flämmingz etc. Fullmechtig , förståndigh Päer Päerssonn , och **ahnklagadhe** Oloff Stille , fordom hennes wälborenheetz tiänare , för dhet
6. för Rätten een ogifft löösskhåna , Charin Erichz dotter som **ahnklagadess** för dett hoon barn födt hadhe och thet sedhan uthi

Figure 2: Concordances displayed for the verb *anklaga* ("accuse") in the graphical user interface.

7 Conclusion

Today historians and other researchers working on older texts have to manually go through large volumes of text when searching for information on for example culture or social structure in historical times. In this paper we have shown that this time-consuming manual effort could be significantly reduced using contemporary natural language processing tools to display only those text segments that may be of interest to the researcher. We have described the development of a tool that automatically identifies verbs in historical Swedish texts using morphological analysis and tagging, and a prototypical graphical user interface, integrating this tool. The results indicate that it is possible to retrieve verbs in Swedish texts from the 17th century with 82% precision and 88% recall, using morphological tools for contemporary Swedish, if the text is normalised into a more modern spelling before the morphological tools are applied (recall may be increased to 92% if a lower precision is accepted).

Adding electronically available dictionaries covering medieval Swedish and 19th century Swedish respectively to the verb extraction tool, did not improve the results as compared to using only contemporary NLP tools. This seems to be partly due to the dictionaries still being in an early stage of development, where lexical coverage is unevenly spread among different word classes, and frequent, irregularly inflected word forms are not covered. It would therefore be interesting to study the results of the historical dictionary lookup, when the dictionaries are more mature.

Since the present extraction tool has been evaluated on one single text, it would also be interesting to explore how these extraction methods should be adapted to handle language variation in texts from different genres and time periods. Due to the lack of spelling conventions, it would also be interesting to see how the extraction process performs on texts from the same period and genre, but written by different authors. Future work also includes experiments on identifying linguistic categories other than verbs.

References

Gösta Bergman. 1995. *Kortfattad svensk språkhistoria*. Prisma Magnum, 5th ed., Stockholm.

Lars Borin, Markus Forsberg, and Lennart Lönngren. 2008. *SALDO 1.0 (Svenskt associationslexikon version 2)*. Språkbanken, University of Gothenburg.

Lars Borin, Dimitrios Kokkinakis, and Leif-Jöran Olsson. 2007. *Naming the Past: Named Entity and Anomacy Recognition in 19th Century Swedish Literature)*. In: Proceedings of the Workshop on Language Technology for Cultural Heritage Data (LaTeCH 2007), pages 1–8. Prague, Czech Republic.

Bra Böcker. 1995. *Nationalencyklopedins ordbok*. Bra Böcker, Höganäs.

Thorsten Brants. 2000. *TnT - A Statistical Part-of-Speech Tagger*. In: Proceedings of the 6th Applied Natural Language Processing Conference (ANLP-00), Seattle, Washington, USA.

Anders Fredrik Dalin. 1850–1855. *Ordbok Öfver svenska språket. Vol I–II*. Stockholm.

Nils Edling. 1937. *Uppländska domböcker. jämte inledning, förklaringar och register utgivna genom Nils Edling*. Uppsala.

Sofia Gustafson-Capková and Britt Hartmann. December 2006. *Manual of the Stockholm Umeå Corpus version 2.0*. Description of the content of the SUC 2.0 distribution, including the unfinished documentation by Gunnel Källgren.

Péter Halácsy, András Kornai, and Csaba Oravecz 2007. *HunPos - an open source trigram tagger*. In: Proceedings of the 45th Annual Meeting of the Association for Computational Linguistics Companion Volume Proceedings of the Demo and Poster Sessions, pages 209–212. Association for Computational Linguistics, Prague, Czech Republic.

Lennart Lönngren. 1992. *Svenskt associationslexikon, del I–IV*. Department of Linguistics and Philology, Uppsala University.

Beáta B. Megyesi. 2008. *The Open Source Tagger HunPoS for Swedish*. Department of Linguistics and Philology, Uppsala University.

Csaba Oravecz, Bálint Sass, and Eszter Simon 2010. *Semi-automatic Normalization of Old Hungarian Codices*. In: Proceedings of the ECAI 2010 Workshop on Language Technology for Cultural Heritage, Social Sciences, and Humanities (LaTeCH 2010). Pages 55–59. 16 August, 2010 Faculty of Science, University of Lisbon Lisbon, Portugal.

Marco Pennacchiotti and Fabio Massimo Zanzotto 2008. *Natural Language Processing Across Time: An Empirical Investigation on Italian*. In: Aarne Ranta and Bengt Nordström (Eds.): Advances in Natural Language Processing. GoTAL 2008, LNAI Volume 5221, pages 371–382. Springer-Verlag Berlin Heidelberg.

Vitor Rocio, Mário Amado Alves, José Gabriel Lopes, Maria Francisca Xavier, and Graça Vicente. 1999. *Automated Creation of a Partially Syntactically Annotated Corpus of Medieval Portuguese Using Contemporary Portuguese Resources*. In: Proceedings of the ATALA workshop on Treebanks, Paris, France.

Carl Johan Schlyter. 1877. *Ordbok till Samlingen af Sweriges Gamla Lagar*. Lund.

Svenska Akademien. 2006. *Svenska Akademiens ordlista över svenska språket*. Norstedts Akademiska Förlag, Stockholm.

Knut Fredrik Söderwall. 1884–1918. *Ordbok Öfver svenska medeltids-språket, vol I–III*. Lund.

Knut Fredrik Söderwall. 1953–1973. *Ordbok Öfver svenska medeltids-språket, vol IV–V*. Lund.

Ulf Teleman, Staffan Hellberg, and Erik Andersson. 1999. *Svenska Akademiens grammatik*. Norstedts Ordbok, Stockholm.

Topic Modeling on Historical Newspapers

Tze-I Yang
Dept. of Comp. Sci. & Eng.
University of North Texas
tze-iyang@my.unt.edu

Andrew J. Torget
Dept. of History
University of North Texas
andrew.torget@unt.edu

Rada Mihalcea
Dept. of Comp. Sci. & Eng.
University of North Texas
rada@cs.unt.edu

Abstract

In this paper, we explore the task of automatic text processing applied to collections of historical newspapers, with the aim of assisting historical research. In particular, in this first stage of our project, we experiment with the use of topical models as a means to identify potential issues of interest for historians.

1 Newspapers in Historical Research

Surviving newspapers are among the richest sources of information available to scholars studying peoples and cultures of the past 250 years, particularly for research on the history of the United States. Throughout the nineteenth and twentieth centuries, newspapers served as the central venues for nearly all substantive discussions and debates in American society. By the mid-nineteenth century, nearly every community (no matter how small) boasted at least one newspaper. Within these pages, Americans argued with one another over politics, advertised and conducted economic business, and published articles and commentary on virtually all aspects of society and daily life. Only here can scholars find editorials from the 1870s on the latest political controversies, advertisements for the latest fashions, articles on the latest sporting events, and languid poetry from a local artist, all within one source. Newspapers, in short, document more completely the full range of the human experience than nearly any other source available to modern scholars, providing windows into the past available nowhere else.

Despite their remarkable value, newspapers have long remained among the most underutilized historical resources. The reason for this paradox is quite simple: the sheer volume and breadth of information available in historical newspapers has, ironically, made it extremely difficult for historians to go through them page-by-page for a given research project. A historian, for example, might need to wade through tens of thousands of newspaper pages in order to answer a single research question (with no guarantee of stumbling onto the necessary information).

Recently, both the research potential and problem of scale associated with historical newspapers has expanded greatly due to the rapid digitization of these sources. The National Endowment for the Humanities (NEH) and the Library of Congress (LOC), for example, are sponsoring a nationwide historical digitization project, *Chronicling America*, geared toward digitizing all surviving historical newspapers in the United States, from 1836 to the present. This project recently digitized its one millionth page (and they project to have more than 20 million pages within a few years), opening a vast wealth of historical newspapers in digital form.

While projects such as *Chronicling America* have indeed increased access to these important sources, they have also increased the problem of scale that have long prevent scholars from using these sources in meaningful ways. Indeed, without tools and methods capable of handling such large datasets – and thus sifting out meaningful patterns embedded within them – scholars find themselves confined to performing only basic word searches across enormous collections. These simple searches can, indeed, find stray information scattered in unlikely places. Such rudimentary search tools, however, become increasingly less useful to researchers as datasets continue to grow in size. If a search for a particular term yields 4,000,000 results, even those search results produce a dataset far too large for any single scholar to analyze in a meaningful way using traditional methods. The age of abundance, it turns out, can simply overwhelm historical scholars, as the sheer volume of available digitized historical newspapers is beginning to do.

In this paper, we explore the use of topic modeling, in an attempt to identify the most important and potentially interesting topics over a given period of time. Thus, instead of asking a historian to look through thousands of newspapers to identify what may be interesting topics, we take a reverse approach, where we first automatically cluster the data into topics, and then provide these automatically identified topics to the historian so she can narrow her scope to focus on the individual patterns in the dataset that are most applicable to her research. Of more utility would be where the modeling would reveal unexpected topics that point towards unusual patterns previously unknown, thus help shaping a scholar's subsequent research.

The topic modeling can be done for any periods of time, which can consist of individual years or can cover several years at a time. In this way, we can see the changes in the discussions and topics of interest over the years. Moreover, pre-filters can also be applied to the data prior to the topic modeling. For instance, since research being done in the History department at our institution is concerned with the "U. S. cotton economy," we can use the same approach to identify the interesting topics mentioned in the news articles that talk about the issue of "cotton."

2 Topic Modeling

Topic models have been used by Newman and Block (2006) and Nelson (2010)[1] on newspaper corpora to discover topics and trends over time. The former used the probabilistic latent semantic analysis (pLSA) model, and the latter used the latent Dirichlet allocation (LDA) model, a method introduced by Blei et al. (2003). LDA has also been used by Griffiths and Steyvers (2004) to find research topic trends by looking at abstracts of scientific papers. Hall et al. (2008) have similarly applied LDA to discover trends in the computational linguistics field. Both pLSA and LDA models are probabilistic models that look at each document as a mixture of multinomials or topics. The models decompose the document collection into groups of words representing the main topics. See for instance Table 1, which shows two topics extracted from our collection.

Topic
worth price black white goods yard silk made ladies wool lot inch week sale prices pair suits fine quality
state states bill united people men general law government party made president today washington war committee country public york

Table 1: Example of two topic groups

Boyd-Graber et al. (2009) compared several topic models, including LDA, correlated topic model (CTM), and probabilistic latent semantic indexing (pLSI), and found that LDA generally worked comparably well or better than the other two at predicting topics that match topics picked by the human annotators. We therefore chose to use a parallel threaded SparseLDA implementation to conduct the topic modeling, namely UMass Amherst's MAchine Learning for LanguagE Toolkit (MALLET)[2] (McCallum, 2002). MALLET's topic modeling toolkit has been used by Walker et al. (2010) to test the effects of noisy optical character recognition (OCR) data on LDA. It has been used by Nelson (2010) to mine topics from the Civil War era newspaper *Dispatch*, and it has also been used by Blevins (2010) to examine general topics and to identify emotional moments from Martha Ballards Diary.[3]

3 Dataset

Our sample data comes from a collection of digitized historical newspapers, consisting of newspapers published in Texas from 1829 to 2008. Issues are segmented by pages with continuous text containing articles and advertisements. Table 2 provides more information about the dataset.

[1] http://americanpast.richmond.edu/dispatch/

[2] http://mallet.cs.umass.edu/

[3] http://historying.org/2010/04/01/

Property	
Number of titles	114
Number of years	180
Number of issues	32,745
Number of pages	232,567
Number of tokens	816,190,453

Table 2: Properties of the newspaper collection

3.1 Sample Years and Categories

From the wide range available, we sampled several historically significant dates in order to evaluate topic modeling. These dates were chosen for their unique characteristics (detailed below), which made it possible for a professional historian to examine and evaluate the relevancy of the results.

These are the subcategories we chose as samples:

- **Newspapers from 1865-1901:** During this period, Texans rebuilt their society in the aftermath of the American Civil War. With the abolition of slavery in 1865, Texans (both black and white) looked to rebuild their post-war economy by investing heavily in cotton production throughout the state. Cotton was considered a safe investment, and so Texans produced enough during this period to make Texas the largest cotton producer in the United States by 1901. Yet overproduction during that same period impoverished Texas farmers by driving down the market price for cotton, and thus a large percentage went bankrupt and lost their lands (over 50 percent by 1900). As a result, angry cotton farmers in Texas during the 1890s joined a new political party, the Populists, whose goal was to use the national government to improve the economic conditions of farmers. This effort failed by 1896, although it represented one of the largest third-party political revolts in American history.

  This period, then, was dominated by the rise of cotton as the foundation of the Texas economy, the financial failures of Texas farmers, and their unsuccessful political protests of the 1890s as cotton bankrupted people across the state. These are the issues we would expect to emerge as important topics from newspapers in this category. This dataset consists of 52,555 pages over 5,902 issues.

- **Newspapers from 1892:** This was the year of the formation of the Populist Party, which a large portion of Texas farmers joined for the U. S. presidential election of 1892. The Populists sought to have the U. S. federal government become actively involved in regulating the economy in places like Texas (something never done before) in order to prevent cotton farmers from going further into debt. In the 1892 election, the Populists did surprisingly well (garnering about 10 percent of the vote nationally) and won a full 23 percent of the vote in Texas. This dataset consists of 1,303 pages over 223 issues.

- **Newspapers from 1893:** A major economic depression hit the United States in 1893, devastating the economy in every state, including Texas. This exacerbated the problem of cotton within the states economy, and heightened the efforts of the Populists within Texas to push for major political reforms to address these problems. What we see in 1893, then, is a great deal of stress that should exacerbate trends within Texas society of that year (and thus the content of the newspapers). This dataset consists of 3,490 pages over 494 issues.

- **Newspapers from 1929-1930:** These years represented the beginning and initial onset in the United States of the Great Depression. The United States economy began collapsing in October 1929, when the stock market crashed and began a series of economic failures that soon brought down nearly the entire U. S. economy. Texas, with its already shaky economic dependence on cotton, was as devastated as any other state. As such, this period was marked by discussions about how to save both the cotton economy of Texas and about possible government intervention into the economy to prevent catastrophe. This dataset consists of 6,590 pages over 973 issues.

Throughout this era, scholars have long recognized that cotton and the economy were the dominating issues. Related to that was the rise and fall

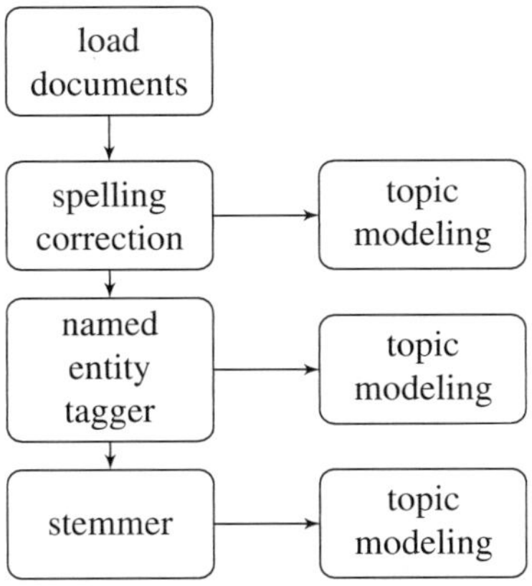

Figure 1: Work flow

of the Populist Party during the 1890s, as farmers sought to use the political system as a means of dealing with their economic problems. As such, we would expect to see these concerns as major (perhaps dominating) topics in the newspapers from the time.

3.1.1 "Cotton" data

Within the date ranges listed above, we also select all mentions of the topic "cotton" – as pertaining to possible discussion relevant to the "U. S. cotton economy." Cotton was the dominating economic force in Texas throughout this period, and historians have long recognized that issues related to the crop wielded tremendous influence on the political, social, and economic development of the state during this era. Problems related to cotton, for example, bankrupted half of all Texas farmers between 1865 and 1900, and those financial challenges pushed farmers to create a major new political party during the 1890s.

3.2 Data Processing

Before applying topic modeling on our data, some pre-processing steps were applied. Some challenges in processing the dataset come from errors introduced by the OCR processing, missing punctuations, and unclear separation between different articles on the same page. Multi-stage pre-processing of the dataset was performed to reduce these errors, as illustrated in Figure 1.

The first phase to reduce errors starts with spelling correction, which replaces words using the Aspell dictionary and de-hyphenates words split across lines. Suggested replacements are used if they are within the length normalized edit distance of the originals. An extra dictionary list of location names is used with Aspell.

Next, the spelling corrected dataset is run through the Stanford Named Entity Recognizer (NER).[4] Stanford NER system first detects sentences in the data then labels four classes of named entities: PERSON, ORGANIZATION, LOCATION, and MISCELLANEOUS (Finkel et al., 2005). The model used in conjunction with the tagger is provided by the software and was trained on the CoNLL 2003 training data using distributional similarity features. The output is then massaged so that entities with multiple words would stay together in the topic modeling phase.

Property	**# of Unique**	**# of Total**
LOC entities	1,508,432	8,620,856
ORG entities	6,497,111	14,263,391
PER entities	2,846,906	12,260,535
MISC entities	1,182,845	3,594,916
Named entities	12,035,294	38,739,698

Table 3: Properties of the newspaper collection after named entity recognition

Lastly, the words that are not tagged as named entities pass through an English stemmer while the named entities stay unchanged. We are using the Snowball stemmer.[5]

At the end of each of the pre-processing stage, we extract subsets from the data corresponding to the sample years mentioned earlier (1865-1901, 1892, 1893, and 1929-1930), which are then used for further processing in the topic modeling phase.

We made cursory comparisons of the outputs of the topic modeling at each of the three stages (spelling correction, NER, stemming). Table 4 shows sample topic groups generated at the three stages. We found that skipping the named entity tagging and stemming phases still gives comparable results. While the named entity tags may give us additional information ("dallas" and "texas" are locations), tagging the entire corpus takes up a large slice of processing time. Stemming after tagging

[4] http://nlp.stanford.edu/software/
[5] http://snowball.tartarus.org

Topic: spell
worth fort city texas county gazette tex special state company dallas time made yesterday night business line railroad louis
Topic: spell + NER
city county texas_location company yesterday night time today worth made state morning fort special business court tex dallas_location meeting
Topic: spell + NER + stemmer
state counti citi texas_location year ani time made worth fort peopl good line special tex land busi work compani

Table 4: Comparison of the three topic output stages: Each entry contains the top terms for a single topic

may collapse multiple versions of a word together, but we found that the stemmed words are very hard to understand such as the case of "business" becoming "busi". In future work, we may explore using a less aggressive stemmer that only collapses plurals, but so far the first stage output seems to give fairly good terms already. Thus, the rest of the paper will discuss using the results of topic modeling at the spelling correction stage.

4 Historical Topics and Trends

We are interested in automatically discovering general topics that appear in a large newspaper corpus. MALLET is run on each period of interest to find the top one general topic groups. We use 1000 iterations with stopword removal. An extra stopword list was essential to remove stopwords with errors introduced by the OCR process. Additionally, we run MALLET on the 1865-1901 dataset to find the top ten topic groups using 250 iterations.

In addition, we also find the topics more strongly associated with "cotton." The "cotton" examples are found by extracting each line that contains an instance of "cotton" along with a window of five lines on either side. MALLET is then run on these "cotton" examples to find the top general topic groups over 1000 iterations with stopword removal.

5 Evaluation and Discussion

The topic modeling output was evaluated by a historian (the second author of this paper), who specializes in the U.S.-Mexican borderlands in Texas and is an expert in the historical chronology, events, and language patterns of our newspaper collection. The evaluator looked at the output, and determined for each topic if it was relevant to the period of time under consideration.

The opinion from our expert is that the topic modeling yielded highly useful results. Throughout the general topics identified for our samples, there is a consistent theme that a historian would expect from these newspapers: a heavy emphasis on the economics of cotton. For example, we often see words like "good," "middling," and "ordinary," which were terms for evaluating the quality of a cotton crop before it went to market. Other common terms, such as "crop," "bale," "market," and "closed" (which suggests something like "the price *closed* at X") evoke other topics of discussion of aspects of the buying and selling of cotton crops.

Throughout the topics, market-oriented language is the overwhelming and dominate theme throughout, which is exactly what our expert expected as a historian of this region and era. You can see, for example, that much of the cotton economy was geared toward supplies the industrial mills in England. The word "Liverpool," the name of the main English port to where Texas cotton was shipped, appears quite frequently throughout the samples. As such, these results suggest a high degree of accuracy in identifying dominate and important themes in the corpus.

Within the subsets of these topics, we find more fine-grained patterns that support this trend, which lend more credence to the results.

Table 5 summarizes the results for each of the three analyzes, with accuracy calculated as follows: $Accuracy(\text{topics}) = \frac{\text{\# of relevant topics}}{\text{total \# of topics}}$ $Accuracy(\text{terms}) = \frac{\text{\# of relevant terms in all topics}}{\text{total \# of terms in all topics}}$. Tables 6, 7 and 8 show the actual analyzes.

5.1 Interesting Finding

Our historian expert found the topic containing "houston april general hero san" for the 1865-1901 general results particularly interesting and hypothesized that they may be referring to the Battle of San Jacinto. The Battle of San Jacinto was the final fight in the Texas Revolution of 1836, as Texas sought to free themselves from Mexican rule. On April 21, 1836, General Sam Houston led about 900

Topics	**Explanation**
black* price* worth* white* goods* yard* silk* made* lot* week ladies wool* inch* ladles* sale* prices* pair* suits* fine*	Reflects discussion of the market and sales of goods, with some words that relate to cotton and others that reflect other goods being sold alongside cotton (such as wool).
state* people* states* bill* law* made united* party* men* country* government* county* public* president* money* committee* general* great question*	Political language associated with the political debates that dominated much of newspaper content during this era. The association of the topic "money" is particularly telling, as economic and fiscal policy were particularly important discussion during the era.
clio worth mid city alie fort lino law lour lug thou hut fur court dally county anil tort iron	Noise and words with no clear association with one another.
tin inn mid tint mill* till oil* ills hit hint lull win hut ilia til ion lot lii foi	Mostly noise, with a few words associated with cotton milling and cotton seed.
texas* street* address* good wanted houston* office* work city* sale main* house* apply man county* avenue* room* rooms* land*	These topics appear to reflect geography. The inclusion of Houston may either reflect the city's importance as a cotton market or (more likely) the large number of newspapers from the collection that came from Houston.
worth* city* fort* texas* county* gazette tex* company* dallas* miss special yesterday night time john state made today louis*	These topics appear to reflect geography in north Texas, likely in relation to Fort Worth and Dallas (which appear as topics) and probably as a reflection that a large portion of the corpus of the collection came from the Dallas/Ft. Worth area.
houston* texas* today city* company post* hero* general* night morning york men* john held war* april* left san* meeting	These topics appear to an unlikely subject identified by the modeling. The words `Houston`, `hero`, `general`, `april` and `san` (perhaps part of `San Jacinto`) all fit together for a historian to suggest a sustained discussion in the newspapers of the April 1836 Battle of San Jacinto, when General Sam Houston defeated Santa Anna of Mexico in the Texas Revolution. This is entirely unexpected, but the topics appear to fit together closely. That this would rank so highly within all topics is, too, a surprise. (Most historians, for example, have argued that few Texans spent much time memorializing such events until after 1901. This would be quite a discovery if they were talking about it in such detail before 1901.)
man time great good men years life world long made people make young water woman back found women work	Not sure what the connections are here, although the topics clearly all fit together in discussion of the lives of women and men.
market* cotton* york* good* steady* closed* prices* corn* texas* wheat* fair* stock* choice* year* lower* receipts* ton* crop* higher*	All these topics reflect market-driven language related to the buying and selling cotton and, to a much smaller extent, other crops such as corn.
tube tie alie time thaw art ton ion aid ant ore end hat ire aad lour thee con til	Noise with no clear connections.

Table 6: 10 topic groups found for the 1865-1901 main set. Asterisks denote meaningful topic terms.

Period	Topics	Explanation
1865-1901	texas* city* worth* houston* good* county* fort* state* man* time* made* street* men* work* york today company great people	These keywords appear to be related to three things: (1) geography (reflected in both specific places like `Houston` and `Fort Worth` and more general places like `county`, `street`, and `city`), (2) discussions of people (`men` and `man`) and (3) time (`time` and `today`).
1892	texas* worth* gazette* city* tex* fort* county* state* good* march* man* special* made* people* time* york men days feb	As with the 1865-1901 set, these keywords also appear to be related to three things: (1) geography, (2) discussions of people and (3) time.
1893	worth* texas* tin* city* tube* clio* time* alie* man* good* fort* work* made street year men county state tex	As with the 1865-1901 set, these keywords also appear to be related to three things: (1) geography, (2) discussions of people and (3) time.
1929-1930	tin* texas* today* county* year* school* good* time* home* city* oil* man* men* made* work* phone night week sunday	As with the 1865-1901 set, these keywords also appear to be related to three things: (1) geography, (2) discussions of people and (3) time. The time discussion here appears to be heightened, and the appearance of economic issues for Texas (`oil`) makes sense in the context of the onset of the Great Depression in 1929-30.

Table 7: Main topics for years of interest for the main set

Period	Topics	Explanation
1865-1901	cotton* texas* good* crop* bales* county* york* houston* spot middling* year* corn* market* worth* oil* closed* special* ordinary* today	All market-oriented language that reflects all aspects of the cotton market, in particular the evaluation of cotton quality. The geography of New York (`york`) and Houston could reflect their importance in the cotton market or (just as important) sources of news and information (with Houston being a central producer of the newspapers in our corpus).
1892	cotton* bales* spot gazette* special* march middling* ordinary* steady* closed* futures* lots* good* texas* sales* feb low* ton* oil*	Market-oriented language that reflects, in particular, the buying and selling of cotton on the open market. The inclusion of February and March 1892, in the context of these other words associated with the selling of cotton, suggest those were important months in the marketing of the crop for 1892.
1893	cotton* ordinary* texas* worth* belt middling* closed* year bales* good* route* crop* city* cents* spot oil* corn* low* return*	Market-oriented language focused on the buying and selling of cotton.
1929-1930	cotton* texas* county crop* year good* today* york* points* oil* market* farm* made* seed* state* price* tin bales* july*	Market-oriented language concerning cotton. What is interesting here is the inclusion of words like `state`, `market`, and `price`, which did not show up in the previous sets. The market-language here is more broadly associated with the macro-economic situation (with explicit references to the `market` and `price`, which seems to reflect the heightened concern at that time about the future of the cotton market with the onset of the Great Depression and what role the `state` would play in that.

Table 8: Main topics for the `cotton` subset

		Accuracy	
	Topic Groups	Topics	Terms
General	Ten for 1865-1901	60%	45.79% (74.56%)
General	One for 1865-1901	100%	73.68%
General	One for 1892	100%	78.95%
General	One for 1893	100%	63.16%
General	One for 1929-1930	100%	78.95%
Cotton	One for 1865-1901	100%	89.47%
Cotton	One for 1892	100%	84.21%
Cotton	One for 1893	100%	84.21%
Cotton	One for 1929-1930	100%	84.21%

Table 5: Accuracy of topic modeling: In parenthesis is the term accuracy calculated using relevant topics only.

Texans against Mexican general Antonio Lopez de Santa Anna. Over the course of an eighteen minute battle, Houston's forces routed Santa Anna's army. The victory at San Jacinto secured the independence of Texas from Mexico and became a day of celebration in Texas during the years that followed.

Most historians have argued that Texas paid little attention to remembering the Battle of San Jacinto until the early twentieth century. These topic modeling results, however, suggest that far more attention was paid to this battle in Texas newspapers than scholars had previously thought.

We extracted all the examples from the corpus for the years 1865-1901 that contain ten or more of the top terms in the topic and also contain the word "jacinto". Out of a total of 220 snippets that contain "jacinto", 125 were directly related to the battle and its memory. 95 were related to other things. The majority of these snippets came from newspapers published in Houston, which is located near San Jacinto, with a surge of interest in the remembrance of the battle around the Aprils of 1897-1899.

6 Conclusions

In this paper, we explored the use of topical models applied on historical newspapers to assist historical research. We have found that we can automatically generate topics that are generally good, however we found that once we generated a set of topics, we cannot decide if it is mundane or interesting without an expert and, for example, would have been oblivious to the significance of the San Jacinto topic. We agree with Block (2006) that "topic simulation is only a tool" and have come to the conclusion that it is essential that an expert in the field contextualize these topics and evaluate them for relevancy.

We also found that although our corpus contains noise from OCR errors, it may not need expensive error correction processing to provide good results when using topic models. We may explore combining the named entity tagged data with a less aggressive stemmer and, additionally, evaluate the usefulness of not discarding the unstemmed words but maintaining their association with their stemmed counterpart.

Acknowledgment

We would like to thank Jon Christensen and Cameron Blevins from Stanford, who have been working with us on the larger project, "Mapping Historical Texts: Combining Text-Mining and Geo-Visualization to Unlock the Research Potential of Historical Newspapers", which subsumes the work we have presented in this paper. This work has been partly supported by the NEH under Digital Humanities Start-Up Grant (HD-51188-10). Any views, findings, conclusions or recommendations expressed in this publication do not necessarily represent those of the National Endowment for the Humanities.

References

[Blei et al.2003] David M. Blei, Andrew Y. Ng, and Michael I. Jordan. 2003. Latent dirichlet allocation. *The Journal of Machine Learning Research*, 3:993–1022.

[Blevins2010] Cameron Blevins. 2010. Topic Modeling Martha Ballard's Diary.

[Block2006] Sharon Block. 2006. Doing More with Digitization: An Introduction to Topic Modeling of Early American Sources. *Common-Place*, 6(2), January.

[Boyd-Graber et al.2009] Jonathan Boyd-Graber, Jordan Chang, Sean Gerrish, Chong Wang, and David M. Blei. 2009. Reading tea leaves: How humans interpret topic models. In *Proceedings of the 23rd Annual Conference on Neural Information Processing Systems.*

[Finkel et al.2005] Jenny Rose Finkel, Trond Grenager, and Christopher Manning. 2005. Incorporating non-local information into information extraction systems by gibbs sampling. In *Proceedings of the 43nd Annual Meeting of the Association for Computational Linguistics (ACL 2005)*, pages 363–370.

[Griffiths and Steyvers2004] Thomas L. Griffiths and Mark Steyvers. 2004. Finding scientific topics. *Proceedings of the National Academy of Sciences of the United States of America*, 101(Suppl 1):5228.

[Hall et al.2008] David Hall, Daniel Jurafsky, and Christopher Manning. 2008. Studying the History of Ideas Using Topic Models. In *Proceedings from the EMNLP 2008: Conference on Empirical Methods in Natural Language Processing*, October.

[McCallum2002] Andrew Kachites McCallum. 2002. MALLET: A Machine Learning for Language Toolkit.

[Nelson2010] Robert K. Nelson. 2010. Mining the *Dispatch*.

[Newman and Block2006] David J. Newman and Sharon Block. 2006. Probabilistic topic decomposition of an eighteenth-century American newspaper. *Journal of the American Society for Information Science and Technology*, 57(6):753–767.

[Walker et al.2010] Daniel D. Walker, William B. Lund, and Eric K. Ringger. 2010. Evaluating models of latent document semantics in the presence of OCR errors. In *Proceedings of the 2010 Conference on Empirical Methods in Natural Language Processing*, pages 240–250. Association for Computational Linguistics.

From Once Upon a Time to Happily Ever After: Tracking Emotions in Novels and Fairy Tales

Saif Mohammad
Institute for Information Technology
National Research Council Canada
Ottawa, Ontario, Canada, K1A 0R6
saif.mohammad@nrc-cnrc.gc.ca

Abstract

Today we have access to unprecedented amounts of literary texts. However, search still relies heavily on key words. In this paper, we show how sentiment analysis can be used in tandem with effective visualizations to quantify and track emotions in both individual books and across very large collections. We introduce the concept of emotion word density, and using the Brothers Grimm fairy tales as example, we show how collections of text can be organized for better search. Using the Google Books Corpus we show how to determine an entity's emotion associations from co-occurring words. Finally, we compare emotion words in fairy tales and novels, to show that fairy tales have a much wider range of emotion word densities than novels.

1 Introduction

Literary texts, such as novels, fairy tales, fables, romances, and epics have long been channels to convey emotions, both explicitly and implicitly. With widespread digitization of text, we now have easy access to unprecedented amounts of such literary texts. Project Gutenberg provides access to 34,000 books (Lebert, 2009).[1] Google is providing access to n-gram sequences and their frequencies from more than 5.2 million digitized books, as part of the *Google Books Corpus (GBC)* (Michel et al., 2011a).[2] However, techniques to automatically access and analyze these books still rely heavily on key word searches alone. In this paper, we show how sentiment analysis can be used in tandem with effective visualizations to quantify and track emotions in both individual books and across very large collections. This serves many purposes, including:

1. *Search*: Allowing search based on emotions. For example, retrieving the darkest of the Brothers Grimm fairy tales, or finding snippets from the Sherlock Holmes series that build the highest sense of anticipation and suspense.
2. *Social Analysis*: Identifying how books have portrayed different people and entities over time. For example, what is the distribution of emotion words used in proximity to mentions of women, race, and homosexuals. (Similar to how Michel et al. (2011b) tracked fame by analyzing mentions in the Google Books Corpus.)
3. *Comparative analysis of literary works, genres, and writing styles*: For example, is the distribution of emotion words in fairy tales significantly different from that in novels? Do women authors use a different distribution of emotion words than their male counterparts? Did Hans C. Andersen use emotion words differently than Beatrix Potter?
4. *Summarization*: For example, automatically generating summaries that capture the different emotional states of the characters in a novel.
5. *Analyzing Persuasion Tactics*: Analyzing emotion words and their role in persuasion (Mannix, 1992; Bales, 1997).

In this paper, we describe how we use a large word–emotion association lexicon (described in Section

[1] Project Gutenberg: http://www.gutenberg.org
[2] *GBC*: http://ngrams.googlelabs.com/datasets

3.1) to create a simple emotion analyzer (Section 3.2). We present a number of visualizations that help track and analyze the use of emotion words in individual texts and across very large collections, which is especially useful in Applications 1, 2, and 3 described above (Section 4). We introduce the concept of emotion word density, and using the Brothers Grimm fairy tales as an example, we show how collections of text can be organized for better search (Section 5). Using the Google Books Corpus we show how to determine emotion associations portrayed in books towards different entities (Section 6). Finally, for the first time, we compare a collection of novels and a collection of fairy tales using an emotion lexicon to show that fairy tales have a much wider distribution of emotion word densities than novels.

The emotion analyzer recognizes words with positive polarity (expressing a favorable sentiment towards an entity), negative polarity (expressing an unfavorable sentiment towards an entity), and no polarity (neutral). It also associates words with joy, sadness, anger, fear, trust, disgust, surprise, anticipation, which are argued to be the eight basic and prototypical emotions (Plutchik, 1980).

This work is part of a broader project to provide an affect-based interface to Project Gutenberg. Given a search query, the goal is to provide users with relevant plots presented in this paper, as well as ability to search for text snippets from multiple texts that have high emotion word densities.

2 Related work

Over the last decade, there has been considerable work in sentiment analysis, especially in determining whether a term has a positive or negative polarity (Lehrer, 1974; Turney and Littman, 2003; Mohammad et al., 2009). There is also work in more sophisticated aspects of sentiment, for example, in detecting emotions such as anger, joy, sadness, fear, surprise, and disgust (Bellegarda, 2010; Mohammad and Turney, 2010; Alm et al., 2005; Alm et al., 2005). The technology is still developing and it can be unpredictable when dealing with short sentences, but it has been shown to be reliable when drawing conclusions from large amounts of text (Dodds and Danforth, 2010; Pang and Lee, 2008).

Automatic analysis of emotions in text has so far had to rely on small emotion lexicons. The WordNet Affect Lexicon (WAL) (Strapparava and Valitutti, 2004) has a few hundred words annotated with associations to a number of affect categories including the six Ekman emotions (joy, sadness, anger, fear, disgust, and surprise).[3] General Inquirer (GI) (Stone et al., 1966) has 11,788 words labeled with 182 categories of word tags, including positive and negative polarity.[4] We use the NRC Emotion Lexicon (Mohammad and Yang, 2011; Mohammad and Turney, 2010), a large set of human-provided word–emotion association ratings, in our experiments.[5]

Empirical assessment of emotions in literary texts has sometimes relied on human annotation of the texts, but this has restricted the number of texts analyzed. For example, Alm and Sproat (2005) annotated 22 Brothers Grimm fairy tales to show that fairy tales often began with a neutral sentence and ended with a happy sentence. Here we use out-of-context word–emotion associations and analyze individual texts to very large collections. We rely on information from many words to provide a strong enough signal to overcome individual errors due to out-of-context annotations.

3 Emotion Analysis

3.1 Emotion Lexicon

The NRC Emotion Lexicon was created by crowdsourcing to Amazon's Mechanical Turk, and it is described in (Mohammad and Yang, 2011; Mohammad and Turney, 2010); we briefly summarize below.

The 1911 *Roget Thesaurus* was used as the source for target terms.[6] Only those thesaurus words that occurred more than 120,000 times in the Google n-gram corpus were annotated for version 0.92 of the lexicon which we use for the experiments described in this paper.[7]

The *Roget's Thesaurus* groups related words into about a thousand categories, which can be thought of

[3]WAL: http://wndomains.fbk.eu/wnaffect.html

[4]GI: http://www.wjh.harvard.edu/~inquirer

[5]Please send an e-mail to saif.mohammad@nrc-cnrc.gc.ca to obtain the latest version of the NRC Emotion Lexicon.

[6]Roget's Thesaurus: www.gutenberg.org/ebooks/10681

[7]The Google N-gram Corpus is available through the Linguistic Data Consortium.

as coarse senses or concepts (Yarowsky, 1992). If a word is ambiguous, then it is listed in more than one category. Since a word may have different emotion associations when used in different senses, word-sense level annotations were obtained by first asking an automatically generated word-choice question pertaining to the target:

Q1. Which word is closest in meaning to *shark* (target)?

- *car*
- *tree*
- *fish*
- *olive*

The near-synonym for Q1 is taken from the thesaurus, and the distractors are randomly chosen words. This question guides the annotator to the desired sense of the target word. It is followed by ten questions asking if the target is associated with positive sentiment, negative sentiment, anger, fear, joy, sadness, disgust, surprise, trust, and anticipation. The questions were phrased exactly as described in Mohammad and Turney (2010).

If an annotator answers Q1 incorrectly, then information obtained from the remaining questions is discarded. Thus, even though there were no gold standard correct answers to the emotion association questions, likely incorrect annotations were filtered out. About 10% of the annotations were discarded because of an incorrect response to Q1.

Each term was annotated by 5 different people. For 74.4% of the instances, all five annotators agreed on whether a term is associated with a particular emotion or not. For 16.9% of the instances four out of five people agreed with each other. The information from multiple annotators for a particular term was combined by taking the majority vote. The lexicon has entries for about 24,200 word–sense pairs. The information from different senses of a word was combined by taking the union of all emotions associated with the different senses of the word. This resulted in a word-level emotion association lexicon for about 14,200 word types.

3.2 Text Analysis

Given a target text, the system determines which of the words exist in our emotion lexicon and calculates ratios such as the number of words associated with an emotion to the total number of emotion words in the text. This simple approach may not be reliable in determining if a particular sentence is expressing a certain emotion, but it is reliable in determining if a large piece of text has more emotional expressions

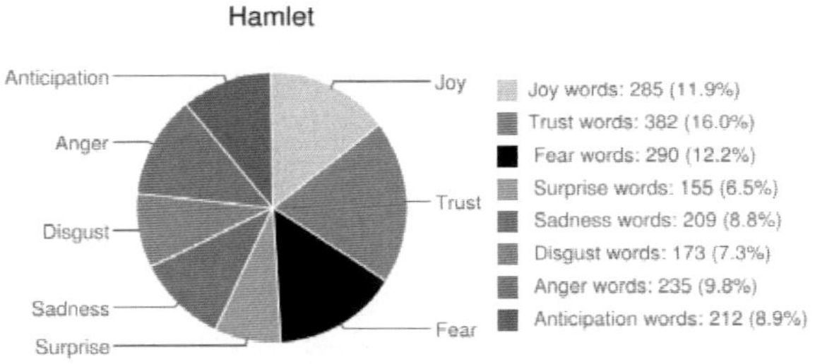

Figure 1: **Emotions pie chart** of Shakespeare's tragedy *Hamlet*. (Text from Project Gutenberg.)

Figure 2: **Emotions pie chart** of Shakespeare's comedy *As you like it*. (Text from Project Gutenberg.)

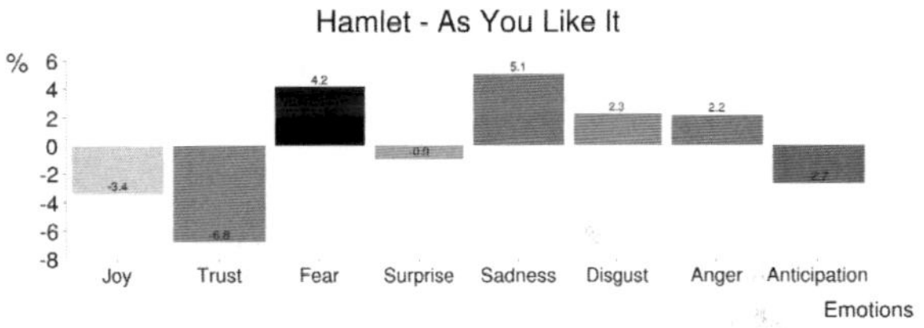

Figure 3: Difference in percentage scores for each of the eight basic emotions in *Hamlet* and *As you like it*.

compared to others in a corpus. Example applications include clustering literary texts based on the distributions of emotion words, analyzing gender-differences in email (Mohammad and Yang, 2011), and detecting spikes in anger words in close proximity to mentions of a target product in a twitter stream (Díaz and Ruz, 2002; Dubé and Maute, 1996).

4 Visualizations of Emotions

4.1 Distributions of Emotion Words

Figures 1 and 2 show the percentages of emotion words in Shakespeare's famous tragedy, *Hamlet*, and his comedy, *As you like it*, respectively. Figure 3 conveys the difference between the two novels even more explicitly by showing only the difference in percentage scores for each of the emotions. Emo-

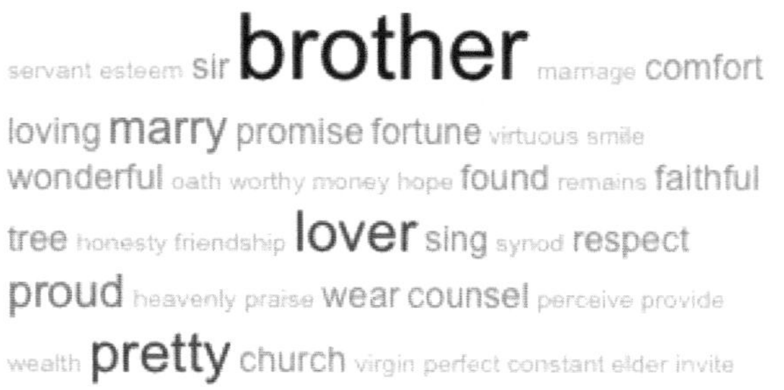

Figure 4: *Hamlet - As You Like It*: relative-salience word cloud for trust words.

Figure 5: *Hamlet - As You Like It*: relative-salience word cloud for sadness words.

tions are represented by colours as per a study on word–colour associations (Mohammad, 2011).

Observe how one can clearly see that *Hamlet* has more fear, sadness, disgust, and anger, and less joy, trust, and anticipation. The bar graph is effective at conveying the extent to which an emotion is more prominent in one text than another, but it does not convey the source of these emotions. Therefore, we calculate the *relative salience* of an emotion word w across two target texts T_1 and T_2:

$$\text{RelativeSalience}(w|T_1, T_2) = \frac{f_1}{N_1} - \frac{f_2}{N_2} \qquad (1)$$

Where, f_1 and f_2 are the frequencies of w in T_1 and T_2, respectively. N_1 and N_2 are the total number of word tokens in T_1 and T_2. Figures 4 and 5 depict snippets of relative-salience word clouds of trust words and sadness words across *Hamlet* and *As You Like it*. Our emotion analyzer uses Google's freely available software to create word clouds.[8]

[8]Google word cloud: http://visapi-gadgets.googlecode.com/svn/trunk/wordcloud/doc.html

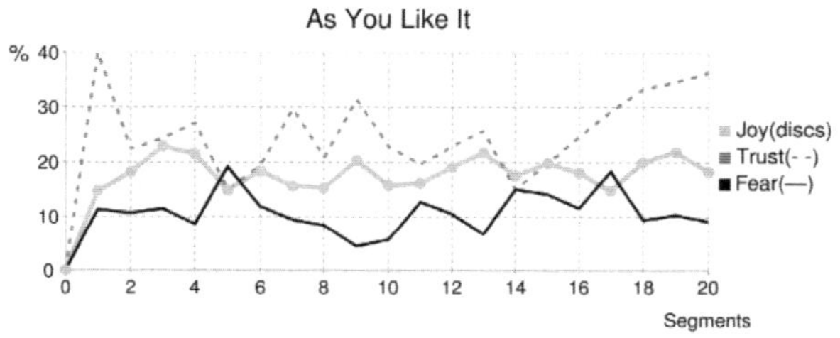

Figure 6: Timeline of the emotions in *As You Like It*.

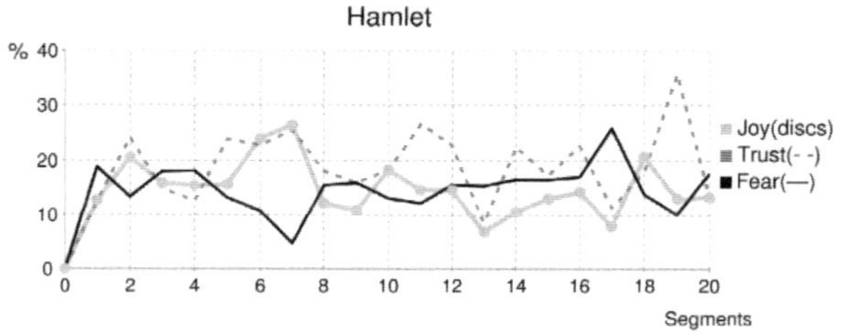

Figure 7: Timeline of the emotions in *Hamlet*.

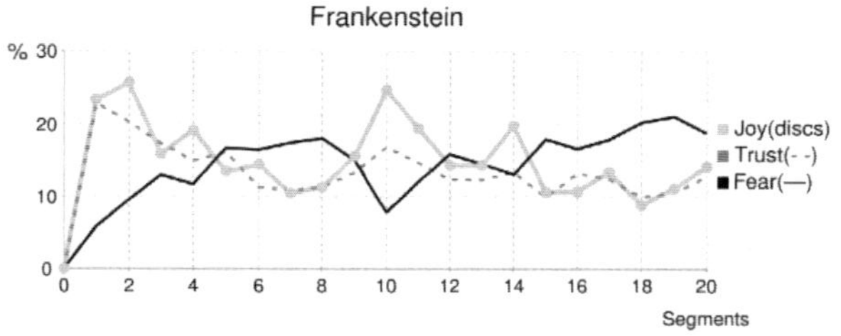

Figure 8: Timeline of the emotions in *Frankenstein*.

4.2 Flow of Emotions

Literary researchers as well as casual readers may be interested in noting how the use of emotion words has varied through the course of a book. Figure 6, 7, and 8 show the flow of joy, trust, and fear in *As You Like it* (comedy), *Hamlet* (tragedy), and *Frankenstein* (horror), respectively. As expected, the visualizations depict the novels to be progressively more dark than the previous ones in the list. Also that *Frankenstein* is much darker in the final chapters.

5 Emotion Word Density

Apart from determining the relative percentage of different words, the use of emotion words in a book can also be quantified by calculating the number of emotion words one is expected to see on reading every X words. We will refer to this metric as *emotion word density*. All emotion densities reported in this paper are for $X = 10,000$. The dotted line in Figure 9 shows the negative word density plot of 192 fairy tales collected by Brothers Grimm. The joy

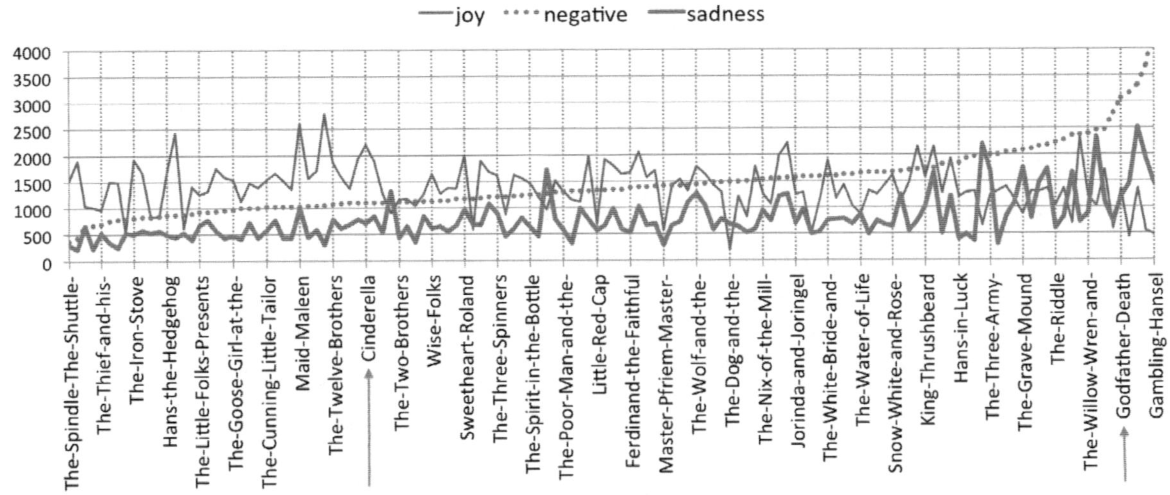

Figure 9: The Brothers Grimm fairy tales arranged in increasing order of negative word density (number of negative words in every 10,000 words). The plot is of 192 stories but the x-axis has labels for only a few due to lack of space. A user may select any two tales, say *Cinderella* and *Godfather Death* (follow arrows), to reveal Figure 10.

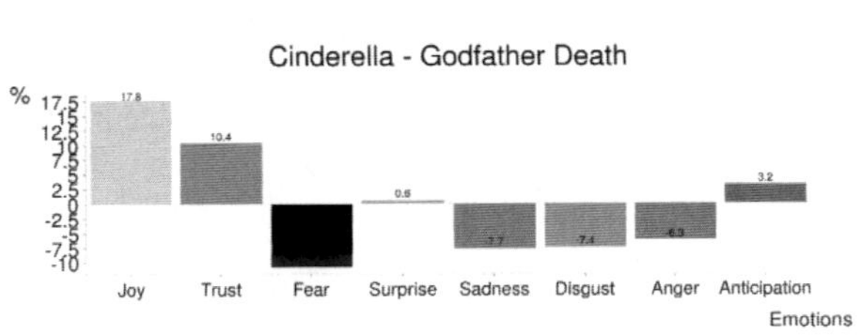

Figure 10: The difference in percentages of emotion words across *Cinderella* and *Godfather Death*.

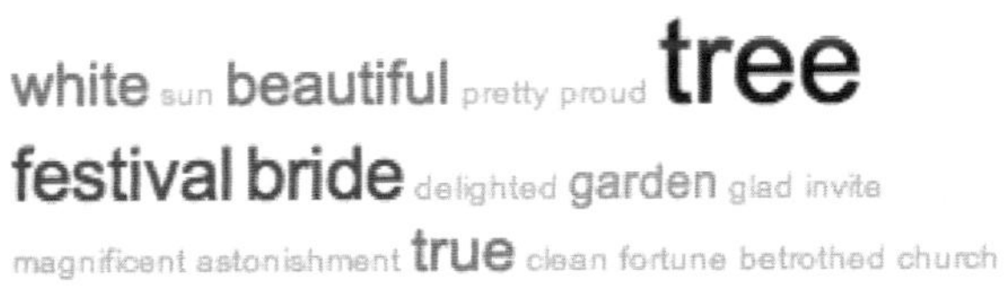

Figure 11: *Cinderella - Godfather Death*: Relative salience word cloud of joy.

and sadness word densities are also shown—the thin and thick lines, respectively. A person interested in understanding the use of emotion words in the fairy tales collected by Brothers Grimm can further select any two fairy tales from the plot, to reveal a bar graph showing the difference in percentages of emotions in the two texts. Figure 10 shows the difference bar graph of *Cinderella* and *Godfather Death*. Figures 11 depicts the relative-salience word cloud of joy words across the two fairy tales. The relative-salience word cloud of fear included: *death, ill, beware, poverty, devil, astray, risk, illness, threatening, horrified* and *revenge*.

6 Emotions Associated with Targets

Words found in proximity of target entities can be good indicators of emotions associated with the targets. Google has released n-gram frequency data from all the books they have scanned up to July 15, 2009.[9] The data consists of 5-grams along with the number of times they were used in books published in every year from 1600 to 2009. We analyzed the 5-gram files (about 800GB of data) to quantify the emotions associated with different target entities. We ignored data from books published before 1800 as that period is less comprehensively covered by Google books. We chose to group the data into five-year bins, though other groupings are reasonable as well. Given a target entity of interest, the system identifies all 5-grams that contain the target word, identifies all the emotion words in those n-grams (other than the target word itself), and calculates percentages of emotion words.

Figure 12 shows the percentage of fear words in the n-grams of different countries. Observe, that there is a marked rise of fear words around World War I (1914–1918) for Germany, America, and China. There is a spike for China around 1900, likely due to the unrest leading up to the Boxer Rebellion (1898–1901).[10] The 1810–1814 spike for

[9]Google books data: http://ngrams.googlelabs.com/datasets.
[10]http://en.wikipedia.org/wiki/Boxer_Rebellion

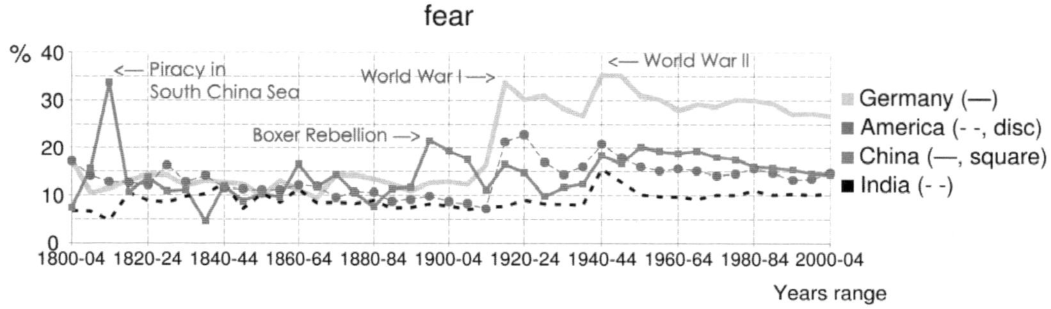

Figure 12: Percentage of **fear** words in close proximity to occurrences of *America, China, Germany,* and *India* in books from the year 1800 to 2004. Source: 5-gram data released by Google.

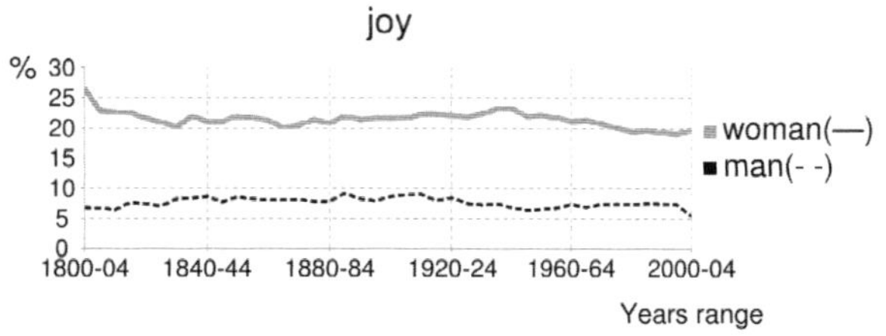

Figure 13: Percentage of **joy** words in close proximity to occurrences of *man* and *woman* in books.

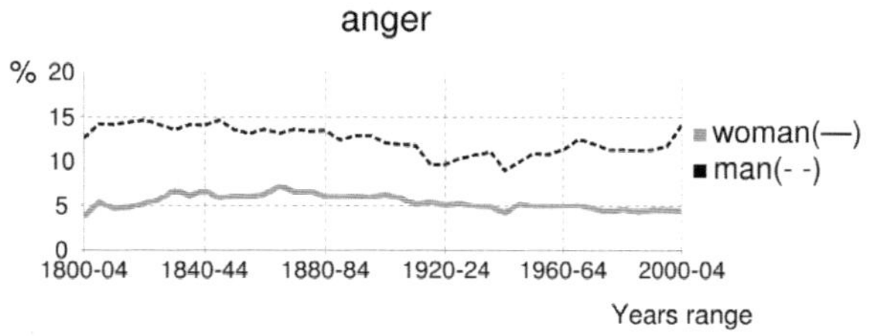

Figure 14: Percentage of **anger** words in close proximity to occurrences of *man* and *woman* in books.

China is probably correlated with descriptions of piracy in the South China Seas, since the era of the commoner-pirates of mid-Qing dynasty came to an end in 1810.[11] India does not see a spike during World War I, but has a spike in the 1940's probably reflecting heightened vigor in the independence struggle (Quit India Movement of 1942[12]) and growing involvement in World War II (1939–1945).[13]

Figures 13 shows two curves for the percentages of joy words in 5-grams that include *woman* and *man*, respectively. Figures 14 shows similar curves for anger words.

[11]http://www.iias.nl/nl/36/IIAS_NL36_07.pdf

[12]http://en.wikipedia.org/wiki/Quit_India_Movement

[13]http://en.wikipedia.org/wiki/India_in_World_War_II

7 Emotion Words in Novels vs. Fairy Tales

Novels and fairy tales are two popular forms of literary prose. Both forms tell a story, but a fairy tale has certain distinct characteristics such as (a) archetypal characters (peasant, king) (b) clear identification of good and bad characters, (c) happy ending, (d) presence of magic and magical creatures, and (d) a clear moral (Jones, 2002). Fairy tales are extremely popular and appeal to audiences through emotions—they convey personal concerns, subliminal fears, wishes, and fantasies in an exaggerated manner (Kast, 1993; Jones, 2002; Orenstein, 2003). However, there have not been any large-scale empirical studies to compare affect in fairy tales and novels. Here for the first time, we compare the use of emotion-associated words in fairy tales and novels using a large lexicon.

Specifically, we are interested in determining whether: (1) fairy tales on average have a higher emotional density than novels, (2) different fairy tales focus on different emotions such that some fairy tales have high densities for certain emotion, whereas others have low emotional densities for those same emotions.

We used the Corpus of English Novels (CEN) and the Fairy Tale Corpus (FTC) for our experiments.[14] The Corpus of English Novels is a collection of 292 novels written between 1881 and 1922 by 25 British and American novelists. It was compiled from Project Gutenberg at the Catholic University of Leuven by Hendrik de Smet. It consists of about 26 million words. The Fairy Tale Corpus (Lobo and Martins de Matos, 2010) has 453 stories, close to 1 million words, downloaded from Project Guten-

[14]CEN: https://perswww.kuleuven.be/~u0044428/cen.htm
FTC: https://www.l2f.inesc-id.pt/wiki/index.php/Fairy_tale_corpus

	anger		anticip.		disgust		fear		joy		sadness		surprise		trust	
	mean	σ	mean	σ	mean	σ	mean	σ	mean	σ	mean	σ	mean	σ	mean	σ
CEN	746	162	1230	126	591	135	975	225	1164	196	785	159	628	93	1473	190
FTC	749	393	1394	460	682	460	910	454	1417	467	814	443	680	325	1348	491

Table 1: Density of emotion words in novels and fairy tales: number of emotion words in every 10,000 words.

berg. Even though many fairy tales have a strong oral tradition, the stories in this collection were compiled, translated, or penned in the 19th century by the Brothers Grimm, Beatrix Potter, and Hans C. Andersen to name a few.

We calculated the polarity and emotion word density of each of the novels in CEN and each of the fairy tales in FTC. Table 1 lists the mean densities as well as standard deviation for each of the eight basic emotions in the two corpora. We find that the mean densities for anger and sadness across CEN and FTC are not significantly different. However, fairy tales have significantly higher anticipation, disgust, joy, and surprise densities when compared to novels ($p < 0.001$). On the other hand, they have significantly lower trust word density than novels. Further, the standard deviations for all eight emotions are significantly different across the two corpora ($p < 0.001$). The fairy tales, in general, have a much larger standard deviation than the novels. Thus for each of the 8 emotions, there are more fairy tales than novels having high emotion densities and there are more fairy tales than novels having low emotion densities.

Table 2 lists the mean densities as well as standard deviation for negative and positive polarity words in the two corpora. The table states, for example, that for every 10,000 words in the CEN, one can expect to see about 1670 negative words. We find that fairy tales, on average, have a significantly lower number of negative terms, and a significantly higher number of positive words ($p < 0.001$).

In order to obtain a better sense of the distribution of emotion densities, we generated histograms by counting all texts that had emotion densities between 0–99, 100–199, 200–399, and so on. A large standard deviation for fairy tales could be due to one of at least two reasons: (1) the histogram has a bimodal distribution—most of the fairy tales have extreme emotion densities (either much higher than that of the novels, or much smaller). (2) the histogram approaches a normal distribution such that more fairy tales than novels have extreme emotion densities. Figures 15 through 20 show histograms comparing novels and fairy tales for positive and negative polarities, as well as for a few emotions. Observe that fairy tales do not have a bimodal distribution, and case (2) holds true.

	negative		positive	
	mean	σ	mean	σ
CEN	1670	243	2602	278
FTC	1543	613	2808	726

Table 2: Density of polarity words in novels and fairy tales: number of polar words in every 10,000 words.

8 Conclusions and Future Work

We presented an emotion analyzer that relies on the powerful word–emotion association lexicon. We presented a number of visualizations that help track and analyze the use of emotion words in individual texts and across very large collections. We introduced the concept of emotion word density, and using the Brothers Grimm fairy tales as an example, we showed how collections of text can be organized for better search. Using the Google Books Corpus we showed how to determine emotion associations portrayed in books towards different entities. Finally, for the first time, we compared a collection of novels and a collection of fairy tales using the emotion lexicon to show that fairy tales have a much wider distribution of emotion word densities than novels.

This work is part of a broader project to provide an affect-based interface to Project Gutenberg. Given a search query, the goal is to provide users with relevant plots presented in this paper. Further, they will be able to search for snippets from multiple texts that have strong emotion word densities.

Acknowledgments

Grateful thanks to Peter Turney and Tara Small for many wonderful ideas. Thanks to Tony (Wenda) Yang for creating an online emotion analyzer.

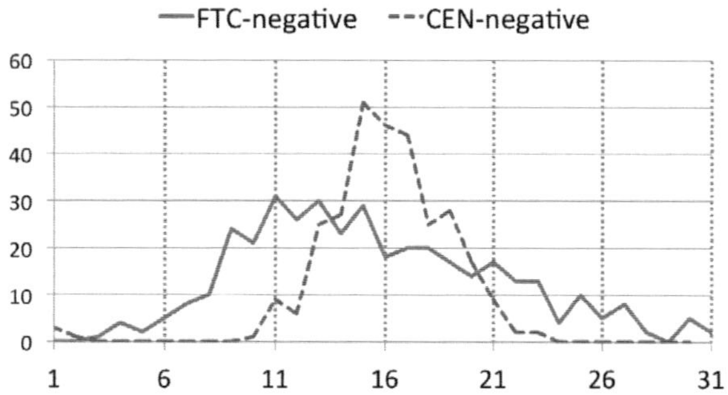

Figure 15: Histogram of texts with different negative word densities. On the x-axis: 1 refers to density between 0 and 100, 2 refers to 100 to 200, and so on.

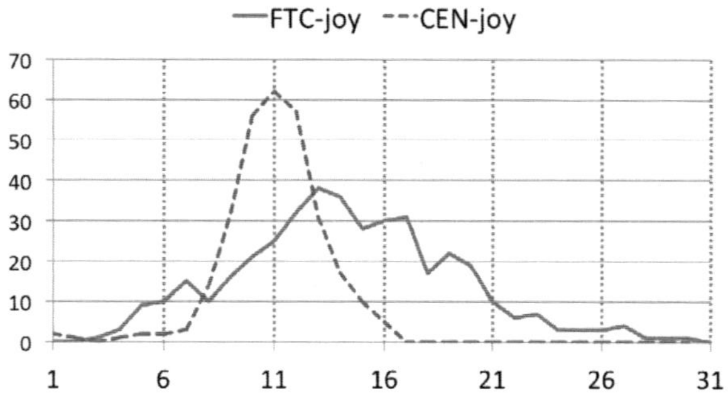

Figure 16: Histogram of texts with different joy word densities.

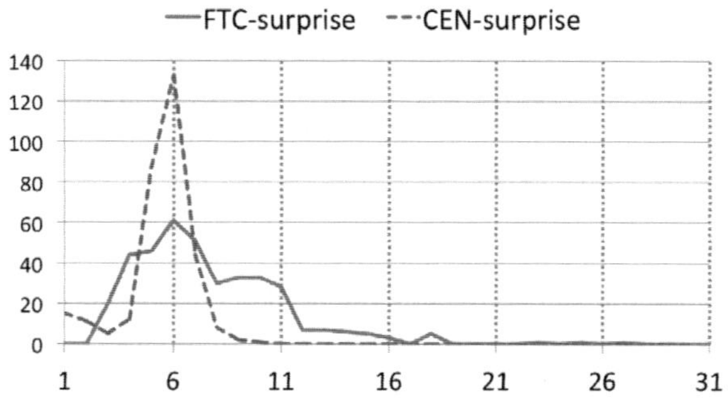

Figure 17: Histogram of texts with different surprise word densities.

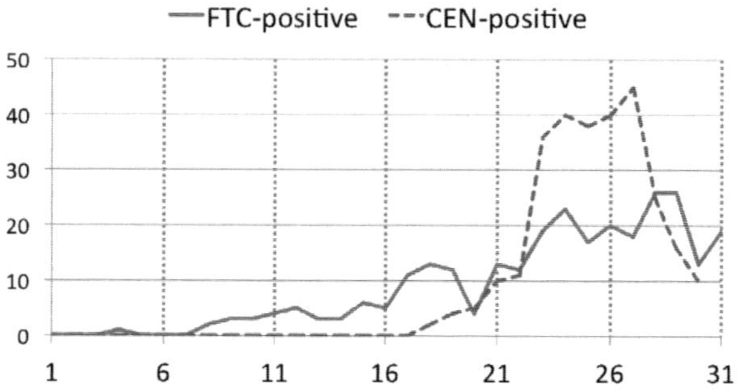

Figure 18: Histogram of texts with different positive word densities. On the x-axis: 1 refers to density between 0 and 100, 2 refers to 100 to 200, and so on.

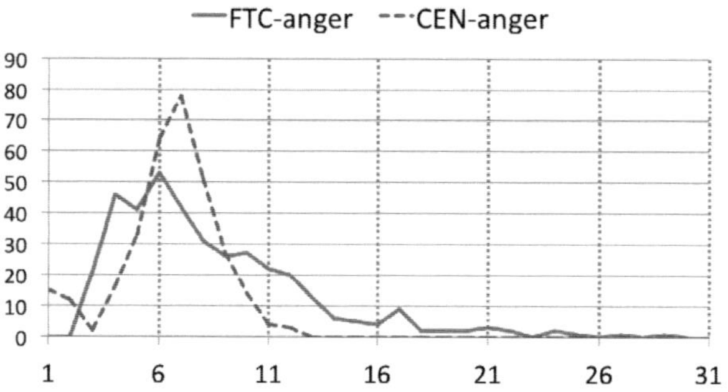

Figure 19: Histogram of texts with different anger word densities.

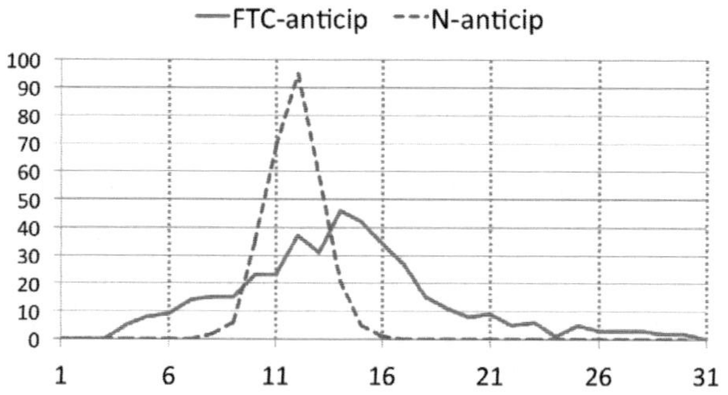

Figure 20: Histogram of texts with different anticip word densities.

References

Cecilia O. Alm and Richard Sproat, 2005. *Emotional sequencing and development in fairy tales*, pages 668–674. Springer.

Cecilia Ovesdotter Alm, Dan Roth, and Richard Sproat. 2005. Emotions from text: Machine learning for text-based emotion prediction. In *Proceedings of the Joint Conference on HLT–EMNLP*, Vancouver, Canada.

Richard Bales. 1997. *Persuasion in the French personal novel: Studies of Chateaubriand, Constant, Balzac, Nerval, and Fromentin*. Summa Publications, Birmingham, Alabama.

Jerome Bellegarda. 2010. Emotion analysis using latent affective folding and embedding. In *Proceedings of the NAACL-HLT 2010 Workshop on Computational Approaches to Analysis and Generation of Emotion in Text*, Los Angeles, California.

Ana B. Casado Díaz and Francisco J. Más Ruz. 2002. The consumers reaction to delays in service. *International Journal of Service Industry Management*, 13(2):118–140.

Peter Dodds and Christopher Danforth. 2010. Measuring the happiness of large-scale written expression: Songs, blogs, and presidents. *Journal of Happiness Studies*, 11:441–456. 10.1007/s10902-009-9150-9.

Laurette Dubé and Manfred F. Maute. 1996. The antecedents of brand switching, brand loyalty and verbal responses to service failure. *Advances in Services Marketing and Management*, 5:127–151.

Steven Swann Jones. 2002. *The Fairy Tale: The Magic Mirror of the Imagination*. Routledge.

Verena Kast. 1993. *Through Emotions to Maturity: Psychological Readings of Fairy Tales*. Fromm Intl.

Marie Lebert. 2009. *Project Gutenberg (1971–2009)*. Benediction Classics.

Adrienne Lehrer. 1974. *Semantic fields and lexical structure*. North-Holland, American Elsevier, Amsterdam, NY.

Paula Vaz Lobo and David Martins de Matos. 2010. Fairy tale corpus organization using latent semantic mapping and an item-to-item top-n recommendation algorithm. In *Language Resources and Evaluation Conference - LREC 2010, European Language Resources Association (ELRA)*, Malta.

Patrick Mannix. 1992. *The rhetoric of antinuclear fiction: Persuasive strategies in novels and films*. Bucknell University Press, Associated University Presses, London.

Jean-Baptiste Michel, Yuan K. Shen, Aviva P. Aiden, Adrian Veres, Matthew K. Gray, The Google Books Team, Joseph P. Pickett, Dale Hoiberg, Dan Clancy, Peter Norvig, Jon Orwant, Steven Pinker, Martin A. Nowak, and Erez L. Aiden. 2011a. Quantitative Analysis of Culture Using Millions of Digitized Books. *Science*, 331(6014):176–182.

Jean-Baptiste Michel, Yuan Kui Shen, Aviva Presser Aiden, Adrian Veres, Matthew K. Gray, The Google Books Team, Joseph P. Pickett, Dale Hoiberg, Dan Clancy, Peter Norvig, Jon Orwant, Steven Pinker, Martin A. Nowak, and Erez Lieberman Aiden. 2011b. Quantitative analysis of culture using millions of digitized books. *Science*, 331(6014):176–182.

Saif M. Mohammad and Peter D. Turney. 2010. Emotions evoked by common words and phrases: Using mechanical turk to create an emotion lexicon. In *Proceedings of the NAACL-HLT 2010 Workshop on Computational Approaches to Analysis and Generation of Emotion in Text*, LA, California.

Saif M. Mohammad and Tony (Wenda) Yang. 2011. Tracking sentiment in mail:
how genders differ on emotional axes. In *Proceedings of the ACL 2011 Workshop on Computational Approaches to Subjectivity and Sentiment Analysis (WASSA)*, Portland, OR, USA.

Saif M. Mohammad, Cody Dunne, and Bonnie Dorr. 2009. Generating high-coverage semantic orientation lexicons from overtly marked words and a thesaurus. In *Proceedings of Empirical Methods in Natural Language Processing (EMNLP-2009)*, pages 599–608, Singapore.

Saif M. Mohammad. 2011. Even the abstract have colour: Consensus in wordcolour associations. In *Proceedings of the 49th Annual Meeting of the Association for Computational Linguistics: Human Language Technologies*, Portland, OR, USA.

Catherine Orenstein. 2003. *Little Red Riding Hood Uncloaked: Sex, Morality, And The Evolution Of A Fairy Tale*. Basic Books.

Bo Pang and Lillian Lee. 2008. Opinion mining and sentiment analysis. *Foundations and Trends in Information Retrieval*, 2(1–2):1–135.

Robert Plutchik. 1980. A general psychoevolutionary theory of emotion. *Emotion: Theory, research, and experience*, 1(3):3–33.

Philip Stone, Dexter C. Dunphy, Marshall S. Smith, Daniel M. Ogilvie, and associates. 1966. *The General Inquirer: A Computer Approach to Content Analysis*. The MIT Press.

Carlo Strapparava and Alessandro Valitutti. 2004. Wordnet-Affect: An affective extension of WordNet. In *Proceedings of the 4th International Conference on Language Resources and Evaluation (LREC-2004)*, pages 1083–1086, Lisbon, Portugal.

Peter Turney and Michael Littman. 2003. Measuring praise and criticism: Inference of semantic orientation from association. *ACM Transactions on Information Systems (TOIS)*, 21(4):315–346.

David Yarowsky. 1992. Word-sense disambiguation using statistical models of Roget's categories trained on large corpora. In *Proceedings of the 14th International Conference on Computational Linguistics (COLING-92)*, pages 454–460, Nantes, France.

Author Age Prediction from Text using Linear Regression

Dong Nguyen **Noah A. Smith** **Carolyn P. Rosé**
Language Technologies Institute
Carnegie Mellon University
Pittsburgh, PA 15213, USA
{dongn,nasmith,cprose}@cs.cmu.edu

Abstract

While the study of the connection between discourse patterns and personal identification is decades old, the study of these patterns using language technologies is relatively recent. In that more recent tradition we frame author age prediction from text as a regression problem. We explore the same task using three very different genres of data simultaneously: blogs, telephone conversations, and online forum posts. We employ a technique from domain adaptation that allows us to train a joint model involving all three corpora together as well as separately and analyze differences in predictive features across joint and corpus-specific aspects of the model. Effective features include both stylistic ones (such as POS patterns) as well as content oriented ones. Using a linear regression model based on shallow text features, we obtain correlations up to 0.74 and mean absolute errors between 4.1 and 6.8 years.

1 Introduction

A major thrust of research in sociolinguistics is to understand the connection between the way people use language and their community membership, where community membership can be construed along a variety of dimensions, including age, gender, socioeconomic status and political affiliation. A person is a member of a multiplicity of communities, and thus the person's identity and language are influenced by many factors.

In this paper we focus on the relationship between age and language use. Recently, machine learning methods have been applied to determine the age of persons based on the language that they utter. Studies of the stylistic and content-based features that predict age or other personal characteristics yield new insights into the connection between discourse and identity. However, that connection is known to be highly contextual, such as whether the data were collected synchronously or asynchronously, through typed or spoken interaction, or whether participants can see one another or not. Recent work in the area of domain adaptation raises awareness about the effect of contextual factors on the generality of text prediction models.

Our first contribution to this literature is an investigation of age prediction using a multi-corpus approach. We present results and analysis across three very different corpora: a blog corpus (Schler et al., 2006), a transcribed telephone speech corpus (Cieri et al., 2004) and posts from an online forum on breast cancer. By using the domain adaptation approach of Daumé III (2007), we train a model on all these corpora together and separate the global features from corpus-specific features that are associated with age.

A second contribution is the investigation of age prediction with age modeled as a continuous variable rather than as a categorical variable. Most prior research on age prediction has framed this as a two-class or three-class classification problem (e.g., Schler et al., 2006 and Garera and Yarowsky, 2009). In our work, modeling age as a continuous variable is interesting not only as a more realistic representation of age, but also for practical benefits of joint modeling of age across corpora since the boundaries for discretizing age into a categorical variable in prior work have been chosen heuristically and in a corpus-dependent way, making it hard to compare performance across different kinds of data.

In the remainder of the paper, we first discuss related work and present and compare the different datasets. We then outline our approach and results. We conclude with discussion and future work.

2 Related work

Time is an important factor in sociolinguistic analysis of language variation. While a thorough review of this work is beyond the scope of this paper, Eckert (1996) gives an overview of the literature on age as a sociolinguistic variable. Linguistic variation can occur as an individual moves through life, or as a result of changes in the community itself as it moves through time. As an added complexity, Argamon et al. (2007) found connections between language variation and age and gender. Features that were used with increasing age were also used more by males for any age. Features that were used with decreasing age were used more by females. In other work, the same features that distinguish male and female writing also distinguish non-fiction and fiction (Argamon et al., 2003). Thus, the separate effects of age, time period, gender, topic, and genre may be difficult to tease apart in naturalistic data where many of these variables are unknown.

Recently, machine learning approaches have been explored to estimate the age of an author or speaker using text uttered or written by the person. This has been modeled as a classification problem, in a similar spirit to sociolinguistic work where age has been investigated in terms of differences in distributions of characteristics between cohorts. In the sociolinguistic literature, cohorts such as these are determined either *etically* (arbitrary, but equal age spans such as decades) or *emically* (related to life stage, such as adolescence etc.). In machine learning research, these cohorts have typically been determined for practical reasons relating to distribution of age groups within a corpus, although the boundaries sometimes have also made sense from a life stage perspective. For example, researchers have modeled age as a two-class classification problem with boundaries at age 40 (Garera and Yarowsky, 2009) or 30 (Rao et al., 2010). Another line of work has looked at modeling age estimation as a three-class classification problem (Schler et al., 2006; Goswami et al., 2009), with age groups of 13-17, 23-27 and 33-42. In addition to machine learning experiments, other researchers have published statistical analyses of differences in distribution related to age and language and have found similar patterns.

As an example of one of these studies, Pennebaker and Stone (2003) analyzed the relationship between language use and aging by collecting data from a large number of previous studies. They used LIWC (Pennebaker et al., 2001) for analysis. They found that with increasing age, people tend to use more positive and fewer negative affect words, more future-tense and less past-tense, and fewer self-references. Furthermore, a general pattern of increasing cognitive complexity was seen. Barbieri (2008) uses key word analysis to analyze language and age. Two groups (15–25 and 35–60) were compared. Analysis showed that younger speakers' talk is characterized by slang and swear words, indicators of speaker stance and emotional involvement, while older people tend to use more modals.

Age classification experiments have been conducted on a wide range of types of data, including blogs (Schler et al., 2006; Goswami et al., 2009), telephone conversations (Garera and Yarowsky, 2009), and recently Twitter (Rao et al., 2010). Effective features were both content features (such as unigrams, bigrams and word classes) as well as stylistic features (such as part-of-speech, slang words and average sentence length). These separate published studies present some commonalities of findings. However, based on these results from experiments conducted on very different datasets, it is not possible to determine how generalizable the models are. Thus, there is a need for an investigation of generalizability specifically in the modeling of linguistic variation related to age, which we present in this paper.

Age classification from speech data has been of interest for many years. Recently, age regression using speech features has been explored (Spiegl et al., 2009). Spiegel's system obtained a mean absolute error of approximately 10 years using support vector regression. Van Heerden et al. (2010) explore combining regression estimates to improve age classification. As far as we are aware, we are the first to publish results from a regression model that directly predicts age using textual features.

3 Data description

We explore three datasets with different characteristics. The data was divided into a training, development and test set. Statistics are listed in Table 1.

3.1 Blog corpus

In August 2004 Schler et al. (2006) crawled blogs from `blogger.com`. Information such as gender and age were provided by the users in their respective profiles. Users were divided into three age groups, and each group had an equal number of female and male bloggers. In our experiments, every document consists of all posts from a particular blogger.

3.2 Fisher telephone corpus

The Fisher corpus (Cieri et al., 2004) contains transcripts of telephone conversations. People were randomly assigned to pairs, and for (almost) every person, characteristics such as gender and age were recorded. Furthermore, for each conversation a topic was assigned. The data was collected beginning December 2002 and continued for nearly one year. In our experiments, we aggregate the data for each person.

3.3 Breast cancer forum

We drew data from one of the most active online forums for persons with breast cancer.[1] All posts and user profiles of the forum were crawled in January 2011. Only a small proportion of users had indicated their age in their profile. We manually annotated the age of approximately 200 additional users with less common ages by looking manually at their posts. An author's age can often be annotated because users tend to make references to their age when they introduce themselves or when telling their treatment history (e.g., *I was diagnosed 2 years ago when I was just 38*). Combining this with the date of the specific post, a birth year can be estimated. Because a person's data can span multiple years, we aggregate all the data per year for each person. Each person was assigned randomly to one of the data splits, to make sure all documents representing the same person appeared in only one split. The dataset contains posts from October 2002 until January 2011.

[1] `http://community.breastcancer.org`

Figure 1: Comparison of age frequency in datasets.

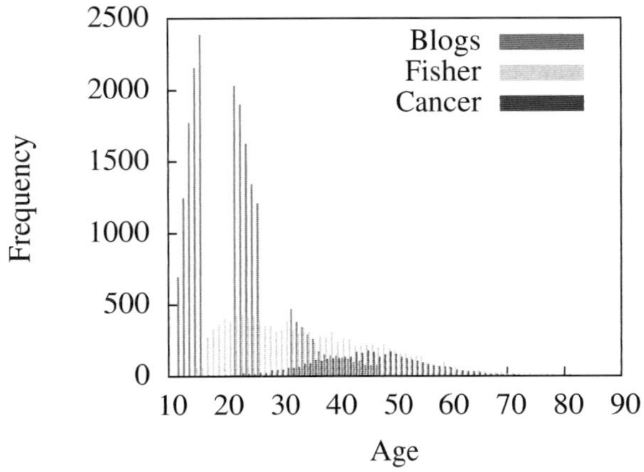

3.4 Dataset comparison and statistics

The datasets differ in several respects: specificity (general topics versus breast cancer), modality of interaction (telephone conversations versus online forum versus blog post), age distribution, and amount of data per person. The blog and Fisher dataset contain approximately equal amounts of males and females, while the breast cancer dataset is heavily biased towards women.

A comparison of the age distributions of the three corpora is given in Figure 1. The Fisher dataset has the most uniform distribution across the ages, while the blog data has a lot of young persons and the breast cancer forum has a lot of older people. The youngest person in our dataset is 13 years old and the oldest is 88. Note that our blog corpus contains gaps between different age categories, which is an artifact of the experimental approach used by the people who released this dataset (Schler et al., 2006).

Because all datasets were created between 2002 and 2011, we are less likely to observe results due to cohort effects (changes that occur because of collective changes in culture, such as use of the Internet).

Table 1: Datasets statistics.

	Blogs		Fisher		Cancer		
Data	**#docs**	**avg #tokens**	**#docs**	**avg #tokens**	**#docs**	**avg #tokens**	**#persons**
Training	9,660	13,042	5,957	3,409	2,330	22,719	1,269
Development	4,830	13,672	2,977	3,385	747	32,239	360
Test	4,830	13,206	2,980	3,376	797	26,952	368

4 Experimental setup

4.1 Linear regression

Given an input vector $\mathbf{x} \in \mathbb{R}^m$, where $x_1, \ldots, x_m$ represent features (also called independent variables or predictors), we find a prediction $\hat{y} \in \mathbb{R}$ for the age of a person $y \in \mathbb{R}$ using a linear regression model: $\hat{y} = \beta_0 + \mathbf{x}^\top \boldsymbol{\beta}$ where β_0 and $\boldsymbol{\beta}$ are the parameters to estimate. Usually, the parameters are learned by minimizing the sum of squared errors. In order to strive for a model with high explanatory value, we use a linear regression model with Lasso (also called L_1) regularization (Tibshirani, 1996). This minimizes the sum of squared errors, but in addition adds a penalty term $\lambda \sum_{j=1}^{m} |\beta_j|$. λ is a constant and can be found by optimizing over the development data. As a result, this method delivers sparse models. We use OWLQN to optimize the regularized empirical risk (Andrew and Gao, 2007; Gao et al., 2007). We evaluate the models by reporting the correlation and mean absolute error (MAE).

4.2 Joint model

To discover which features are important across datasets and which are corpus-specific, we train a model on the data of all corpora using the feature representation proposed by Daumé III (2007). Using this model, the original feature space is augmented by representing each individual feature as 4 new features: a global feature and three corpus-specific features, specifically one for each dataset. Thus for every feature f, we now have f_{global}, f_{blogs}, f_{fisher} and f_{cancer}. For every instance, only the global and the one specific corpus feature are set. For example for a particular feature value x_j for the blog dataset we would have $\langle x_j, x_j, 0, 0\rangle$. If it would appear in the cancer dataset we would have $\langle x_j, 0, 0, x_j\rangle$. Because the resulting model using L_1 regression only selects a small subset of the features, some features may only appear either as global features or as corpus-specific features in the final model.

4.3 Overview different models

Besides experimenting with the joint model, we are also interested in the performance using only the discovered global features. This can be achieved by applying the weights for the global features directly as learned by the joint model, or retraining the model on the individual datasets using only the global features. In summary, we have the following models:

- INDIV: Models trained on the three corpora individually.
- JOINT: Model trained on all three corpora with features represented as in Daumé III (2007).
- JOINT-Global: Using the learned JOINT model but only keeping the global features.
- JOINT-Global-Retrained: Using the discovered global features by the JOINT model, but *retrained* on each specific dataset.

4.4 Features

4.4.1 Textual features

We explore the following textual features; all features are frequency counts normalized by the length (number of tokens) of the document.

- *Unigrams.*
- *POS unigrams* and *bigrams*. Text is tagged using the Stanford POS tagger (Toutanova et al., 2003).
- *LIWC* (Pennebaker et al., 2001). This is a word counting program that captures word classes such as inclusion words (*LIWC-incl:* "with," "and," "include," etc.), causation words (*LIWC-cause:* "because," "hence," etc.), and stylistic characteristics such as percentage of words longer than 6 letters (*LIWC-Sixltr*).

Figure 2: Scatterplot of true and predicted age.

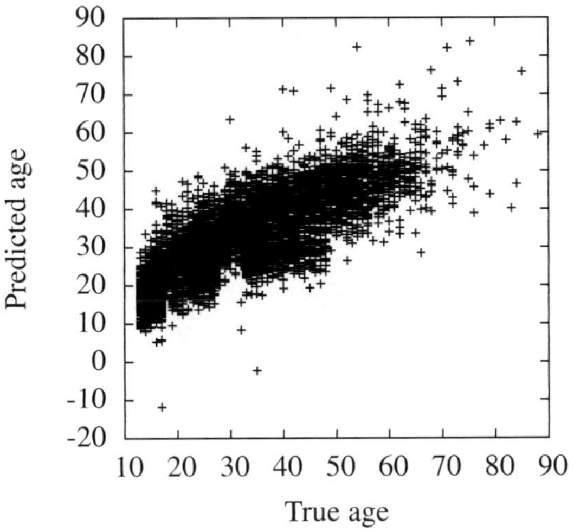

4.4.2 Gender

Because the gender of a person also influences how age is reflected in a person's text or speech (e.g. Argamon et al. (2007)), we add a binary feature for the gender of the person (Male = 1, Female = 0). This feature is only known for the blog and Fisher dataset. For the breast cancer dataset the gender is not known, but we assume they are all women.

5 Results and discussion

As discussed, we experiment with four different models. We explore three different feature sets: only unigrams, only POS, and the full feature set. The results are presented in Table 2. The most important features using the JOINT model with the full feature set (condition 10) are presented in Table 3.

5.1 Quantitative analysis

Overall, similar performance is obtained on the Fisher and blog datasets. The highest correlations were achieved on the Fisher dataset, with a best correlation of $r = 0.742$. This gives an r^2 value of 0.551, indicating that 55% of the variance can be explained by the model. However, a higher mean absolute error (MAE) was observed compared to the blog dataset. This may be caused by the larger spread in distribution of ages in the Fisher dataset. The lowest correlations were observed on the cancer dataset. This is probably caused by the small amount of training instances, the noisy text, and the fact that the ages lie very close to each other.

Overall, the joint model using all features performed best (condition 10). In Figure 2 a plot is presented that relates the true and predicted ages for this condition. We find that for the high ages there are more instances with high errors, probably caused by the small amount of training data for the extreme ages.

We find the correlation metric to be very sensitive to the amount of data. For example, when computing the correlation over the aggregated results of all corpora, we get a much higher correlation (0.830), but the MAE (5.345) is closer to that computed over the individual datasets. However, the MAE is dependent on the age distributions in the corpus, which can be observed by contrasting the MAE on the runs of the Fisher and cancer dataset. This thus suggests that these two measures are complementary and both are useful as evaluation metrics for this task.

For most experiments the joint models show improvement over the individual models. Returning to our question of generality, we can make several observations. First, performance decreases significantly when only using the global features (comparing JOINT and JOINT-Global-retrained), confirming that corpus-specific features are important. Second, learned weights of global features are reasonably generalizable. When using the full feature set, retraining the global features on the corpora directly only gives a slight improvement (e.g. compare conditions 11 and 12). Third, the bias term (β_0) is very corpus-specific and has a big influence on the MAE. For example, when comparing conditions 11 and 12, the correlations are very similar but the MAEs are much lower when the model is retrained. This is a result of adjusting the bias term to the specific dataset. For example the bias term of the model trained on only the blog dataset is 22.45, compared to the bias of 46.11 when trained on the cancer dataset.

In addition, we observe better performance in the cancer dataset when retraining the model using only the global features compared to the initial feature set. This suggests that using the global features might have been an effective method for feature selection to prevent overfitting on this small dataset.

Table 2: Results on the test set, reported with Pearson's correlation (r) and mean absolute error (MAE).

			Blogs		Fisher		Cancer	
ID	**Model**	**#Features**	***r***	**MAE**	***r***	**MAE**	***r***	**MAE**
			Unigrams					
1	INDIV	56,440	0.644	4.236	0.715	7.145	0.426	7.085
2	JOINT	56,440	0.694	4.232	0.723	7.066	0.530	**6.537**
3	JOINT-Global	656	0.605	5.800	0.628	10.370	0.461	16.632
4	JOINT-Global-retrained	656	0.658	4.409	0.675	7.529	0.498	6.797
			POS					
5	INDIV	4,656	0.519	5.095	0.553	8.635	0.150	7.699
6	JOINT	4,656	0.563	4.899	0.549	8.657	0.035	8.449
7	JOINT-Global	110	0.495	6.332	0.390	12.232	0.151	19.454
8	JOINT-Global-retrained	110	0.519	5.095	0.475	9.187	0.150	7.699
			All features					
9	INDIV	61,416	**0.699**	**4.144**	0.731	6.926	0.462	6.943
10	JOINT	61,416	0.696	4.227	**0.742**	**6.835**	**0.535**	6.545
11	JOINT-Global	510	0.625	5.295	0.650	11.982	0.459	17.472
12	JOINT-Global-retrained	510	0.629	4.633	0.651	7.862	0.490	6.876

5.2 Feature analysis

The most important features using the JOINT model with the full feature set (condition 10) are presented in Table 3. Features associated with a young age have a negative weight, while features associated with old age have a positive weight. For almost all runs and evaluation metrics the full feature set gives the best performance. However, looking at the performance increase, we observe that the unigram only baseline gives strong results. Overall, both stylistic as well as content features are important. For content features, we see that references to family (e.g., "granddaughter" versus "son") as well as to daily life (e.g., "school" versus "job") are very predictive.

Although the performance using only POS tags is lower, reasonable correlations are obtained using only POS tags. In Table 3 we see many POS features associated with old age. This is confirmed when analyzing the whole feature set selected by the JOINT model (condition 10). In this model 510 features are nonzero, 161 of which are POS patterns. Of these, 43 have a negative weight, and 118 have a positive weight. This thus again suggests that old age is characterized more by syntactic effects than young age.

Most important features are consistent with observations from previous research. For example, in the Fisher dataset, similar to findings from classification experiments by Garera and Yarowsky (2009), the word "well" is most predictive of older age. "Like" has the highest association with younger age. This agrees with observations by Barbieri (2008). As was also observed by others, "just" is highly associated with young persons. Consistent with literature that males generally "sound older" than they truly are (Argamon et al., 2007, and others), our male speaker feature has a high negative weight. And, in agreement with previous observations, younger people use more swear words and negative emotions.

The differences between the corpora are reflected in the features that have the most weight. The effective features in the Fisher dataset are more typical of conversational settings and effective features in the cancer dataset are about being pregnant and having kids. Features associated with the blog dataset are typical of the story telling nature of many blog posts.

Comparing the extracted corpus-specific features with the features selected when training on the individual corpora, we do see evidence that the JOINT model separates general versus specific features. For example, the most important features associated with young people in the cancer dataset when only training on the cancer dataset (condition 9) are: *LIWC - Emoticons*, *LIWC - Pronoun*, definitely,

Table 3: Most important features in the JOINT model with all features (condition 10).

(a) Features for younger people.

Global		**Blogs**		**Fisher**		**Cancer**	
like	-1.295	you	-0.387	actually	-0.457	LIWC-Emotic.	-0.188
gender-male	-0.539	went	-0.310	mean	-0.343	young	-0.116
LIWC-School	-0.442	fun	-0.216	everyone	-0.273	history	-0.092
just	-0.354	school	-0.192	definitely	-0.273	mom	-0.087
LIWC-Anger	-0.303	but	-0.189	mom	-0.230	ultrasound	-0.083
LIWC-Cause	-0.290	LIWC-Comma	-0.152	student	-0.182	kids	-0.071
mom	-0.290	go	-0.142	pretty	-0.137	age	-0.069
so	-0.271	POS-vbp nn	-0.116	POS-lrb cd	-0.135	mum	-0.069
definitely	-0.263	thats	-0.115	LIWC-Swear	-0.134	POS-sym rrb	-0.069
LIWC-Negemo	-0.256	well	-0.112	huge	-0.126	discharge	-0.063

(b) Features for older people.

Global		**Blogs**		**Fisher**		**Cancer**	
years	0.601	LIWC - Job	0.514	well	1.644	POS - dt	0.713
POS - dt	0.485	son	0.267	LIWC - WC	0.855	POS - md vb	0.450
LIWC - Incl	0.483	kids	0.228	POS - uh prp	0.504	POS - nn	0.369
POS - prp vbp	0.337	years	0.178	retired	0.492	LIWC - Negate	0.327
granddaughter	0.332	work	0.147	POS - prp vbp	0.430	POS - nn vbd	0.321
grandchildren	0.293	wife	0.142	said	0.404	POS - nnp	0.304
had	0.277	husband	0.137	POS - cc fw	0.358	us	0.287
daughter	0.272	meds	0.112	son	0.353	all	0.266
grandson	0.245	dealing	0.096	subject	0.319	good	0.248
ah	0.243	weekend	0.094	POS - cc cc	0.316	POS - cc nn	0.222

mom, mum, really, *LIWC - Family*, *LIWC - Humans*, thank, and she. The difference in age distribution is reflected in the feature weights. In the JOINT model, the bias term is 24.866. Because most of the persons in the cancer dataset are older, the features associated with young age in the cancer dataset have much lower weights compared to the other datasets.

Because our goal is to compare features across the corpora, we have not exploited corpus-specific features. For example, thread or subforum features could be used for the breast cancer corpus, and for the Fisher dataset, one could add features that exploit the conversational setting of the data.

5.3 Examples

We present examples of text of younger and older persons and connect them to the learned model. The examples are manually selected to illustrate strengths and weaknesses of the model.

5.3.1 Younger people

We first present some examples of text by young persons. The following is an example of a 17-year old in the blog dataset, the system predicted this to be from a 16.48-year-old:

> *I can't sleep, but this time I have school tommorow, so I have to try I guess. My parents got all pissed at me today because I forgot how to do the homework [...]. Really mad, I ended it pissing off my mom and [...] NOTHING! Damn, when I'm at my cousin's I have no urge to use the computer like I do here, [...].*

This example matches with important features determined by the system, containing references to school and parents, and usage of swearing and anger words.

The following are selected turns (T) by a 19-year old (system prediction: 17.37 years) in a conversation in the Fisher dataset.

> *T: yeah it's too i just just freaked out [...]*
> *T: that kinda sucks for them*
> *T: they were they were like going crazy [...]*
> *T: it's like against some law to like*

The text has many informal words such as "kinda" and well as many occurrences of the word "like."

This example is from a 19-year old from the cancer dataset. The system's prediction was far off, estimating an age of 35.48.

> *Im very young and an athlete and I really do not want to look disfigured, especially when I work so hard to be fit. I know it sounds shallow, but Im young and hope to [...] my husband one day :) [...] My grandmother died of breast cancer at 51, and my mother is currently dealing with a cancerous tumor on her ovaries.*

Besides explicit references to being "very young," the text is much more formal than typical texts, making it a hard example.

5.3.2 Older people

The following is a snippet from a 47-year-old (system prediction: 34.42 years) in the blog dataset.

> *[...]In the weeks leading up to this meeting certain of the managers repeatedly asserted strong positions. [...] their previous (irresponsible yet non-negotiable) opinions[...] Well, today's my first Father's day [...]. Bringing a child into this world is quite a responsibility especially with all the fears and challenges we face. [...]*

This matches some important features such as references to jobs, as well as having kids. The many references to the word "father" in the whole text might have confused the model. The following are selected turns (T) by a 73-year old (system prediction: 73.26 years) in a conversation in the Fisher dataset.

> *T: ah thoughts i'm retired right now*
> *T: i i really can't ah think of anyth- think of i would ah ah change considerably ah i'm i'm very i've been very happily married and i have ah three children and six grandchildren*
> *T: yeah that's right well i i think i would do things more differently fair- fairly recently than a long time ago*

This example contains references to being retired and having grandchildren, as well as many usages of "ah". The following is an example of a 70-year old (system prediction: 71.53 years) in the cancer dataset.

> *[...] I was a little bit fearful of having surgery on both sides at once (reduction and lift on the right, tissue expander on the left) [...] On the good side, my son and family live near the plastic surgeon's office and the hospital, [...], at least from my son and my granddaughter [...]*

6 Conclusion

We presented linear regression experiments to predict the age of a text's author. As evaluation metrics, we found correlation as well as mean absolute error to be complementary and useful measures. We obtained correlations up to 0.74 and mean absolute errors between 4.1 and 6.8 years. In three different corpora, we found both content features and stylistic features to be strong indicators of a person's age. Even a unigram only baseline already gives strong performance and many POS patterns are strong indicators of old age. By learning jointly from all of the corpora, we were able to separate generally effective features from corpus-dependent ones.

Acknowledgments

The authors would like to thank the anonymous reviewers for feedback, Michael Heilman for the regression code, and other members of the ARK group for help running the experiments. This work was funded by NSF grants CAREER IIS-1054319 to N.A.S. and IIS-0968485 to C.P.R.

References

Galen Andrew and Jianfeng Gao. 2007. Scalable training of l_1-regularized log-linear models. In *Proc. of ICML*.

Shlomo Argamon, Moshe Koppel, Jonathan Fine, and Anat R. Shimoni. 2003. Gender, genre, and writing style in formal written texts. *Text*, 23(3):321–346.

Shlomo Argamon, Moshe Koppel, James Pennebaker, and Jonathan Schler. 2007. Mining the blogosphere: age, gender, and the varieties of self-expression.

Federica Barbieri. 2008. Patterns of age-based linguistic variation in American English. *Journal of Sociolinguistics*, 12(1):58–88.

Christopher Cieri, David Miller, and Kevin Walker. 2004. The Fisher corpus: a resource for the next generations of speech-to-text. In *Proc. of LREC*, pages 69–71.

Hal Daumé III. 2007. Frustratingly easy domain adaptation. In *Proc. of ACL*.

Penelope Eckert. 1996. Age as a sociolinguistic variable. In *The Handbook of Sociolinguistics*. Oxford: Blackwell.

Jianfeng Gao, Galen Andrew, Mark Johnson, and Kristina Toutanova. 2007. A comparative study of parameter estimation methods for statistical natural language processing. In *Proc. of ACL*.

Nikesh Garera and David Yarowsky. 2009. Modeling latent biographic attributes in conversational genres. In *Proc. of ACL-IJCNLP*.

Sumit Goswami, Sudeshna Sarkar, and Mayur Rustagi. 2009. Stylometric analysis of bloggers' age and gender. In *Proc. of ICWSM*.

James W. Pennebaker and Lori D. Stone. 2003. Words of wisdom: Language use over the lifespan. *Journal of Personality and Social Psychology*, 85:291–301.

James W. Pennebaker, Roger J. Booth, and Martha E. Francis, 2001. *Linguistic Inquiry and Word Count (LIWC): A Computerized Text Analysis Program.*

Delip Rao, David Yarowsky, Abhishek Shreevats, and Manaswi Gupta. 2010. Classifying latent user attributes in Twitter. In *Proc. of SMUC*.

Jonathan Schler, Moshe Koppel, Shlomo Argamon, and James Pennebaker. 2006. Effects of age and gender on blogging. In *Proceedings of the AAAI Spring Symposia on Computational Approaches to Analyzing Weblogs*.

Werner Spiegl, Georg Stemmer, Eva Lasarcyk, Varada Kolhatkar, Andrew Cassidy, Blaise Potard, Stephen Shum, Young Chol Song, Puyang Xu, Peter Beyerlein, James Harnsberger, and Elmar Nöth. 2009. Analyzing features for automatic age estimation on cross-sectional data. In *Proc. of INTERSPEECH*.

Robert Tibshirani. 1996. Regression shrinkage and selection via the lasso. *Journal of the Royal Statistical Society Series B (Methodological)*, 58(1):267–288.

Kristina Toutanova, Dan Klein, Christopher D. Manning, and Yoram Singer. 2003. Feature-rich part-of-speech tagging with a cyclic dependency network. In *Proc. of NAACL-HLT*.

Charl van Heerden, Etienne Barnard, Marelie Davel, Christiaan van der Walt, Ewald van Dyk, Michael Feld, and Christian Muller. 2010. Combining regression and classification methods for improving automatic speaker age recognition. In *Proc. of ICASSP*.

A Study of Academic Collaboration in Computational Linguistics with Latent Mixtures of Authors

Nikhil Johri, Daniel Ramage
Department of Computer Science
Stanford University
Stanford, CA, USA

Daniel A. McFarland
School of Education
Stanford University
Stanford, CA, USA

Daniel Jurafsky
Department of Linguistics
Stanford University
Stanford, CA, USA

{njohri2,dramage,dmcfarla,jurafsky}@stanford.edu

Abstract

Academic collaboration has often been at the forefront of scientific progress, whether amongst prominent established researchers, or between students and advisors. We suggest a theory of the different types of academic collaboration, and use topic models to computationally identify these in Computational Linguistics literature. A set of *author-specific* topics are learnt over the ACL corpus, which ranges from 1965 to 2009. The models are trained on a per year basis, whereby only papers published up until a given year are used to learn that year's author topics. To determine the collaborative properties of papers, we use, as a metric, a function of the cosine similarity score between a paper's term vector and each author's topic signature in the year preceding the paper's publication. We apply this metric to examine questions on the nature of collaborations in Computational Linguistics research, finding that significant variations exist in the way people collaborate within different subfields.

1 Introduction

Academic collaboration is on the rise as single authored work becomes less common across the sciences (Rawlings and McFarland, 2011; Jones et al., 2008; Newman, 2001). In part, this rise can be attributed to the increasing specialization of individual academics and the broadening in scope of the problems they tackle. But there are other advantages to collaboration, as well: they can speed up production, diffuse knowledge across authors, help train new scientists, and are thought to encourage greater innovation. Moreover, they can integrate scholarly communities and foster knowledge transfer between related fields. But all collaborations aren't the same: different collaborators contribute different material, assume different roles, and experience the collaboration in different ways. In this paper, we present a new frame for thinking about the variation in collaboration types and develop a computational metric to characterize the distinct contributions and roles of each collaborator within the scholarly material they produce.

The topic of understanding collaborations has attracted much interest in the social sciences over the years. Recently, it has gained traction in computer science, too, in the form of social network analysis. Much work focuses on studying networks formed via citations (Radev et al., 2009; White and Mccain, 1998), as well as co-authorship links (Nascimento et al., 2003; Liu et al., 2005). However, these works focus largely on the graphical structure derived from paper citations and author co-occurrences, and less on the textual content of the papers themselves. In this work, we examine the nature of academic collaboration using text as a primary component.

We propose a theoretical framework for determining the types of collaboration present in a document, based on factors such as the number of established authors, the presence of unestablished authors and the similarity of the established authors' past work to the document's term vector. These collaboration types attempt to describe the nature of co-authorships between students and advisors (e.g. "apprentice" versus "new blood") as well as those solely between established authors in the field. We present a decision diagram for classifying papers into these types, as well as a description of the intuition behind each collaboration class.

We explore our theory with a computational method to categorize collaborative works into their collaboration types using an approach based on topic modeling, where we model every paper as a latent mixture of its authors. For our system, we use Labeled-LDA (LLDA (Ramage et al., 2009)) to train models over the ACL corpus for every year of the words best attributed to each author in all the papers they write. We use the resulting author signatures as a basis for several metrics that can classify each document by its collaboration type.

We qualitatively analyze our results by examining the categorization of several high impact papers. With consultation from prominent researchers and textbook writers in the field, we demonstrate that our system is able to differentiate between the various types of collaborations in our suggested taxonomy, based only on words used, at low but statistically significant accuracy. We use this same similarity score to analyze the ACL community by sub-field, finding significant deviations.

2 Related Work

In recent years, popular topic models such as Latent Dirichlet Allocation (Blei et al., 2003) have been increasingly used to study the history of science by observing the changing trends in term based topics (Hall et al., 2008), (Gerrish and Blei, 2010). In the case of Hall et al., regular LDA topic models were trained over the ACL anthology on a per year basis, and the changing trends in topics were studied from year to year. Gerrish and Blei's work computed a measure of influence by using Dynamic Topic Models (Blei and Lafferty, 2006) and studying the change of statistics of the language used in a corpus.

These models propose interesting ideas for utilizing topic modeling to understand aspects of scientific history. However, our primary interest, in this paper, is the study of academic collaboration between different authors; we therefore look to learn models for authors instead of only documents. Popular topic models for authors include the Author-Topic Model (Rosen-Zvi et al., 2004), a simple extension of regular LDA that adds an additional author variable over the topics. The Author-Topic Model learns a distribution over words for each topic, as in regular LDA, as well as a distribution over topics for each author. Alternatively, Labeled LDA (Ramage et al., 2009), another LDA variation, offers us the ability to directly model authors as topics by considering them to be the topic labels for the documents they author.

In this work, we use Labeled LDA to directly model probabilistic term 'signatures' for authors. As in (Hall et al., 2008) and (Gerrish and Blei, 2010), we learn a new topic model for each year in the corpus, allowing us to account for changing author interests over time.

3 Computational Methodology

The experiments and results discussed in this paper are based on a variation of the LDA topic model run over data from the ACL corpus.

3.1 Dataset

We use the ACL anthology from years 1965 to 2009, training over 12,908 papers authored by over 11,355 unique authors. We train our per year topic models over the entire dataset; however, when evaluating our results, we are only concerned with papers that were authored by multiple individuals as the other papers are not collaborations.

3.2 Latent Mixture of Authors

Every abstract in our dataset reflects the work, to some greater or lesser degree, of all the authors of that work. We model these degrees explicitly using a latent mixture of authors model, which takes its inspiration from the learning machinery of LDA (Blei et al., 2003) and its supervised variant Labeled LDA (Ramage et al., 2009). These models assume that documents are as a mixture of 'topics,' which themselves are probability distributions over the words in the vocabulary of the corpus. LDA is completely unsupervised, assuming that a latent topic layer exists and that each word is generated from one underlying topic from this set of latent topics. For our purposes, we use a variation of LDA in which we assume each document to be a latent mixture of its *authors*. Unlike LDA, where each document draws a multinomial over all topics, the latent mixture of authors model we use restricts a document to only sample from topics corresponding to its authors. Also, unlike models such as the Author-Topic Model (Rosen-Zvi et al., 2004), where authors are modeled as distributions over latent topics, our model associates each author to exactly one topic, modeling authors directly as distributions over words.

Like other topic models, we will assume a generative process for our collection of D documents from a vocabulary of size V. We assume that each document d has N_d terms and M_d authors from a set of authors A. Each author is described by a multinomial distribution β_a over words V, which is initially unobserved. We will recover for each document a hidden multinomial $\theta^{(d)}$ of length M_d that describes which mixture of authors' best describes the document. This multinomial is in turn drawn from a symmetric Dirichlet distribution with parameter α restrict to the set of authors $\lambda^{(d)}$ for that paper. Each document's words are generated by first picking an author z_i from $\theta^{(d)}$ and then drawing a word from the corresponding author's word distribution. Formally, the generative process is as follows:

- For each author a, generate a distribution β_a over the vocabulary from a Dirichlet prior μ
- For each document d, generate a multinomial mixture distribution $\theta^{(d)} \sim Dir(\alpha.\mathbf{1}_{\lambda^{(d)}})$
- For each document d,
  - For each $i \in \{1, ..., N_d\}$
    - Generate $z_i \in \{\lambda_1^{(d)}, ..., \lambda_{M_d}^{(d)}\} \sim Mult(\theta^{(d)})$
    - Generate $w_i \in \{1, ..., V\} \sim Mult(\beta_{z_i})$

We use Gibbs sampling to perform inference in this model. If we consider our authors as a label space, this model is equivalent to that of Labeled LDA (Ramage et al., 2009), which we use for inference in our model, using the variational objective in the open source implementation[1]. After inference, our model discovers the distribution over terms that best describes that author's work in the presence of other authors. This distribution serves as a 'signature' for an author and is dominated by the terms that author uses frequently across collaborations. It is worth noting that this model constrains the learned 'topics' to authors, ensuring directly interpretable results that do not require the interpretation of a latent topic space, such as in (Rosen-Zvi et al., 2004).

To imbue our model with a notion of time, we train a separate LLDA model for each year in the corpus, training on only those papers written before and during the given year. Thus, we have separate 'signatures' for each author for each year, and each signature only contains information for the specific author's work up to and including the given year. Table 1 contains examples of such term signatures computed for two authors in different years. The top terms and their fractional counts are displayed.

4 Studying Collaborations

There are several ways one can envision to differentiate between types of academic collaborations. We focus on three factors when creating collaboration labels, namely:

- Presence of unestablished authors
- Similarity to established authors
- Number of established authors

If an author whom we know little about is present on a collaborative paper, we consider him or her to be a new author. We threshold new authors by the number of papers they have written up to the publication year of the paper we are observing. Depending on whether this number is below or above a threshold value, we consider an author to be *established* or *unestablished* in the given year.

Similarity scores are measured using the trained LLDA models described in Section 3.2. For any given paper, we measure the similarity of the paper to one of its (established) authors by calculating the cosine similarity of the author's signature in the year preceding the paper's publication to the paper's term-vector.

Using the aforementioned three factors, we define the following types of collaborations:

- **Apprenticeship Papers** are authored by one or more established authors and one or more unestablished authors, such that the similarity of the paper to more than half of the established authors is high. In this case, we say that the new author (or authors) was an apprentice of

[1] http://nlp.stanford.edu/software/tmt/

Philipp Koehn, 2002		Philipp Koehn, 2009		Fernando Pereira, 1985		Fernando Pereira, 2009	
Terms	Counts	Terms	Counts	Terms	Counts	Terms	Counts
word	3.00	translation	69.78	grammar	14.99	type	40.00
lexicon	2.00	machine	34.67	phrase	10.00	phrase	30.89
noun	2.00	phrase	26.85	structure	7.00	free	23.14
similar	2.00	english	23.86	types	6.00	grammar	23.10
translation	1.29	statistical	19.51	formalisms	5.97	constraint	23.00
purely	0.90	systems	18.32	sharing	5.00	logical	22.41
accuracy	0.90	word	16.38	unification	4.97	rules	21.72

Table 1: Example term 'signatures' computed by running a Labeled LDA model over authors in the ACL corpus on a per year basis: top terms for two authors in different years are shown alongside their fractional counts.

the established authors, continuing in their line of work.

- **New Blood Papers** are authored by one established author and one or more unestablished authors, such that the similarity of the paper to the established author is low. In this case, we say that the new author (or authors) provided new ideas or worked in an area that was dissimilar to that which the established author was working in.
- **Synergistic Papers** are authored only by established authors such that it does not heavily resemble any authors' previous work. In this case, we consider the paper to be a product of synergy of its authors.
- **Catalyst Papers** are similar to synergistic ones, with the exception that unestablished authors are also present on a Catalyst Paper. In this case, we hypothesize that the unestablished authors were the catalysts responsible for getting the established authors to work on a topic dissimilar to their previous work.

The decision diagram in Figure 1 presents an easy way to determine the collaboration type assigned to a paper.

5 Quantifying Collaborations

Following the decision diagram presented in Figure 1 and using similarity scores based on the values returned by our latent author mixture models (Section 3.2), we can deduce the collaboration type to assign to any given paper. However, absolute categorization requires an additional thresholding of author similarity scores. To avoid the addition of an arbitrary threshold, instead of directly categorizing papers, we rank them based on the calculated similarity scores on three different spectra. To facilitate ease of interpretation, the qualitative examples we present are drawn from high PageRank papers as calculated in (Radev et al., 2009).

5.1 The MaxSim Score

To measure the similarity of authors' previous work to a paper, we look at the cosine similarity between the term vector of the paper and each author's term signature. We are only interested in the highest cosine similarity score produced by an author, as our categories do not differentiate between papers that are similar to one author and papers that are similar to multiple authors, as long as high similarity to any single author is present. Thus, we choose our measure, the MaxSim score, to be defined as: $\max_{a \in est} cos(a_{sig}, paper)$

We choose to observe the similarity scores only for established authors as newer authors will not have enough previous work to produce a stable term signature, and we vary the experience threshold by year to account for the fact that there has been a large increase in the absolute number of papers published in recent years.

Depending on the presence of new authors and the number of established authors present, each paper can be placed into one of the three spectra: the Apprenticeship-New Blood spectrum, the Synergy spectrum and the Apprenticeship-Catalyst spectrum. Apprenticeship and Low Synergy papers are those with high MaxSim scores, while low scores indicate New Blood, Catalyst or High Synergy papers.

5.2 Examples

The following are examples of high impact papers as they were categorized by our system:

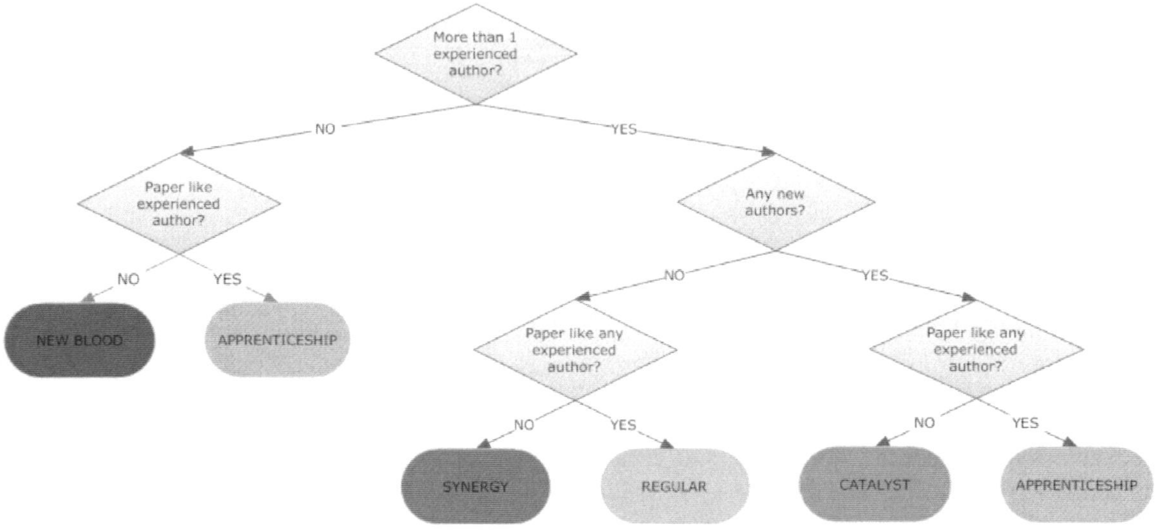

Figure 1: Decision diagram for determining the collaboration type of a paper. A minimum of 1 established author is assumed.

5.2.1 Example: Apprenticeship Paper

Improvements in Phrase-Based Statistical Machine Translation (2004)
by Richard Zens and Hermann Ney
This paper had a high MaxSim score, indicating high similarity to established author Hermann Ney. This categorizes the paper as an Apprenticeship Paper.

5.2.2 Example: New Blood Paper

Thumbs up? Sentiment Classification using Machine Learning Techniques (2002)
by Lillian Lee, Bo Pang and Shivakumar Vaithyanathan
This paper had a low MaxSim score, indicating low similarity to established author Lillian Lee. This categorizes the paper as a New Blood Paper, with new authors Bo Pang and Shivakumar Vaithyanathan. It is important to note here that new authors do not necessarily mean young authors or grad students; in this case, the third author on the paper was experienced, but in a field outside of ACL.

5.2.3 Example: High Synergy Paper

Catching the Drift: Probabilistic Content Models, with Applications to Generation and Summarization (2003)
by Regina Barzilay and Lillian Lee
This paper had low similarity to both established authors on it, making it a highly synergistic paper. Synergy here indicates that the work done on this paper was mostly unlike work previously done by either of the authors.

5.2.4 Example: Catalyst Paper

Answer Extraction (2000)
by Steven Abney, Michael Collins, Amit Singhal
This paper had a very low MaxSim score, as well as the presence of an unestablished author, making it a Catalyst Paper. The established authors (from an ACL perspective) were Abney and Collins, while Singhal was from outside the area and did not have many ACL publications. The work done in this paper focused on information extraction, and was unlike that previously done by either of the ACL established authors. Thus, we say that in this case, Singhal played the role of the catalyst, getting the other two authors to work on an area that was outside of their usual range.

5.3 Evaluation

5.3.1 Expert Annotation

To quantitatively evaluate the performance of our system, we prepared a subset of 120 papers from among the highest scoring collaborative papers based on the PageRank metric (Radev et al., 2009). Only those papers were selected which had at least a single established author. One expert in the field was asked to annotate each of these papers as being either similar or dissimilar to the established authors' prior work given the year of publication, the title of the publication and its abstract.

We found that the MaxSim scores of papers labeled as being similar to the established authors were, on average, higher than those labeled as dissimilar. The average MaxSim score of papers annotated as low MaxSim collaboration types (High Synergy, New Blood or Catalyst papers) was 0.15488, while that of papers labeled as high MaxSim types (Apprentice or Low Synergy papers) had a mean MaxSim score of 0.21312. The MaxSim scores of the different sets were compared using a t-test, and the difference was found to be statistically significant with a two-tailed p-value of 0.0041.

Framing the task as a binary classification problem, however, did not produce very strong results. The breakdown of the papers and success rates (as determined by a tuned threshold) can be seen in Table 3. The system had a relatively low success rate of 62.5% in its binary categorization of collaborations.

5.3.2 First Author Prediction

Studies have suggested that authorship order, when not alphabetical, can often be quantified and predicted by those who do the work (Sekercioglu, 2008). Through a survey of all authors on a sample of papers, Slone (1996) found that in almost all major papers, "the first two authors are said to account for the preponderance of work". We attempt to evaluate our similarity scores by checking if they are predictive of first author.

Though similarity to previous work is only a small contributor to determining author order, we find that using the metric of cosine similarity between author signatures and papers performs significantly better at determining the first author of a paper than random chance. Of course, this feature alone isn't extremely predictive, given that it's guaranteed to give an incorrect solution in cases where the first author of a paper has never been seen before. To solve the problem of first author prediction, we would have to combine this with other features. We chose two other features - an alphabetical predictor, and a predictor based on the frequency of an author appearing as first author. Although we don't show the regression, we do explore these two other features and find that they are also predictive of author order.

Predictor Feature	Accuracy
Random Chance	37.35%
Author Signature Similarity	45.23%
Frequency Estimator	56.09%
Alphabetical Ordering	43.64%

Table 2: Accuracy of individual features at predicting the first author of 8843 papers

Table 2 shows the performance of our prediction feature alongside the others. The fact that it beats random chance shows us that there is some information about authorial efforts in the scores we have computed.

6 Applications

A number of questions about the nature of collaborations may be answered using our system. We describe approaches to some of these in this section.

6.1 The Hedgehog-Fox Problem

From the days of the ancient Greek poet Archilochus, the Hedgehog-Fox analogy has been frequently used (Berlin, 1953) to describe two different types of people. Archilochus stated that "The fox knows many things; the hedgehog one big thing." A person is thus considered a 'hedgehog' if he has expertise in one specific area and focuses all his time and resources on it. On the other hand, a 'fox' is a one who has knowledge of several different fields, and dabbles in all of them instead of focusing heavily on one.

We show how, using our computed similarity scores, one can discover the hedgehogs and foxes of Computational Linguistics. We look at the top 100 published authors in our corpus, and for each author, we compute the average similarity score the author's signature has to each of his or her papers. Note that we start taking similarity scores into account only after an author has published 5 papers, thereby allowing the author to stablize a signature in the corpus and preventing the signature from being boosted by early papers (where author similarity would be artificially high, since the author was new).

We present the authors with the highest average similarity scores in Table 4. These authors can be

Collaboration Type	True Positives	False Positives	Accuracy
New Blood, Catalyst or High Synergy Papers	43	23	65.15%
Apprentice or Low Synergy Papers	32	22	59.25%
Overall	75	45	62.50%

Table 3: Evaluation based on annotation by one expert

considered the hedgehogs, as they have highly stable signatures that their new papers resemble. On the other hand, Table 5 shows the list of foxes, who have less stable signatures, presumably because they move about in different areas.

Author	Avg. Sim. Score
Koehn, Philipp	0.43456
Pedersen, Ted	0.41146
Och, Franz Josef	0.39671
Ney, Hermann	0.37304
Sumita, Eiichiro	0.36706

Table 4: Hedgehogs - authors with the highest average similarity scores

Author	Avg. Sim. Score
Marcus, Mitchell P.	0.09996
Pustejovsky, James D.	0.10473
Pereira, Fernando C. N.	0.14338
Allen, James F.	0.14461
Hahn, Udo	0.15009

Table 5: Foxes - authors with the lowest average similarity scores

6.2 Similarity to previous work by sub-fields

Based on the different types of collaborations discussed in, a potential question one might ask is which sub-fields are more likely to produce *apprentice* papers, and which will produce *new blood* papers. To answer this question, we first need to determine which papers correspond to which sub-fields. Once again, we use topic models to solve this problem. We first filter out a subset of the 1,200 highest page-rank collaborative papers from the years 1980 to 2007. We use a set of topics built by running a standard LDA topic model over the ACL corpus, in which each topic is hand labeled by experts based on the top terms associated with it. Given these topic-term distributions, we can once again use the cosine similarity metric to discover the highly associated

Topic	Score
Statistical Machine Translation	0.2695
Prosody	0.2631
Speech Recognition	0.2511
Non-Statistical Machine Translation	0.2471
Word Sense Disambiguation	0.2380

Table 6: Topics with highest MaxSim scores (papers are more similar to the established authors' previous work)

Topic	Score
Question Answering	0.1335
Sentiment Analysis	0.1399
Dialog Systems	0.1417
Spelling Correction	0.1462
Summarization	0.1511

Table 7: Topics with lowest MaxSim scores (papers are less similar to the established authors' previous work)

topics for each given paper from our smaller subset, by choosing topics with cosine similarity above a certain threshold δ (in this case 0.1).

Once we have created a paper set for each topic, we can measure the 'novelty' for each paper by looking at their MaxSim score. We can now find the average MaxSim score for each topic. This average similarity score gives us a notion of how similar to the established author (or authors) a paper in the sub field usually is. Low scores indicate that new blood and synergy style papers are more common, while higher scores imply more non-synergistic or apprenticeship style papers. This could indicate that topics with lower scores are more open ended, while those with higher scores require more formality or training. The top five topics in each category are shown in Tables 6 and 7. The scores of the papers from the two tables were compared using a t-test, and the difference in the scores of the two tables was found to be very statistically significant with a two-tailed p value $<< 0.01$.

7 Discussion and Future Work

Once we have a robust way to score different kinds of collaborations in ACL, we can begin to use these scores as a quantitative tool to study phonemena in the computational linguistics community. With our current technique, we discovered a number of negative results; however, given that our accuracy in binary classification of categories is relatively low, we cannot state for sure whether these are true negative results or a limitation of our model.

7.1 Tentative Negative Results

Among the questions we looked into, we found the following results:

- There was no signal indicating that authors who started out as new blood authors were any more or less likely to survive than authors who started out as apprentices. Survival was measured both by the number of papers eventually published by the author as well as the year of the author's final publication; however, calculations by neither measure correlated with the MaxSim scores of the authors' early papers.

- Each author in the corpus was labeled for gender. Gender didn't appear to differentiate how people collaborated. In particular, there was no difference between men and women based on how they started their careers. Women and men are equally likely to begin as new blood authors as they are to begin as apprentices.

- On a similar note, established male authors are equally likely to partake in new blood or apprentice collaborations as their female counterparts.

- No noticeable difference existed between average page rank scores of a certain categorization of collaborative papers (e.g. high synergy papers vs. low synergy papers).

It is difficult to conclusively demonstrate negative results, particularly given that our MaxSim scores are by themselves not particularly strong discriminators in the binary classification tasks. We consider these findings to be tentative and an opportunity to explore in the future.

8 Conclusion

Not everything we need to know about academic collaborations can be found in the co-authorship graph. Indeed, as we have argued, not all types of collaborations are equal, as embodied by differing levels of seniority and contribution from each co-author. In this work, we have taken a first step toward computationally modeling these differences using a latent mixture of authors model and applied it to our own field, Computational Linguistics. We used the model to examine how collaborative works differ by authors and subfields in the ACL anthology. Our model quantifies the extent to which some authors are more prone to being 'hedgehogs,' whereby they heavily focus on certain specific areas, whilst others are more diverse with their fields of study and may be analogized with 'foxes.'

We also saw that established authors in certain subfields have more deviation from their previous work than established authors in different subfields. This could imply that the former fields, such as 'Sentiment Analysis' or 'Summarization,' are more open to new blood and synergistic ideas, while other latter fields, like 'Statistical Machine Translation' or 'Speech Recognition' are more formal or require more training. Alternatively, 'Summarization' or 'Sentiment Analysis' could just still be younger fields whose language is still evolving and being influenced by other subareas.

This work takes a first step toward a new way of thinking about the contributions of individual authors based on their network of areas. There are many design parameters that still exist in this space, including alternative text models that take into account richer structure and, hopefully, perform better at discriminating between the types of collaborations we identified. We intend to use the ACL anthology as our test bed for continuing to work on textual models of collaboration types. Ultimately, we hope to apply the lessons we learn on modeling this familiar corpus to the challenge of answering large-scale questions about the nature of collaboration as embodied by large scale publication databases such as ISI and Pubmed.

Acknowledgments

This research was supported by NSF grant NSF-0835614 CDI-Type II: What drives the dynamic creation of science? We thank our anonymous reviewers for their valuable feedback and the members of the Stanford Mimir Project team for their insights and engagement.

References

Isaiah Berlin. 1953. *The hedgehog and the fox: An essay on Tolstoy's view of history*. Simon & Schuster.

David M. Blei and John D. Lafferty. 2006. Dynamic topic models. In *Proceedings of the 23rd international conference on Machine learning*, ICML '06, pages 113–120, New York, NY, USA. ACM.

David M. Blei, Andrew Y. Ng, and Michael I. Jordan. 2003. Latent dirichlet allocation. *J. Mach. Learn. Res.*, 3:993–1022.

Sean M. Gerrish and David M. Blei. 2010. A language-based approach to measuring scholarly impact. In *Proceedings of the 26th International Conference on Machine Learning*.

David Hall, Daniel Jurafsky, and Christopher D. Manning. 2008. Studying the history of ideas using topic models. In *Proceedings of the Conference on Empirical Methods in Natural Language Processing*, EMNLP '08, pages 363–371, Stroudsburg, PA, USA. Association for Computational Linguistics.

B. F. Jones, S. Wuchty, and B. Uzzi. 2008. Multi-university research teams: Shifting impact, geography, and stratification in science. *Science*, 322:1259–1262, November.

Xiaoming Liu, Johan Bollen, Michael L. Nelson, and Herbert Van de Sompel. 2005. Co-authorship networks in the digital library research community. *Information Processing & Management*, 41(6):1462 – 1480. Special Issue on Infometrics.

Mario A. Nascimento, Jörg Sander, and Jeffrey Pound. 2003. Analysis of sigmod's co-authorship graph. *SIGMOD Rec.*, 32:8–10, September.

M. E. J. Newman. 2001. From the cover: The structure of scientific collaboration networks. *Proceedings of the National Academy of Science*, 98:404–409, January.

Dragomir R. Radev, Pradeep Muthukrishnan, and Vahed Qazvinian. 2009. The acl anthology network corpus. In *Proceedings of the 2009 Workshop on Text and Citation Analysis for Scholarly Digital Libraries*, NLPIR4DL '09, pages 54–61, Stroudsburg, PA, USA. Association for Computational Linguistics.

Daniel Ramage, David Hall, Ramesh Nallapati, and Christopher D. Manning. 2009. Labeled lda: a supervised topic model for credit attribution in multi-labeled corpora. In *Proceedings of the 2009 Conference on Empirical Methods in Natural Language Processing: Volume 1 - Volume 1*, EMNLP '09, pages 248–256.

Craig M. Rawlings and Daniel A. McFarland. 2011. Influence flows in the academy: Using affiliation networks to assess peer effects among researchers. *Social Science Research*, 40(3):1001 – 1017.

Michal Rosen-Zvi, Thomas Griffiths, Mark Steyvers, and Padhraic Smyth. 2004. The author-topic model for authors and documents. In *Proceedings of the 20th conference on Uncertainty in artificial intelligence*, UAI '04, pages 487–494.

Cagan H. Sekercioglu. 2008. Quantifying coauthor contributions. *Science*, 322(5900):371.

RM Slone. 1996. Coauthors' contributions to major papers published in the ajr: frequency of undeserved coauthorship. *Am. J. Roentgenol.*, 167(3):571–579.

Howard D. White and Katherine W. Mccain. 1998. Visualizing a discipline: An author co-citation analysis of information science. *Journal of the American Society for Information Science*, 49:1972–1995.

Author Index